Fishing Lures

FIELD GUIDE

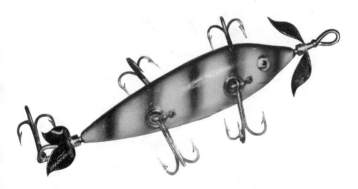

Carl F. Luckey & Clyde Harbin Sr.

Edited by Dennis Thornton
Designed by Wendy Wendt

700 East State Street • Iola, WI 54990-0001
715-445-2214 • 888-457-2873
www.krause.com

Please call or write for our free catalog of publications.
To place an order or obtain a free catalog please call 800-258-0929.

Library of Congress Catalog Number: 2003105295
ISBN: 0-87349-692-2
Printed in the United States of America

Fishing Lure Field Guide

INTRODUCTION

A fishing lure is a device usually made of wood or plastic, bearing a hook and a way to tie it to a line, made in such a way as to deceive a fish into thinking it to be a delicacy worthy of pursuit. The result, with luck, is a bit of good eating.

To a collector, a pristine and antique lure has the additional appeal of being worthy of pursuit to add it to a collection. Many of the older lures have acquired value many times their original purchase price as collectors seek them out. Who wouldn't want a rare 1912 Heddon Dowagiac Minnow as the centerpiece of his or her collection?

This Field Guide is a distillation of information from the *Old Fishing Lures & Tackle* book first put together by Carl F. Luckey in 1980 and currently in its sixth edition. Luckey died in 1998 and his work is being continued by longtime collaborator Clyde A. Harbin Sr., better known as "The Bassman." The book and the membership of the National Fishing Lure Collectors Club are at the heart of the lure collection hobby that has reached thousands of enthusiasts.

The focus of this book is primarily manufactured artificial lures used since the earliest days of their production in the United States. There are only a few artificial flies in the listings, nor will you find many metal or metal spinner type lures. The majority of information presented is about fishing lures made beginning around 1890-1900 and ending in the early 1970s.

Think about how many thousands of anglers have tried to think of a "better mousetrap" in those 70 or 80 years. Most producers of plugs experimented with myriad designs in the continuing battle to make the "secret weapon."

The producers are represented by hundreds of operations, from the one-man shop to the large manufacturer, that have come and gone during this time. The types of lures range from the sublime to the ridiculous, from the ineffective to the explosively successful fish-getter. Every single one of them, if you believe the ads, has been the proverbial secret weapon to overcome the fickle tastes of our fishy foes.

EVOLUTION OF AMERICAN FISHING TACKLE

PRE-COLONIAL TIMES

1. The Indians used their hands, traps, spears, and lights at night. Light could be said to be one of the first artificial "lures."

2. American Indians as well as primitive peoples of other parts of the world used a "Gorge," the crude forerunner of today's barbed hook. The gorge is a straight bar made of bone, shell, stone, or wood, sometimes with a groove around it near the center for tying a line. It was inserted lengthwise in the bait. When the fish swallowed the bait, the line was tugged and the gorge became lodged lengthwise in the fish.

3. Eskimos and Indians used artificial lures made of ivory or bone. They were customarily used as decoys while ice fishing and/or spear fishing.

4. Eskimos and Indians used gill nets and seines.

18th CENTURY

First appearance of fishing for sport in America. Sport fishing probably pre-dates this era, but it was likely to be European aristocrats who brought their fly fishing gear with them.

1800-1810

First appearance of the Phantom Minnow in America.
George Snyder made the first "Kentucky Reels."

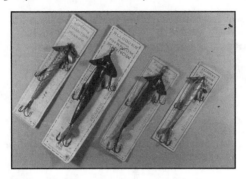

1835-1840

The first commercial manufacture of "Kentucky Reels" by the
Meeks Brothers.

1844-1925

The development of the "Henshall Rod."

1848

Julio T. Buel began commercial manufacture of the spoon lure. He
is credited with its invention. Buel was actually fishing with his
invention as early as 1821 and made many for friends and neigh-
bors over the years.

1852

Julio T. Buel - First U.S. patent on spinner bait.

1859

First known patent for a lure that mentions wood as possible
  material for the lure body. Riley Haskell, Painesville, Ohio.

1874

First granted patent for an artificial lure specifying the use of wood
  for the lure body. Patented May 26, 1874, by David Huard and
  Charles M. Dunbar of Ashland, Wis.

1876

Early manufactured artificial lure incorporating wood as a compo-
  nent. Listed in U.S. patent records as patented by H.C. Brush,
  Aug. 22, 1876.

1880

First known granted patent for an artificial lure specifying glass for
  the lure body. J. Irgens, Sept. 7, 1880.

1883

Patent for "artificial bait" called The Flying Hellgrammite by Harry Comstock, Fulton, N.Y., Jan. 30, 1883.

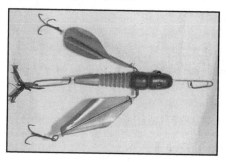

1883

Patent granted to Earnest F. Pflueger for artificial lures coated with luminous paint for fishing at night.

1885

The development of the "Chicago Rod".

1890

The beginning of widespread bait casting in the United States. Although the bait-casting reel was invented about 75 years previously, it wasn't until the 1890s that casting plugs were born in the U.S.

1869-1898

James Heddon is generally credited with the first artificial lure we know as the "plug" today.

1900-1905

The beginnings of major plug manufacturers in the United States.

1907

The first appearance of jointed wooden plugs—the "K and K Animated Minnows."

1910-1920

The first widespread use of luminous paint on plugs began sometime during this period. Pflueger was given the first patent on a luminous lure on Feb. 3, 1883.

1912

The first water sonic plugs appeared, probably the 1912 "Diamond Wiggler."

1914

The first appearance of fluted plugs, probably the Lockhart "Wobbler Wizard." It was followed by the Wilson "Fluted Wobbler" around 1917.

1914

The Detroit Glass Minnow Tube was introduced; the first of the few and rare glass fishing lures.

1915

First appearance of a self-illuminated plug to use a battery-operated bulb. It was called "Dr. Wasweyler's Marvelous Electric Glow Casting Minnow."

1917

Earliest known advertisement of a lure made of celluloid. The first advertisement found was in a May 1917 issue of National Sportsman magazine. It was for an Al Foss "Oriental Wiggler" æa pork rind minnow. Soon after, his ads began to say Pyralin instead of celluloid. These may be the first plastic lures.

1922

The Vesco Bait Company of New York City advertised baits and spoons made of Dupont Pyralin. One of the first plastic plugs.

1932

Heddon introduced its "Fish Flesh" plastic lure. The first lures were produced in the No. 9100 and No. 9500 (Vamp) series. Soon thereafter came plastic "Spooks."

1940

Appearance of the first American-built spinning reels.

Anatomy of a Lure

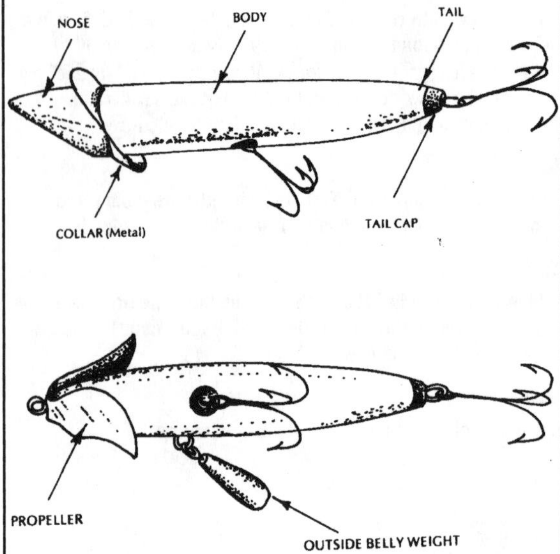

NOSE

BODY

TAIL

COLLAR (Metal)

TAIL CAP

PROPELLER

OUTSIDE BELLY WEIGHT

Anatomy of a Lure

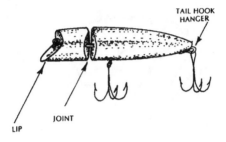

TAIL HOOK HANGER

JOINT

LIP

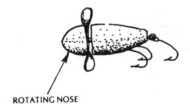

ROTATING NOSE

Anatomy of a Lure

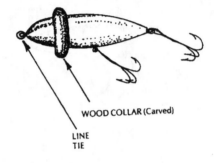

WOOD COLLAR (Carved)

LINE
TIE

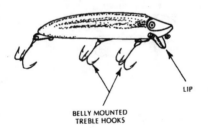

LIP

BELLY MOUNTED
TREBLE HOOKS

Types of Propellers

Various Types of Propellers

Al Foss style propeller spinner

F. C. Woods style propeller spinner

Clark and Keeling Expert style.

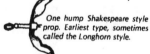

One hump Shakespeare style prop. Earliest type, sometimes called the Longhorn style.

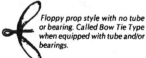

Floppy prop style with no tube or bearing. Called Bow Tie Type when equipped with tube and/or bearings.

Types of Propellers

Various Types of Propellers

The Shakespeare smooth edge (no hump) prop. Latest style. Note the three types of bearings they are found with.

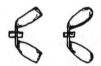

Two styles inexpensive tube type props found on various lures.

Types of Propellers

Various Types of Propellers

Creek Chub style propeller . . .r-
ner. Found with several (at least
two) washer type loose bearings
to stabilize it.

Style used on early Holzwarth
Experts and on later Rhodes
and earliest Shakespeare
wooden minnows.

Earth South Bend and
Shakespeare (only a few used)
two hump props.

Bow Tie type. Same as the Floppy Prop above but has tube
and bearing. Location of the
tube and bearing is found
reversed also.

Winchester style tail propeller
spinner.

Types of Hook Hangers

Screw hook

*Screw eye
(recessed*

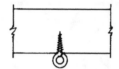

*Screw eye
(found with and without washer)*

*L-Rig
(variation)*

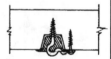

*L-Rig
(Heddon style,
most common)*

Types of Hook Hangers

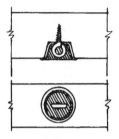

Cup
(Metal up and screw eye)

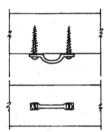

Bar
(one-piece bar)

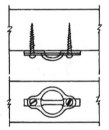

2-Pc surface or toilet seat (First style of heddon two-piece

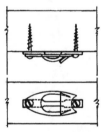

2-Pc surface or flap rig (*Second style of Heddon 2-Pc.)

Types of Hook Hangers

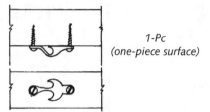

1-Pc
(one-piece surface)

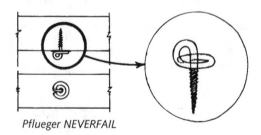

Pflueger NEVERFAIL

**Pflueger used a slightly different type of this
2-PC hanger.*

Styles of Hook-hanger and Line-tie Hardware

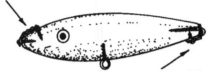

Inch Worm Line Tie

Two-Piece Tail Hook Hanger

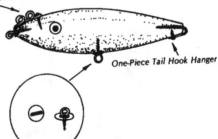

Pig Tail Line Tie

One-Piece Tail Hook Hanger

Detail of the Screw Eye and Washer style hook hanger

Styles of Hook-hanger and Line-tie Hardware

Heddon's patented Dummy Double detachable double hook

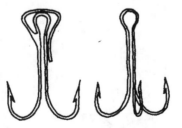

F. C. Woods patented detachable double and treble hooks

Styles of Hook-hanger and Line-tie Hardware

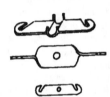

Three styles of plate hardware used in See-thru Plate Hook Hangers

Gem Clip style hook hanger. Usually utilized with a see-thru type.

The Creek Chub convertible metal lip, three choices and two line tie options

Hints for Buying, Selling, Trading

1. Arm yourself with knowledge. Get and study every piece of printed information you can get your paws on.
2. Cooperation builds better collections, good friends, and sources. Ask for help from knowledgeable collectors and, after you get established, give an edge to those who helped you in the beginning.
3. If you find you have a treasure, don't be greedy, be fair. If you don't deal fairly you may find many of your sources drying up.
4. If you find you have made a bad deal, don't worry over it ælearn from it. Turn lemons into lemonade by knowing better next time.
5. Always make an offer. Nothing ventured, nothing gained. Remember one man's trash is another man's treasure.
6. Honest mistakes are made. If you have built up a good rapport with and a good reputation among your collector friends, most mistakes can be rectified. Keep in mind, however, that it is not possible to make all your deals mutually fair, only mutually acceptable. Don't squawk if you find later the deal wasn't so good. You can't win them all.

One note about the way the values are presented in this book. They are presented as "Collector Value Range." In many cases the range is quite wide. All the value ranges in this book are for lures in very good to mint condition. Any in less than very good condition will fall out the lower side range.

Condition Grading

   The National Fishing Lure Collectors Club (NFLCC) has established a code of ethics for members. Part of that code is the NFLCC Standard Lure Grading System. The code states, in part, that the system "... should be used on all sale and bid lists and verbal discussions of tackle grading. Bid or sale lists should include a minimum of five-day return privilege." It is a 1 to 10 grading system. If the numerical scale condition needs further clarification, it states that a 1/2 can be added. Also, a (+) or (-) can be added to a regular description. For example, "AVG+" means better than "Average" but not quite up to "Good."

Numerical Scale of Condition	Description/condition	
10	NEW-IN-BOX (NIB)	Used with original box or carton.
9	MINT (M)	Unused without box or carton.
8	EXCELLENT (EXC)	Very little age or no age cracks; very minor defects.
7	VERY GOOD (VG)	Little age cracks; some minor defects.
5-6	GOOD (G)	Some age cracks; starting to chip, small defects.
3-4	AVERAGE (AVG)	Some paint loss and/or chipping; showing age.
2	FAIR (F)	Major paint loss and/or defects; much chipping.
1	POOR (P)	Parts missing, poor color and/or major chipping.
0	REPAINT (R)	Original paint covered over in part or all.

James Heddon and Sons

Dowagiac, Michigan
Will T. Heddon, 1870-1955
James Heddon, 1845-1911
Charles Heddon, 1874-1941

The Heddon Company began humbly and became one of the giants of the tackle industry in its 80-plus years. James Heddon started the company in about 1897. Its lures are among those most prized by collectors.

The following pages list the old Heddon lures by ascending catalog series and date where possible. There were three notable early lures: the Heddon hand-carved frog, the model of the original Dowagiac bait, and the model of the first Heddon wooden bait.

James Heddon's Wooden Frog c. 1898

Body length: approximately 3"

James Heddon carved this plug for himself and a few others for friends, therefore it is extremely rare and valuable. **$18,000-$25,000**

Wooden Frog.

The Dowagiac Underwater c. 1903

Body length: 2 3/8"

Several early versions evolved into the No. 100. The earliest version has marine brass hardware, no eyes, nose-mounted pro-peller, and tiny round-blade tail spinner. It has no name or trade markings. The earliest version has a lead weight swung from beneath the belly. Later versions have the weight inside the body. The hook hangers have cup hardware. **$1,500-$2,500**

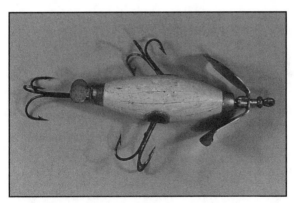

1903 Dowagiac Underwater.

Dowagiac "Expert" Surface Lure and The 200 Series c. 1902

Body length: 4 1/2"

First called the "Dowagiac Perfect Surface Casting Bait," the Expert had evolved into the 200 Series by 1912. The 1902 patent describes four features: the metal angling collar, the hook socket, the screw hook or open-eye screw, and the sloped-up nose. The 1902 version is valued at **$5,000**. Later versions of the 200 Series range from **$75-$850**.

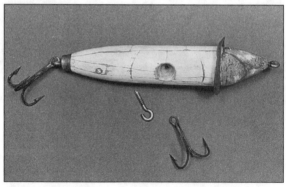

1902 vintage "Expert."

Series No. 1001 RH

These woodpecker-type lures are Heddon products. Information about them is elusive. **$200-$600**

Night-Radiant Moonlight Bait c. 1908-11

Body length: 5"

This plug sports glass eyes, two opposite trebles on the bulbous head, a belly treble, and trailing treble. There is also a 4" version with only three treble hooks. **$2,000-$3,000**

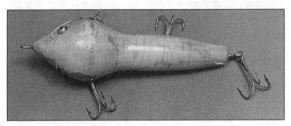

Night-Radiant Moonlight Bait.

Dowagiac Minnow Series "0" and "00"

Pictured in the 1912 Heddon catalog, they were produced with cup and screw hook hardware. The "0" is about 3 3/4" with three trebles and two propellers. The "00" is almost 4" and has five trebles. Colors: white body, red and green; yellow body, red, green, and black; red body, black. **$250-$450**

Dowagiac Minnow No. 100 Series and No. 150 Series

The No. 100 was first found in the 1905 catalog. The 100s and 150s are probably the first shaped-body minnows Heddon produced commercially. The 100s are normally equipped with two opposite-mount side trebles and a trailing treble, while the 150s have five trebles (two on each side). The 100s lasted until about 1942-43, but the 150s continued in production as late as 1953.

The No. 150 has a light green fancy back finish, unmarked nickel props, rear screw eye, screw hangers, and cups of brass. The glass eyes have yellow irises. There are three hand-painted gill marks and three internal belly weights.

No. 150: 3 3/8", 9/10 oz., or 3 3/4", 3/4 oz., aluminum color, solid red, yellow, gold color, fancy sienna yellow, red body, dark blended back, yellow perch; yellow perch, scale finish; frog colors; frog scale finish; green scale finish; red scale finish; goldfish, scale finish; copper, white. **$200-$900**

No. 100, left, later No. 100, right.

The Jeanette Hawley Mohawk

Heddon marketed the Mohawk and the Mohawk Cracker around 1904-05 under Laura Heddon's pen name, Jeanette Hawley. Mohawk: 3 3/5", 7/10 oz., fancy green back; Mohawk Cracker: 2 3/4", 2/3 oz., white body, red eyes, aluminum, red, yellow. **$15,000-$17,500**

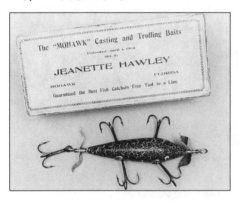

Jeanette Hawley Mohawk

Dowagiac Minnow No. 175 Series

This lure, first found cataloged in 1909, is essentially the same as the No. 150 Series except that it is a 3T model having only two opposite-mounted side trebles. It has the same specifications as the 150s and was available in fancy green back with white belly, rainbow, and blended white (gray back). Earliest models are 3 3/4" long. **$200-$400**

Heddon "Dowagiac" Minnow No. 10 Series

New in the 1912 catalog, this little beauty was 2 3/8" long. It has one single-feathered trailing hook and "... the new Heddon Hexagon form ..." This entry said it was available in a yellow body with red and brown spots, and white body with red and green spots. **$300-$450**

"Dowagiac" Minnow No. 10.

Dowagiac Minnow No. 20 Series

This tiny (1 3/4", 1/2 oz.) plug first appeared in a 1909 Heddon catalog and promptly disappeared, not to turn up in catalogs again until 1922. It is the same size and weight as the Artistic Minnow and has a nose mounted propeller spinner. The No. 20 has three treble hooks, one trailing and one on each side. Colors: fancy back sienna, yellow finish, fancy green back, white, red, gold and silver white in 1909. **$175-$400**

Baby Dowagiac No. 20 Series

The lure was found in a 1952 catalog that featured it as "NEW." The lure is made of wood and is 2 1/2" long, has tacked-on plastic eyes, one-piece surface style hook hangers, and three no. 6 treble hooks. The seven colors or finishes listed are: rainbow; shiner scale; red head, flitter; spotted orange; yellow perch scale; green crackle back; white with red eyes and tail. **$75-$120**

Laguna Runt No. 10 Series

The 1939 catalog states that this is the "same body as the River Runt but without collar" (diving lip). It was made in two models, a sinker and a floater. The colors are exactly the same as the River Runt colors. It was still around in a 2 5/8" wood body, sinking version in 1949. Earliest models: **$85-$175**

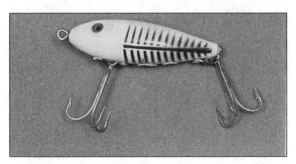

Laguna Runt

Sea Runt Series No. 610

This is essentially the same lure as the Laguna Runt except for the line tie. On the Sea Runt the line tie is placed on top of the nose instead of at the point of the nose. Size: 2 5/8". Colors: white with red head, yellow with red head and white body with red and green spots. **$60-$120**

Walton Feather Tail No. 40 Series

This smaller plug was first found in a 1924 catalog and last found in a 1926 catalog. It has a tail-mounted single hook covered with feathers and a nose-mounted propeller spinner. It has glass eyes, and came in red and white; black body, orange tail; shiner scale, gray tail; and pike scale with green and yellow tail. **$85-$175**

Walton Feather Tail.

Artistic Minnow No. 50 Series

This 1 3/4" lure first appears around 1905 and seems to have been removed from the Heddon line by 1910. It was available in a fancy back sienna-yellow finish and a gold finish. At some point, a gold body with greenish-cast back was added. All metal hardware except the hook is gold plated. The trailing treble is tied with fancy feathers or buck tail and it has glass eyes. Collectors should be aware of the almost identical features of the Artistic Minnow and the Pflueger Simplex. **$150-$300**

Wilder-Dilg

No. 30 Series (Cork)
No. 910 & No. 930 Series (Plastic)

Introduced in the 1923 catalog, this cork-bodied, feathered lure was named after B.F. Wilder and William H. Dilg. In 1939, Heddon changed the body composition from cork to plastic and renamed it the Wilder-Dilg Spook. It was dropped from the line in 1953. It was made in a bass size at 3 1/4" overall and a trout size at 2" overall. The bass size was available in six patterns and the trout size in 12. **$25-$40**

Wilder - Dilg

Drewco Series No. 70

This is a c. 1934 Heddon plastic saltwater lure. It measures 2 1/2" and the colors are white with red and green spots, and white with a red head. **$85-$175**

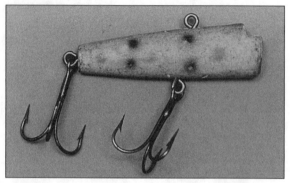

Drewco.

Heddon-Stanley Weedless Pork-Rind Lure Series No. 70

This lure is made of Bakelite and was new about 1923 (changed to Pyraline in 1925). It has glass eyes and is available with or without the wire weed guard and surface attachment. Size: 1 1/8", 5/8 oz. Colors: solid white; white body, red top; solid red; green scale; pike scale; shiner scale. **$25-$50**

Fuzzi-Bug Series No. 74 & No. 75

These flies look like a moth on the water, with beady eyes and fuzzy bodies. Colors: brown body, wings, and hackle; white body and wings, red hackle; gray body, wings, and hackle; solid yellow; dark green body and wings, black hackle; red body and wings, yellow hackle. **$45-$75**

Tiny Tease Series No. 80

The lure first showed up in catalogs in 1928. Size: 1 7/8", 1/10 oz. Colors: Rainbow, white and red, red dace scale; natural scale; shiner scale; brook trout. **$125-$170**. The brook trout finish can bring up to **$200**.

Tiny Tease

Pop-Eye-Frog Series No. 85

The lure was being made as early as 1937. The fly measures
1 5/8" body length and 3 1/2" overall. The single hook has a weed
guard. Colors: green frog and yellow frog. **$25-$75**

Bubble Bug or Bubbling Bug Series No. 90

Called the Bubble Bug on the box, a 1936 catalog listed it as
the Bubbling Bug. Size: 1 3/4"; Colors: white body, red stripes,
white wings; yellow body, black stripes, yellow wings; gold body,
green stripes, green-black wings. **$150-$250**

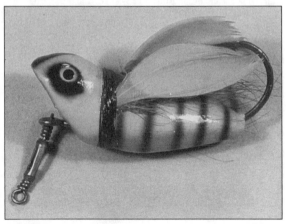

Bubble Bug.

River Runt Series No. 110

New in 1929, the earliest models have the "L-rig" hook hardware. There were subtle body style changes and hook hardware progression over the years. Wood, 2 5/8", 1/2 oz. Colors: Rainbow, white with red head, white with red head and silver specks; solid red, yellow perch scale; red dace scale; silver scale; natural scale; shiner scale; shiner scale with red head; pearl, silver with red head, solid black; silver herring; black with white head, solid white; Allen stripey. **$50-$85**

Re-issue of the wooden River Runt.

River Runt Spook Series No. 9010, Series No. 9110 (Standard), Series No. 9400, Series No. 9430

The Spooks (plastic lures) were introduced in 1932. The plastic line was considerably more versatile with many different models offered such as jointed. The initial colors offered are listed as follows: rainbow, white body with red head, solid red, yellow perch scale, red dace scale, natural scale, shiner scale, green scale, pearl. By 1938 the list had expanded to include: spotted, silver flitter with red head, silver scale, gold fish shore minnow, glow worm, silver shore minnow, black with white head, yellow shore minnow, perch scale, red and white shore minnow, pike scale, black and white shore minnow, red and white water wave, yellow and black water wave, green and black water wave.

The first Spook was a sinking model, but by 1938 Heddon had added a Floating Model, Series No. 9400, and a Jointed River Runt, Series No. 9430. **$20-$30**

River Runt Spook.

Glow Worm River Runt Spook No. 9409GW

This is a luminous River Runt Spook, introduced in the late 1930s. The base color is green. The half moons and dots along the body side are made of glued-on luminous material. **$30-$40**

Salmon River Runt Series No. 8850

This strong, 5 1/2" wooden plug is from the River Runt family. It has a string arrangement in the hook hardware and a different type metal diving lip. **$125-$175**

River Runtie Series No. 750

River Runtie Spook Series No. 950

The 1937 catalog introduced these lures as "Two New Flyrod lures." The Series No. 750 is a 1" wood body lure and the Series No. 950 is transparent plastic. Colors: red and white, perch scale, silver shore minnow, green shore minnow, and red and white shore minnow. River Runtie (wood) **$125-$200**, River Runtie Spook **$20-$30**

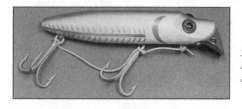

Series No. 950 River Runtie Spook.

Deep Dive River Runt Spook

Go-Deeper River Runt Spook Series DD 9110

Midget Deep Dive and Tiny Deep Dive

Midget Go-Deeper Series DD 9010, Series DD 350

These are "Spook" or plastic deep running River Runts, cataloged 2 1/2", 2 1/4" and 1 3/4" respectively. The belly hook hanger is integrated with the dive lip. Colors: perch, coach dog, red head, green shad, yellow coach dog and black, white shore minnow.

The first Go-Deeper models came out with the second style of the two-piece surface hook hangers. They were offered in a Midget size at 3 1/4" and a Standard size at 3 1/2". Colors: white with red head, shad, pike, green shore minnow, yellow shore minnow, silver shore minnow, red and white shore minnow, black and white shore minnow, natural, rainbow, yellow perch, shiner scale. **$20-$30**

Deep Dive River Runt.

Midget Digit Series No. B-110

The plugs are all wooden with weighted bodies and painted eyes. This is a tiny version of the #110 River Runt and dates to 1941. Size: 1 1/2", 2/5 oz. Colors: white body, spotted; white with red head; black with white head; yellow perch scale; red dace scale; shiner scale; blue pearl; red head with silver flitters; silver scale; black and white shore minnow; yellow shore minnow. **$20-$30**

Torpedo Series No. 120 and No. 130

The 2T model is the normal No. 120, 3" Torpedo. The standard Torpedo No. 130 is larger (4 1/2") and has two belly-mounted treble hooks. All found have L-rig, two-piece, or surface hardware, with the small round-blade floppy Heddon/Stanley propeller spinners. They were offered in catalogs in wood until 1936. Colors: white body, red eyes; yellow perch scale finish; green scale finish; pike scale finish; shiner scale finish; rainbow scale finish; natural scale finish; blue scale finish; rainbow scale, purple back; orange black spots. **$85-$150**

Torpedo Spook

In 1933, when Heddon introduced a plastic "Spook" line it offered the No. 9130 Series Torpedo Spook in a 4 3/4" size and very slim. The wood body Torpedo continued in the line along with the plastic version until plastic had replaced it altogether in 1936. Collector value range: **$15-$30** with the early style hardware.

The Tiny Torpedo is a spinning size at 2 1/8". A 1959 catalog listed the colors available as: Perch, bullfrog, red head with flitter, white with red head, silver shore minnow, yellow shore minnow, red and white shore minnow, and black and white shore minnow. **$15-$30**

Magnum Torpedo.

S.O.S. Wounded Minnow Series No. 140, No. 160 and No. 170

All three sizes have a unique "banana" shape. Lures have a one-piece bar, L-rig, and two-piece hook hangers. The No. 370 is the Musky size. It has the same length as the No. 170 (4 3/4"), but is much heavier. S.O.S. means Swims On Side. All early plugs have glass eyes. They came on the market around 1927-28 and lasted until the 1950s. Sizes: No. 140, 3", 1/2 oz.; No. 160, 3 1/2", 3/5 oz.; No. 170, 4 3/4", 4/5 oz.; No. 370, 4 3/4", 1 1/6 oz. Colors: white with red head, green scale; perch scale; shiner scale; silver scale; dace scale; luminous. **$60-$200**

Heddon-Stanley Pork Rind Lures

Ace - Series No. 190

Queen - Series No. 280

King - Series No. 290

The smallest, the Ace, was the first to be introduced, around 1925. It was available in either nickel or copper finish in four versions: Weedless or Non-Weedless, with or without a fly. By 1927, the other two sizes, the King and Queen, were in the catalogs. Three enamel finishes were added: white and red, pike scale and shiner scale to the back or convex side of the spoon body. There is also a Muskie size, Silver Kill, which is 6 1/2" and in the same finishes. By the 1930s, they had added gold plate to all four and silver flitter to the King and Queen. In 1938, new varieties were called the Devil Ace, Devil King, and Devil Queen, in a beetle design in two colors with contrasting colored buck tails. Colors: yellow and black, white and red, black and yellow, white and black, nickel plate. **$20-$30**

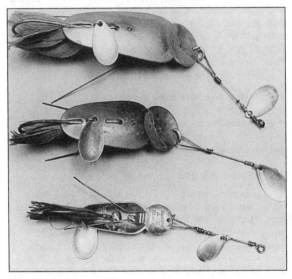

King, top, Queen, middle, Ace.

Wounded Spook Series No. 9140 and Series No. 9160

Introduced in the 1939 catalog, these two lures are 3" and 4 1/4" respectively. The two bear the second style of the Heddon two-piece surface hook hangers and an unmarked floppy propeller spinner at the nose and a slightly different one at the tail. Colors: yellow perch; yellow shore minnow; silver scale; green shore minnow, silver shore minnow; red and white shore minnow. **$15-$20**

Flipper Series No. 140

The Flipper came along about 1927. Size: 3 3/4", 3/4 oz. The lure is missing in listings from 1929 on. The number 140 was then given to the smallest S.O.S. Wounded Minnow, which was added around 1937. All are glass eyed and have L-rig hook hardware. **$125-$200**

The 4 1/4" Flippers have a fatter body, but what makes them unusual is the "Heddon Stanley" marked floppy props. Each has glass eyes and the shallow, big cup and screw eye hook hangers. **$150-$300**

Yowser Spinner Bait Series No. 195

This lure came along about 1935 and only lasted until around 1939. The weight is 4/5 oz. and overall length is 4" without measuring the fancy feather tail. It came in a single-hook version only. Very rare. **$50-$100**

Yowser Spinner Baits

Dowagiac Surface Minnow Series No. 210

This is a short (3 1/2") version of the Series 200 Dowagiac Minnow. It was first available around 1917-20, was gone in 1947-48, and back again in 1949 through 1955. Earliest hook hardware is the L-rig. They are found with no eyes, glass eyes and painted eyes. Colors in 1921: white body with blue head, white body with red head, frog, green scale. In 1936, the colors listed included: luminous with red head; brown mouse with leather ears, whiskers, and tail, and gray mouse with ears, whiskers, and tail.

The No. 210 was reintroduced in a plastic version in 1975. It lasted until the sale of the company in 1977. Colors for the plastic version were: black, blue head, bone, bull frog, coach dog, silver flitter, silver shad, yellow. Wood: **$50-$100**, plastic **$15-$30**

Dowagiac Surface Minnows No. 210

Experimental Pflueger Lure

It looks as if Pflueger was looking into the possibility of competing with Heddon's No. 210 Dowagiac Minnow. The lure never went into production. It has the Neverfail hardware so that dates it contemporary with the Heddon No. 210. **$200-$300**

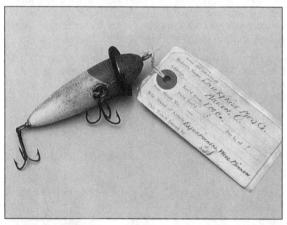

Experimental Lure.

Weedless Widow Series No. 220

The first time this lure was offered was in a 1928 Heddon flyer as the Weedless Wizard (2 1/2", 3 1/4 oz., six colors). It had only a rigid, feathered, single hook on the tail. The 1928 catalog, however, named it the Weedless Widow. In 1930, Heddon made them with a detachable belly double hook addition. Colors: white with red head, bullfrog, green scale, pike scale, shiner scale, and silver scale. There was a Junior offered in 1940 at 2 1/4" in the same colors, and by 1949 this smaller size was the only one available. **$50-$125**

Weedless Widow.

Surface Minny Series No. 260

This scarce lure was in production only a short time. It appeared around 1934 and is absent from the 1936 and subsequent catalogs. It has been found only in the old two-piece hardware. **$200-$300**

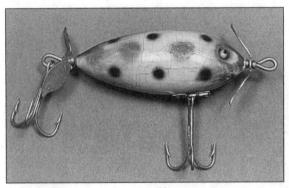

Surface Minny.

Widget Series No. 300

This lure looks like a tiny version of the Tadpolly. It was first found in a 1953 catalog. The line tie is reinforced with a wire connecting it to the hook mount. It is a fly rod lure cataloged at 5/16 oz. and 1 1/4". **$20-$40**

Heddon Surface Minnow Musky Surf Series No. 300

It was called new in a 1905 catalog. The 1905 colors were: rainbow, frog green back, white, aluminum, red, yellow or copper. The early 300s were 4" and had one belly treble with cup hardware and a trailing treble. In 1911, the body had grown a bit fatter and shorter (3 1/2"). It also noted the availability of a 3T model on special order. By 1922, the No. 300 is listed at 3 3/4" and had added two finishes: white body with red and green spots; white body, red eyes. The Musky Surf name appeared in 1927.

The No. 300 Series was around for about 30 years and can be found with a classic progression of Heddon hook hardware from the brass cup to the one-piece surface. All had glass eyes. A 1937 catalog renamed it the Musky Surfusser. It was gone after 1941. **$200-$600**

Musky Surf No. 300.

Hi-Tail Series No. 305

This 1960s plastic lure measures 2" in length. Colors: frog, silver flitter, black, yellow, perch, white with red head. **$20-$30**

Deep 6 Series No. 345 and Series No. 9345

The series numbers have only to do with size. They are 1 3/4" and 2 1/4", respectively. These plastic lures first appeared in the 1965 catalog. They are floating divers. Colors: black, perch, yellow, red head with flitter, spotted orange, natural crab, green shad, coach dog. **$4-$10**

Musky Surface

Musky Surfusser Series No. 350

Apparently this was a short-lived lure in the Heddon line. It is cataloged from 1933 through 1936, but is absent from then on. The upper plug has unmarked big propellers, the same as found on early No. 700s. Colors: spotted, white with red head, green scale, and shiner scale. **$300-$700**

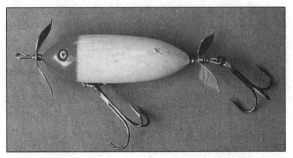

No. 350 Musky Surfusser. Photo courtesy Dennis "Doc" Hyder

Ice Decoy

The earliest catalog entry that could be found for a Heddon Ice Decoy was in 1913. It has a small screw eye line tie, large metal side fins and two additional metal fins (dorsal and ventral) and a natural (wooden) tail. It was listed as 5 1/8" and available in fancy green back with white belly, or yellow perch finish. By 1916, the lure was listed as 4 3/8". By 1923, they had added six more finishes: rainbow, white body with red eyes, green scale, perch scale, shiner scale, and natural scale. They had disappeared from the catalogs by 1928. All have glass eyes and fins are marked Heddon. Bat Wing Model - **$700-$1,200**; Regular Model - **$500-$800**; Ice Spook - **$300-$600**

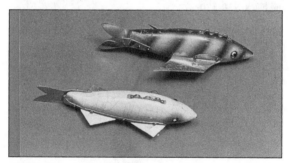

Bat Wing, top, and Regular Model.

Musky Surface Spook Series No. 9170

This 5 1/2", 1 1/2 oz. lure was in the 1934 catalog, and has two large spinners and three sets of treble hooks. Colors: white and red; white with red and black spots; natural pike; shiner scale. **$50-$150**

Fidget

Fidget Feather

Fidget Flasher Series No. 400

These Heddon spinning lures have jointed bodies with metal head plates inscribed Heddon. Colors: red head with white body and black. **$10-$20**

Spinfin Series No. 411, No. 412, and No. 413

The series numbers have only to do with the three sizes of the Spinfin. They were made in 2 1/4", 2 1/2", and 2 5/8" sizes. They may have been made before the early 1950s, but they didn't appear in the catalogs. Colors: Red head, white body; silver flitter; white head, black body; perch scale. **$5-$15**

Gamby Spinners Series No. 421 and Series No. 423

The series numbers have only to do with sizes 2 3/4" and 3 3/4". They were found in a 1957 catalog and nowhere else. Colors: silver, gold, or copper. **$5-$15**

Whis-Purr Series No. 420 and Series No. 425

Listed as "new" in the 1961 catalog, this metal spinning lure was available in two sizes, 3" and 3 1/2", Series #420 and Series #425. Colors: silver with white head and buck tail; gold with yellow head and buck tail. **$5-$15**

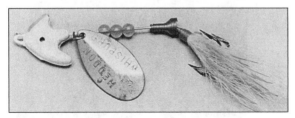

Whis-Purr.

Sonar Series No. 431, Series No. 433, Series No. 435

The 1959 catalog features this lure. The series numbers have only to do with the size. The lures are made of metal and the sizes are 1 7/8", 2 3/8", and 3 1/4". The three holes along the back are line ties. Each hole would take the lure to a different depth on retrieve. Colors: silver finish; yellow; red and white; black; gold finish; perch; gray shad; hot orange. Hot orange and black were not available on the larger Series No. 435. **$5-$15**

Killer Series No. 400

A caption in the 1905 Heddon catalog said the Killer No. 400 resembles the No. 100 Minnow "... excepting that it has but one propeller, is round instead of minnow shaped in body, and is without eyes or other decorations." In 1909, it was called the Dowagiac Minnow, No. 402. Colors: fancy back, rainbow, white. A bucktail and glass eyes were added. **$300-$500**

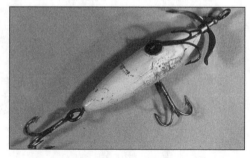

Killer No. 400.

Killer Series No. 450

This is a 1905-vintage lure that is exactly the same as the No. 400 except that it has an additional propeller at the tail. The more belly weights (up to three), the older the lure. Sizes: 2 5/8" and 3". Colors: white, red, yellow, copper, aluminum, white body with red head and tail. **$300-$500**

Multiple Metal Minnow Series No. 500

This lure first shows up in the early 1900s; some say as early as 1909. It didn't last long. It is similar to the No. 500 and No. 600 Series Salt Water Specials. Size: 2 1/2" long and nickel plated; also in a gold finish and a larger, musky version at about 4 3/4". They may also be found with glass eyes. **$300-$600**

Saltwater Special Series No. 500, No. 600, and No. 850

They first appear around 1924 as No. 600 in four sizes and five color designs. By 1925 another series number (No. 500) appeared and the only sizes were No. 500: 1/2 oz., 2"; No. 600 Series: 2 1/2", 3 1/2", 4 1/2" and 5". In 1926, another style was added, the No. 850 Series and No. 800 Series. In 1932, a "plastic" plug identical to the No. 800 Series was introduced as the No. 9600 "Salt Spook." All were gone from catalogs by 1949. Colors: white body with red head; white body, gold speckled, red head; white body, silver speckled, red head; yellow perch scale; white body, red eyes; white body, gold speckled; white body, silver speckled; solid black; shiner scale; aluminum color body, bronze back. **$100-$125**

A variation is the 3 1/2" Florida Special No.10 B. There was also a smaller version, the No.10 S at 2 3/4". These were found only in a 1922 Heddon catalog. **$100-$300**

Wee Willie Series Number Unknown

Called Wee Willie by some collectors, this lure is placed here because of its similarity to the Saltwater Specials. The red head, white body plug is 3 1/2" long and has "HEDDON" stenciled on the belly. The other measures 2 1/8". Each has three internal belly weights and cup/screw hook hardware. **$75-$150**

Wee Willie

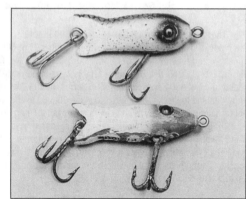

Sea Runt Series No. 610

This lure was introduced as "new" in a 1937 catalog. It is somewhat similar to the #110 River Runt, but has no diving lip and the line tie is located at the top of the nose. Size: 2 5/8", 2/3 oz. Colors: spotted; white with red head; white with silver flitter and red head; silver scale; yellow with red head. **$100-$150**

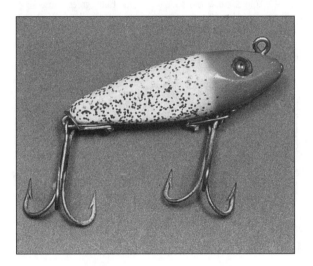

Sea Runt Series No. 610.

Coast Minnow No. 1, No. 2, No. 3, No. 4

Appearing around 1913, the Coast Minnow was available in four sizes. The lure has a flat metal line tie and hook hanger, and rear-mounted propeller spinner. Later models had line tie/tail hook hangers of the twisted through-body wire type. Sizes: No. 1, 4"- 4 1/2", 1 3/4", 2 1/2 oz.; No. 2, 3"-3 1/2", 1 oz.; No. 3, 2 1/2"-2 3/4", 1/2 oz.; No. 4, 5", 2 1/2 oz. Colors: Fancy green back, white body, red and green spots; rainbow, green scale; dark green back, gold speckles. **$600-$900**

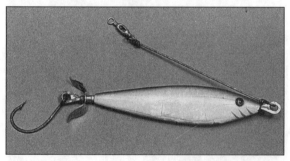

Coast Minnows.

Dowagiac "Muskollonge" Minnow Series No. 700

The 1910 catalog used this spelling for this musky lure, which was made in three treble hook and 5T versions. The 5T was the first to be offered (1909) and is the rarest. The 3T model was introduced in the 1911 catalog and continued to be available until 1928. It has three to four internal belly weights, glass eyes, cup and screw eye hardware and no name on props. Sizes: 4 3/4" and 5 1/2". Colors: fancy back, white belly; fancy green back, white belly, rainbow, fancy sienna back, yellow belly, red sides; yellow perch, white body, red eyes. **$1,500-$2,500**

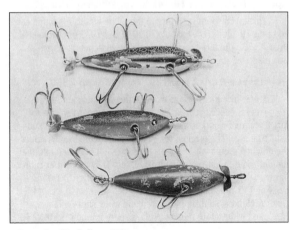

Dowagiac "Muskollonge" Minnows.

Heddon Underwater Minnow No. "747"

VL&A No. 7000

This is a huge 8", 9-oz. version of the Series No. 700. It was never cataloged by Heddon, or sold by them to the public as far as can be determined. It was apparently specially made for the Von Lengerke & Antoine company (VL&A). It appeared in the VL&A catalogs in 1915 and 1916 as available in two finishes: fancy green back and rainbow (green back with red sides blending to white belly). **$2,000-$3,000**

Spoony-Fish Series No. 490, No. 590, No. 790

This metal spoon-type lure in the shape of a fish is found listed in the Heddon trade catalogs of 1930 and 1931 only. It measures 2 3/4". The three series numbers listed denote the sizes it was made in: 2 5/8", 4 1/4", and 5 3/4". **$150-$300**

Punkinseed Series No. 730, 740, 380, and 980

A new lure in 1940 was made in floating and sinking models. It was a real departure from the traditional standard shapes for lures. Made of wood, it was a remarkably realistic looking "sunfish" type lure. The original version has the line tie located under the notched mouth while a short time later it was moved into the mouth. Later, the lure was made in plastic. They can sell extraordinarily high in rare finishes. Sizes: No. 730 (sinking), 2 1/4", 2/3 oz.; No. 740 (floating), 2 1/2", 3/5 oz. Colors: bluegill, crappie, shad, rock bass, sunfish, perch, red and white shore minnow, black and white shore minnow, yellow shore minnow. **$50-$250**

Tiny Punkinseed Series No. 380

The fly rod size was made in plastic in 1947 through 1957. Available colors were shad, bluegill, sunfish, or a crappie finish in the 1947 catalog. The colors had expanded to also include red and white shore minnow and rock bass by 1957. **$50-$200**

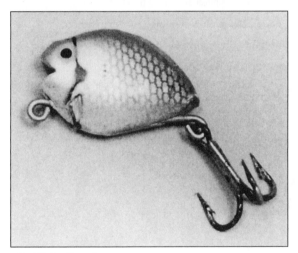

No. 380 Punkinseed.

Punkinseed Spook Series No. 9630

The Punkinseed Spook was featured as new in the 1950 Heddon catalog, with 2 1/8" as the only size listed. The 1 3/4" size showed up in a 1956 catalog. Colors (plastic): shad, crappie, red and white shore minnow, black and white shore minnow, yellow shore minnow, sunfish, bluegill. **$30-$75**

Heddon Swimming Minnow

Dowagiac Swimming Minnow

No. 800 and No. 900

The 800s are sinkers and the 900s are floating divers, first found cataloged in a 1910 edition. The No. 800 is 3 1/4" with a trailing treble only. The No. 900 is 4 1/2" and has a trailing treble and a belly double with a locking pin. Colors: white body, green and red spots; yellow body, green and red spots. No. 800, **$600-$900**; No. 900, **$600-$900**

Triple Teaser Series No. 1000

This unusual lure was first found listed in the 1929 catalog and last seen in the 1933 issue. It was made with either white, red, red and white, or natural buck tail and red or yellow feathered single hook. Each of the little minnow blades have "Heddon Triple Teaser" stamped on them. **$30-$50**

Triple Teaser

Black Sucker Minnow Series No. 1300

This lure was first listed in a 1913 catalog. It was described as 5 3/4", 2 1/2 oz. It has a very dark, almost black back blending down the sides into a light tint of red, ending in white down to the belly. They have been found in rainbow finish and natural scale finish. They are found with cup and two types of L-rig hook hardware, belly treble, side trebles. All found so far have glass eyes. **$2,000-$3,000**

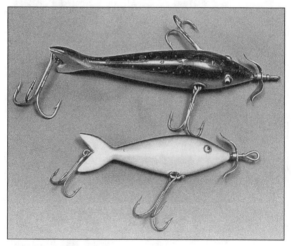

Black Sucker Minnows.

Heddon Dowagiac Minnow Series No. 1400

First found in a 1913 Heddon catalog, it was never listed again. Colors available were white body with red, green, and black spots and yellow body with red, green, and black spots. Body length is 3". There are only six known to exist in collectors' hands. One of them was sold at Lang's 1998 auction for **$9,900**. **$4,000-$6,000**

Dummy Double Series No. 1500

Ballyhooed as new in a 1913 catalog entry, this rare 3 1/4" plug cannot be found listed in catalogs any later than 1916. It uses the hexagonal body of the Series No. 0 Dowagiac Minnow. The lure was first made with the "Football" style side hook hangers, but the 1914 catalog illustrates the lure with an L-rig hanger. "Dummy Double" hooks are one on either side and one trailing. Colors available in 1913: red, white, green spotted. Colors in 1914: 1500, white body, red and green spots; 1501, yellow body, red and green spots; 1502, blended white body, red eyes; 1503, fancy green back, white belly; 1504, blended red; 1505, rainbow; 1509, frog. 1915 Colors: 1500, fancy back; 1501, rainbow; 1502, blended white body, red eyes; 1504, blended red; 1505, yellow body, red and green spots; 1509A, yellow perch; 1509B, spotted frog. **$750-$1,500**

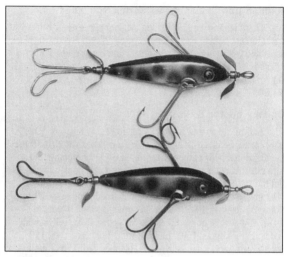

Dummy Double.

Stanley Perfection Weedless Hooks

These are weedless hooks made in several variations and sizes. Variations include a No. 2 with spinner, a No. 2 with buck tail, rigged variously with or without weights on the hook shanks, pork rind attachments, spoons and even one that is meant to be fitted with a live frog. The essential element of each of them is the unique hinged wire weedless hook guard. **$10-$20**

Deep Diving Wiggler Series No. 1600

This lure and the following No.1700 Series were the first Heddon production lures to utilize the L-rig hook hanger patented by Heddon in 1918. Both also sport the 1914-patent inch worm line tie. There are two different 3T configurations, one with two belly trebles and a trailing treble and the other with two opposite-side mounted trebles and a trailing treble. Each has two triangular fins, one mounted horizontally on each side of the head. Each has triple line ties, but they are found with slightly different designs. Most have the L-rig hook hangers, but there is a rare early one with the cup and screw hook hardware. None had eyes. Size: 4 1/2", 3/4 oz. Colors: fancy green back with white belly; white body with red and green spots; white body with red head; yellow body with red and green spots; yellow perch; frog finish; rainbow; shiner scale. **$100-$200**

No. 1600 Wigglers. Photo courtesy Dennis "Doc" Hyder

Near Surface Wiggler Series No. 1700

This lure was first introduced in 1915 and lasted until about 1926. All found so far have had glass eyes. The multiple line tie changed several times over the years. Variations included a double pigtail type line tie fastened at the nose with a screw eye, cup and L-rig hardware, inch worm line tie and L-rig hardware. All of these have reinforcing tail cup hardware although it has been reported that the latest did not have this feature. All have the metal under-nose plate with two side protruding fins. Colors available were the same as listed with the No. 1600 Series Deep Diving Wiggler. Size: 4 1/2", 7/8 oz. **$150-$275** Rare finishes can bring much more. A perfect one in frog scale finish sold for **$1,980** at a Lang auction in 1998.

Midget Crab Wiggler (2 1/2") Series No. 1950

These are smaller versions of the No. 1800 Crab Wiggler. They were introduced in 1915 and 1921 respectively. The earliest had 'U' collars and variable line ties. The last U-collar on this lure (before transition to the later O-collar) can be identified by noting that the script stamped on the collar is larger than on the earlier ones. Later plugs also have a single line tie secured to the body by using the same screw used to hold the center flange of the collar on. The colors are the same as the No. 1800 Crab Wiggler. **$75-$125**

Crab Wiggler Series No. 1800

This reverse-running plug was first introduced in 1915. The earliest models had the variable line tie and 'U' shaped collar. Then came 'O' collars. Sizes: 4 1/2", 9/10 oz.; 3 1/2, 1 oz.; 3 3/4", 7/8 oz.; 4", 7/8 oz. Colors: fancy green back; white body, red and green spots; rainbow; white body with red head; yellow body, green back, red and green spots; yellow perch; imitation frog; imitation crab; green scale finish; red scale finish; goldfish, scale; yellow perch scale finish. **$75-$175**

Crab Wigglers

Deep-O-Diver Series No. 7000

This is an unusual version of the Midget Crab Wiggler. It has the same body with a unique line tie and a different style O-collar metal diving lip that is pointed. It sports only one double hook. New around 1919, it was first made with a pin type pork rind attachment on the body. By 1921, this was integrated into the double hook. This later version came with an imitation pork rind attachment. Size: 2 1/2", 2/3 oz. Colors: white body, red head, white body, greenish black spots; yellow body, black head, green scale finish; red, scale finish; frog, scale finish; goldfish, scale finish; yellow perch, scale finish. **$75-$125**

Deep-O-Divers.

Wiggle King Series No. 2000

The Wiggle King is similar to both the Lucky-13 and the Basser. It probably represents the first stage in the development of both. It came along in 1918. The 3 7/8" Wiggle King has no upper overhang at the top of the carved out head. Colors: white body with red head; white body with spots; rainbow; frog; green scale. **$150-$350**

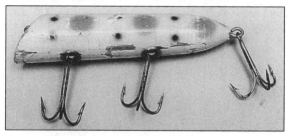

Wiggle King.

Crazy Crawler Series No. 2100

This surface lure first appeared in the Heddon catalog in 1940. It has a startling similarity to the James Donaly "Wow" lure, for which Heddon bought the patent. Sizes: No. 2100, 2 3/4", 3/4 oz., **$50-$90**; No. 2120, 2 1/2", 3/5 oz., **$50-$90**; No. 2150, 3 1/2", 1 oz., **$90-$150** Colors: silver shore minnow, gray mouse, glow worm (luminous lines on belly), bullfrog, red and white shore minnow, yellow with red head, black shore minnow, yellow shore minnow, black with white head, white with red head, luminous white with red wings, chipmunk. (The Glow Worm finish can as much as triple the collector value.)

Crazy Crawler Spook Series No. 9120

The plastic "Spook" version of the classic Crazy Crawler was introduced in the 1957 catalog. It is 2 3/8" and weighs 5/8 oz. A listing and illustration for a 1 3/4" Tiny Crazy Crawler, No. 320 was first found in the 1962 catalog along with the larger one. Colors: bullfrog, yellow with red head, gray mouse, silver shore minnow, black with white head, red and white shore minnow. **$10-$20**

Crazy Crawler Spook.

Sam-Spoon Series No. 2160

This lure was new about 1936 and was in the line regularly into the 1940s. It was available in either a single hook or a treble hook model. Length is 6 1/2" and it was available in Allen stripey, shiner scale, red and white, or plain nickel-plated. **$50-$80**

Lucky-13 Series No. 2400 and No. 2500

The Lucky-13 was preceded by the Wiggle King. They are quite similar, but the Lucky-13 always has a bit of an overhang at the top of the scooped-out nose. The Lucky-13s appeared about 1920 in two sizes, the regular at 3 7/8" and the Junior Lucky-13 at 3". The oldest examples sport cup hardware and follow the classic hardware changes over the years. Colors: white body, red head, green scale finish, red scale finish, frog scale finish, goldfish scale finish, yellow perch scale finish, white body with red and green spots, pike scale, shiner scale, mullet scale, orange with black spots blue scale finish, rainbow, frog scale with red head, shiner scale with red head, silver flitter with red head, natural scale. **$30-$150**

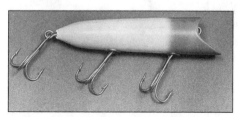

Lucky-13.

Plastic Lucky-13

Heddon began making the Lucky-13 in plastic sometime in the 1950s. Sizes: Lucky-13, 3 3/4", **$5-$10**; Baby Lucky-13, 2 5/8", **$3-$5**; Tiny Lucky-13, 1 7/8", **$3-$10**

Spin-Diver Series No. 3000

New around 1918, this lure disappeared from catalogs after 1926. It has been found with no prop and unmarked lip. A handsome 3T glass-eyed, 4 3/8", nose-spinnered plug, it has been found only in L-rig hardware. Colors: green, red, frog, gold scale, yellow scale finish, fancy green back, white body with red and green spots, rainbow, yellow perch, white body with red spot on tail fin and enamel eyes. **$700-$1,500**. Rare finishes can bring incredible prices. A Spin-Diver in green fancy back finish (crackle-back) brought **$1,650** at a Lang auction in 1998.

Spin-Divers.

Spoony Frog Series No. 3200

New in 1928 and gone from production two years later, this all-metal lure was offered in four color designs: gold-plated, silver-plated, red and white striped, and green frog. They ran belly-up on retrieve. Size: 3", 4/5 oz. **$45-$75**

Little Luny Frog Series No. 3400

One year after Heddon introduced the No. 3500 Luny Frog, it made this lighter, smaller version available. It is also made of Pyralin and subject to the same brittleness. It was available in the same colors as the larger one below. **$75-$125**

Luny Frog Series No. 3500

This interesting bait was introduced in the 1927 catalog and by 1932 it was no longer listed as available. The lure was made of Pyralin and is known to be very brittle. It would shatter into several pieces if cast against rocks or other hard surfaces. They were available with double or treble belly hooks. Size: 4 1/2"; 7/8 oz. Colors: green frog, meadow frog, white body with red head (rare).

$50-$150

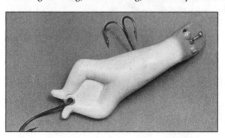

Luny Frog.

Meadow Mouse Series No. 4000

A 1929 catalog states that this was a new plug for that year. The lures are found with and without the name on the River Runt-type diving lip. They are found with almost any combination of hook types, but the first catalog illustration shows a belly double and a trailing single hook option. All have black bead eyes. Size: 2 3/4", 2/3 oz. Colors: brown mouse, gray mouse with white belly, white and red, black body with white head, fur finish brown mouse, fur finish gray mouse, fur finish white mouse. **$50-$100**

Meadow Mouse.

Tad Polly Series No. 5000 and No. 6000

The smaller version (Series No. 5000) was the first to be introduced in 1919 and Series No. 6000 came along in 1920-21 and only lasted for seven or eight years, disappearing after 1929. Series No. 5000 was continuously in production until about 1941.

There are at least two slightly differing body styles to be found; one is a bit fatter than the other. A more significant difference is the metal plate shape and the position of the identifying marks on the plate. The oldest is the "heart shape" or apple-like shape, then came the "bell-shape." The words "Heddon Dowagiac" are arranged in an inverted "V" shape on the bell plate and next, the words are in the upright "V" position, then later rearranged to a curve following the rounded edge of the plate. No. 5000, 3 7/8", 5/8 oz., **$40-$90**; No. 5100 (Runt), 3", 1/2 oz., **$200-$300**; No. 6000, 4 5/8", 3/4 oz., **$40-$90**. Colors: fancy green back, white body with red and green spots, rainbow, white body with red head and tail, yellow perch, frog coloration, green scale finish, red scale finish, frog scale finish, goldfish scale finish, yellow perch scale finish, shiner scale.

Tad Polly lure.

Tad Polly Spook Series No. 9000

Tiny Tad Series No. 390

The 3" plastic Tad Polly Spook floater/diver was new in 1952. Colors: bullfrog, yellow perch scale, golden shiner, silver shore minnow, spotted orange, yellow shore minnow, white with red head, yellow body with red head, red head with flitter, black and white shore minnow, light green scale, silver body, red and black spots. **$10-$20**

The 2 1/8" plastic Tiny Tad spinning lure came along a year later. It was a sinker. Colors: Bullfrog, red head with flitter, golden shiner, yellow perch scale, spotted orange, yellow shore minnow, white with red head, black and white shore minnow. **$5-$15**

Game Fisher Series No. 5500

Baby Game Fisher Series No. 5400

The No. 5500 Game Fisher came out in 1923 and had disappeared from catalogs from 1934 on. The smaller No. 5400 came along about a year later. The Baby Game Fisher was only a two-segment jointed plug. Both were missing from the 1934 and subsequent catalogs. The patent text actually specifies glass eyes, but glass-eyed Game Fishers are seldom found and are considered very rare. Wooden Model, **$20-$40**; Glass-eyed model, no trade data found; German Plastic, no trade data found.

Zaragossa Minnow Series No. 6500

Originating around 1922, the earliest found so far have the L-rig hardware. They continued in production into the 1950s.

Heddon released a series of Centennial Reproductions of some of its classic lures, including the Zaragossa. They are glass eyed and were very nice, but don't be fooled if one is represented as the old lure. The new ones with glass eyes also have the one-piece surface hardware. Size: 4 1/4", 1/2-3/4 oz. Colors: white body, red throat, natural scale finish; red scale finish; frog scale, red eyes; frog, scale finish; goldfish, scale; yellow perch, scale finish; green cracked back; rainbow, white, red eyes; green scale; pike scale; shiner scale; shiner scale, red head, white body, silver specks; white body, red and green spots. Originals: **$90-$150**

Re-issue of the wooden Zaragossa Minnow.

Zara-Spook Series No. 9260

Zara-Spook Jr. Series No. 9240

This plastic lure was introduced in two sizes in the 1939 catalog, 4 1/4" and 3". The lures had the second style of the two Heddon two-piece surface hook hangers. The examples with the one-piece surface hardware would be valued considerably less. Colors: bullfrog, green shore minnow, yellow perch, silver shore minnow, yellow shore minnow, red and white shore minnow. **$25-$50**

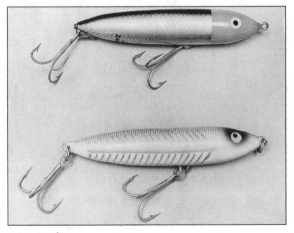

Zara-Spook.

Darting Zara Series No. 6550 and No. 6600

This lure dates back to at least 1928. They were made of wood up until the late 1930s when they became the Zara Spook. No. 6550, 3 3/4", weight unknown; No. 6600, 4 1/2", 5/8 oz. Colors: orange with red spots, bullfrog, green scale, silver scale. **$100-$200**

Darting Zara.

Jointed Darting Zara

A jointed wooden version of the Darting Zara was not found referenced in any Heddon catalogs. A case could be made that it is an altered unjointed Darting Zara except that the paint on the inside of the joint is an exact match to the remaining paint. This is a Heddon production model, be it ever so rare. It measures 4 1/8", has glass eyes, one-piece bar hook hardware, tail spinner, and has "HEDDON" stenciled on the belly. **$150-$250**

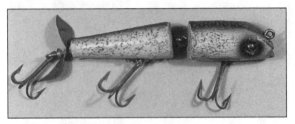

Jointed Darting Zara.

Darting Zara-Spook Series No. 9200 and No. 9210

This plastic version of the Darting Zara was new in 1939. The only size listed was 3 1/4", but the Baby Darting Zara, at 3 1/4", was introduced a year or two later. Colors: bullfrog, silver scale, and silver flitter with red head. Smaller size also has silver shore minnow and yellow shore minnow. **$15-$25**

Flaptail Series No. 7000

Flaptail Jr. Series No. 7110

These two were introduced about 1935. When it was first released it had FLAPTAIL VAMP on its belly. The Flaptail Jr. size is found with both one and two treble hooks. The regular Flaptails have two trebles. No. 7000, 4", 4/5 oz.; No. 7110, 3 1/4", 5/8 oz. Colors: white with red head, frog, green scale, perch scale, pike scale, dace scale, silver scale, gray mouse, brown mouse, chipmunk (fur finish). **$50-$75**

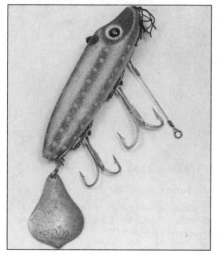

Flaptail.

Flaptail Musky Series No. 7050

New in 1935, this 5 1/4" lure is a heavier, sturdier version of the regular No. 7000 Series Flaptail. It has "Teddy Bear Glass Eyes." Colors: white with red head, copper sheen, natural scale, shiner scale, silver scale, spotted, gray mouse, chipmunk (fur finish). **$75-$150**

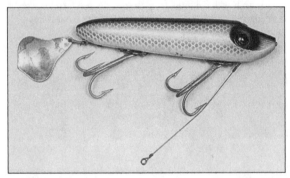

Flaptail Musky.

Flaptail Spook Series No. 7200

Flaptail Spook Jr. Series No. 9700

This is the plastic "Spook" version of the wooden Flaptail. The lures measure 3" and 2 3/4" respectively. They were not found in catalogs after 1953. **$10-$15**

Jointed Vamp Series No. 7300

Swimming Vamp

A 1927 catalog says "... newest member of the Vamp family." The 1928 catalog and those after refer to this lure as "The Swimming Vamp Jointed." The oldest Jointed Vamps can be identified by the single bar type connector at the joint. The newer ones use a two-piece connector. The shorter front section of this jointed lure is considered rare. No. 7300, 4 1/2", 3/4 oz.; 7300 (Classic), 5", 3/4 oz. Colors: rainbow, white body with red head, green scale, perch scale, pike scale, shiner scale, natural scale, rainbow scale, white body with silver specks and red head. **$45-$90**

Jointed Musky Vamp

Giant Jointed Vamp Series No. 7350

This is a jointed version of the No. 7550 Musky Vamp. Prior to 1935, it was called a Jointed Musky Vamp. From 1935 to the 1950s, it is known as the Giant Jointed Vamp. They are all listed as 6" in length, but the lures actually measure longer. Colors are the same as the Musky Vamps. **$75-$135**

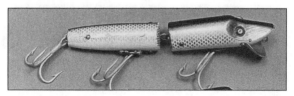

Giant Jointed Vamps.

Baby Vamp Series No.7400

New around 1925, this is essentially the same as the No. 7500 series Vamp, but smaller, at 3 1/2", 1/2 oz. It is occasionally found with the metal lip in the two-piece hook hardware vintage. Colors: white body red and green spots; rainbow; white body with red eyes and tail; green scale; pike scale; shiner scale; mullet scale; orange with black spot; blue scale. **$45-$90**

Vampire/Vamp Series No. 7500

The Vamp was born in 1920 as the Vampire Minnow, first available in 4 1/2", 5/8 oz., and five colors. The very earliest have cup hardware, but the early Vampires are more often found with the "L-rig." Another way to distinguish these early Vampires is by the manner of attaching the diving lip, integrated with the L-rig hook hanger. By 1922, they were all Vamps. The diving lips are marked "Heddon." Colors: white body with red and green spots; rainbow; white body with red eyes and tail; green scale; pike scale; mullet scale; red scale; frog scale; yellow perch scale; orange, black spots; blue scale; silver scale; white with silver specks and red head; luminous with red head and tail; natural scale. **$75-$125**

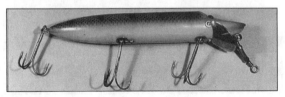

Vampire.

Great Vamp Series No. 7540

Musky Vamp Series No. 7550

Vampire Musky Series No. 7600

The first of these to come along was the 8" model in 1925, with the 6" version shortly thereafter. The large one was gone by about 1930 and the smaller one had disappeared by 1932. The 5" version was in the line from 1937 to 1939. They were made quite large and strong to handle muskies. Colors: White body, red eyes and tail, green scale, pike scale, shiner scale, natural scale, white body with spots. No. 7540, 5", 1 1/3 oz., **$100-$200**; No. 7550, 6", 1 4/5 oz., **$150-$300**; No. 7600, 8", 3 1/4 oz., **$500-$700**

Floating Vamp-Spook

Series No. 9500

Series No. 9750

Jointed Vamp-Spook

Series No. 9730

King Fish Vamp-Spook

Series No. KF9750

Heddon first introduced the plastic "Spook" line of lures in 1932. This was the first of any of the wooden lures listed as available in plastic. It is a hollow floater weighing 3/4 ounce and is 3 3/4" long. The next year saw the catalog introduction of a three-hook floating model, the Series No. 9750 and a Series No. 9730

Jointed Vamp Spook. In 1934, the King Fish model was listed. By 1938, the only two remaining in the catalog were the No. 9750 three hooker and the No. 9730 jointed model. No. 9500, 3 3/4", 3/4 oz.; No. 9750, 3 3/4", 3/4 oz.; No. 9730 (Jtd.), 4 1/2", 4/5 oz.; KF9750, 4 1/2", 1 oz. Colors: rainbow, white with red head, gold flitters with red head, pike scale, shiner scale, silver scale, green scale, yellow perch scale, x-ray green, x-ray silver scale, silver herring. **$35-$110**

Zig-Wag Series No. 8300

Zig-Wag Junior Series No. 8340

King-Zig-Wag Series No. 8350 and 8360

The No. 8300 was the first to come along, in 1928, then the No. 8340 Zig-Wag Junior appeared in 1937. The No. 8360 King-Zig-Wag was last, in 1939. All three were still being offered in the late 1940s and early 1950s. Colors: white body with red head, green frog, green scale, green scale with red head, pike scale, pike scale with red head, shiner scale with red head, natural scale, natural scale with red head, bullfrog, white body with silver specks and red head. No. 8300, 4 1/2", 3/4 oz., **$35-$65**; No. 8340, 3 1/2", 1/2 oz., **$40-$60**; No. 8350, 5", 1 1/8 oz., **$25-$65**; No. 8360, 6", 1 1/2 oz., **$25-$65**

King Zig-Wag

Heddon Basser Series No. 8400 and No. 8500

The original Basser came out in 1922 and was called the Head-On-Basser. These words were stamped on the metal head plate. In 1924, this had been changed to Heddon Basser. The stamped identification has undergone some other style changes over the years, but the words have remained the same. The Basser is another of those that were reissued as Classics around 1965 in wooden body and labeled "Original." Colors: rainbow, white body with red head and tail, white body with silver specks, white body with silver specks and red head, green scale, red scale, frog scale, goldfish scale, yellow perch scale, pike scale, shiner scale, white spotted, mullet scale, orange with black spots, blue scale, luminous, luminous with red head. No. 8400 (Plunking), 3", 5/8 oz., **$100-$150**; No. 8500 (Regular), 4", 3/4 oz., **$25-$60**; No. 8510 (Salmon), 4", 7/8 oz., **$30-$60**; No. 8520 (Salmon or Deluxe), 4 1/2", 7/8 oz., **$30-$60**; No. 8540 (King Basser), 4 1/2", 1 oz., **$35-$75**; No. 8550 (King Basser), 5", 1 1/10 oz., **$50-$90**; No. 9560 (King Basser), 6", 2 1/4 oz., **$50-$90**

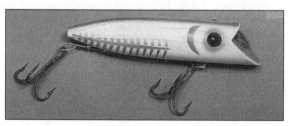

King Basser Series No. 8550.

Basser-Spook

Sea-Basser Spook

Series No. 9850

The plastic version of the Basser was introduced in the 1933 catalog. The Basser-Spook was listed at 3/4 oz., 4 1/4". The Sea-Basser Spook was described as "... special salt-water model, with two heavy double hooks for Salmon and Striped Bass." It may have been a plastic version of the Series No. 8560 King Basser. In the 1934 catalog a second size was added, the Basser-Spook Jr., Series No. 9840 at 3 1/4" and 2/3 oz. Colors: rainbow, shiner scale, red and white, silver flitter with red head, green scale, x-ray green, x-ray silver scale, yellow perch scale. Colors for Sea-Basser Spook Jr: white with red head, yellow perch, shiner scale, shiner herring. **$10-$20**

Shrimpy-Spook Series No. 9000

This lure was introduced in the 1930 Heddon catalog. The hook hardware is the first of the two Heddon styles of two-piece surface types called the "toilet seat" by collectors. It has black bead eyes, an internal belly weight, and measures 4 3/4". There were two colors listed, "White back, Gold Flitter, Red Head" and "Natural Shrimp Transparent Body." The 1931 catalog was the last to list the lure. **$150-$250**

Super Dowagiac

Super Dowagiac Spook

Series No. 9100

This lure is not found cataloged by Heddon in a wood body version. They were introduced in a plastic body model in a 1930 catalog. The body of the wooden model measures 2". It has two-piece hook hanger hardware, painted eyes, and is drilled from the nose and filled with lead. The Spook is considerably longer than the wooden version at 3 1/4". Colors: red and green spots, rainbow, white head and tail with red decorations, perch scale, gold specks with red head, shiner scale. Wood: **$50-$90**; Plastic, **$20-$30**

Super Dowagiac.

Chugger Spook Series No. 9540

The first Chuggers were the No. 9540 Series Chugger Spooks, released in 1938-39. There are several wooden Chuggers in collectors' hands that were purchased in the "Classic" boxes of 1964-65. They are definitely later models because of the eyes and hardware. They are not marked "Original" on the lure body as are the other four classics. Wood: **$40-$80**; Plastic "Spook": **$10-$20**

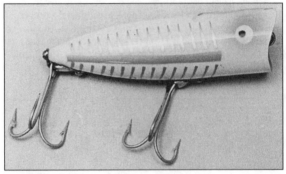

Chugger Spook.

Sea Spook Series No. 9800

This lure was featured as new in the 1930 Heddon catalog. The lure is 3 3/4" with a belly treble hook and one trailing, with the line tie at the nose. That particular lure has the one-piece bar style belly hook hanger. The other one sports the first style of the two, two-piece surface hook hangers collectors call the "toilet seat" style. All have glass eyes. Colors: red and green spots, white head and tail with red decorations, gold speckled with red head, shiner scale. **$50-$100**

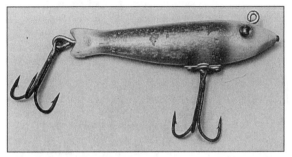

Sea Spook.

Scissortail Series No. 9830

The Scissortail was called "a startlingly new lure" in the 1953 catalog. It is 3 1/8" long, plastic, and has one-piece surface hook hangers and bug eyes. **$15-$30**

Cobra Series No. 9900

This wooden lure was first found in the 1965 catalog. There were several sizes and two types, each with a different Cobra name. Vibra-Flash (glitter) color and size: No. 9905 Baby Cobra, red and white, 3"; No. 9910 Cobra, Gold, 4"; No. 9930 Cobra, perch, 5"; No. 9940 King Cobra, yellow, 8"; No. 9960 Surface Cobra, shad, 4"; No. 9970 Surface Cobra, silver, 5". The Surface Cobra has a propeller spinner fore and aft and the other Cobras have no spinners, but do have a plastic lip at the nose. **$10-$15**

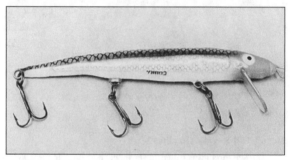

Cobra.

Stingaree Series No. 9930

Tiny Stingaree Series No. 330

This plastic lure first appeared in catalogs in 1957 in a 2 1/2" and a spinning size, the Tiny Stingaree at 1 1/2". This is a unique bait with an up-and-down undulating motion something like a sting ray. The lure was a failure and gone from the catalog the following year. Colors: white with red head, yellow perch scale, red and white shore minnow, bullfrog, black and white shore minnow, yellow shore minnow. **$10-$20**

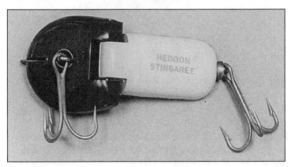

Tiny Stingaree.

Commando

This is a soft plastic lure introduced in 1968. When the fish strikes, the hook is supposed to snap away from the body which then ostensibly runs up the line so "... there is no weight attached to the hook to help your fish throw the plug." The tail portion spins upon retrieve. Size: 4 1/2", 5/8 oz. Colors: purple, green, red and white, gold, blue and silver, black and silver. **$5-$10**

Commando.

Hep Spinners Series No. 460 through No. 464

These series numbers have only to do with the sizes. These are brass-bodied spinners marked "HEP" on the blades. They were available in five sizes: 1 3/4", 2", 2 3/8", 2 5/8" and another, heavier 2 5/8". The colors of the blades were gold finish and silver finish. There were four other finishes that were available only on the lighter 2 5/8" size: smokey black, bullfrog, spotted orange and red and white. **$5-$10**

Spoon Kit and Hep Kit

Heddon marked these attractive little kits of its various spoons and spinners. There are five kits in plastic boxes. Intact they would each be valued at about **$25-$50**

Big Bud

This is not a particularly old lure, but it is seen at just about every tackle show for sale. At 2 3/4", 5/8-ounce, it was brought out by Heddon in 1976-77. It is a novelty plug, but it is listed along with serious lures. **$10-$20**

Big Bud.

Harden's Special

Harden's Star

This lure is a Heddon product, at least in part. In the late 1920s to early 1930s, Walter Harden took a Heddon Zaragossa and modified it for his particular brand of Florida bass fishing. The two versions proved so successful that Heddon put them on the market. Hardens's Special, $300-$400; Harden's Star, **$300-$400**

Harden's Whiz

Both versions have glass eyes and the second style of the two-piece surface hook hangers. Sizes: 4 1/2" and 3 1/2". This is essentially a Heddon Baby Vamp body with floppy props, yellow glass eyes, and two-piece "toilet seat" style hook hardware. **$300-$400**

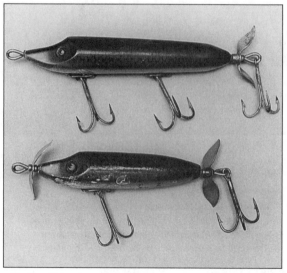

Harden's Whiz.

Creek Chub Bait Company

Garrett, Indiana

The Creek Chub Company began doing business in 1906 in Garrett, Ind. A significant contribution to the industry was its development of the natural scale finish for artificial lures. This finish was offered as early as 1917. The earliest lures lacked eyes, then glass eyes were added. Creek Chub stuck to the use of the cup and screw eye hardware from its initial development. The first hook hardware was the simple screw eye with a flat washer. The earliest metal diving blades were plain with no name stamped on them. Next came the plain lip with its name (CCBCO) and usually a patent date of 9-7-20. The next change was the reinforced lip produced by stamping two parallel ridges in the lip for extra strength.

Creek Chub was sold to the Lazy Ike Corp., Des Moines, Iowa, in 1978.

Creek Chub Ice Decoy

This is a very rare Creek Chub product. Not found in any catalog to date, it is 4 1/2" long including tail fin. It has glass eyes, metal tail fin, and opposite mounted side fins in line with the line tie. The body is that of the Creek Chub Fin Tail Shiner. **$1,000-$1,500**

Ice Decoy.

The Creek Chub Wiggler 1906-1964

This lure came along in 1906. It was illustrated in the 1920 patent for the Creek Chub Bait Co. reversible lip. A 1917 catalog illustrates the lure with no eyes, but a 1918 catalog showed eyes. They have always had the treble hooks, one belly mounted and one trailing. The collector may be reasonably sure he has the earliest version if it has flattened head, no eyes, no name stamped on the lip, and no tail hook metal insert. Size: 3 1/2", 3/4 oz. Colors: natural chub, scale finish, perch with scale finish, dark gold with scale finish, red side minnow with scale finish, white with red head, solid red, goldfish with scale finish, natural mullet with scale finish, green back with scale finish, black with white head, silver flash, frog finish, silver shiner. **$100-$250**

Creek Chub Wiggler.

The Baby Chub 1917-1955

Known in later catalogs as the Baby Chub Wiggler, the 1917 listing shows this plug to be essentially the same as the Creek Chub Wiggler but in a smaller, lighter version. It has the same hook configuration and the reversible metal lip blade is smaller. It is one of the first three lures available from the company. Size: 3 1/2", 3/4 oz. Colors: Natural chub scale finish; perch, scale finish; red side, scale finish; dark gold, scale finish; white with red head; green back, scale finish; solid red; gold finish, scale finish; black with red head; solid red; silver flash; silver shiner, scale finish; natural mullet, scale finish; frog finish. **$75-$200**

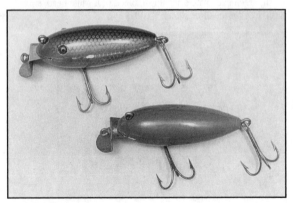

Baby Chubs

The Creek Crab Wigglers or The Crawdad, 300 Series

Baby Crawdad, 400 Series

1917-1964

New in the late 1910s, the Creek Crab Wiggler was renamed The Crawdad by 1920. At first only one size (2 3/4") and one finish (natural crab) was available. In 1919, it added the Baby Crab at 2 1/2" and two more finishes, "Albino" and "Tan Color, Shell Finish." Both sport bead eyes. The "River Peeler" (steel blue shell finish) was added by 1924. A 1917 catalog said this lure was the "Only Bait Without Nickel Plate." It has eight flexible rubber legs protruding from the belly. The regular Crawdad is equipped with two belly trebles and the Baby size has two double hooks. The very earliest of these critters will have painted dive planes with no markings, red eyes, screw eye and washer hook rig. Colors: Natural crab, shell finish; albino finish (white and red); tan color, shell finish; river peeler, steel blue, shell finish; perch scale; silver flash. **$50-$150**

Cray-Z-Fish (Plastic) 1964-1978

Called new in the 1964 catalog, it was last illustrated in the 1968 edition. It remained in the catalog price lists until 1978, indicating it may have remained in production. This lure is the plastic replacement for the Crab Wiggler. The colors were described in the catalog as created especially for the lure and not available on other Creek Chub lures. The size was never listed, only the weight, 1/4 oz. Colors: white with red head, natural crab, shrimp crab, tan crab, silver shad, tiger stripe. **$5-$10**

Open Mouth Shiner 1918-1933

New in 1918, this plug closely resembles a Shiner or Silver-side Minnow. It has a cut-out notch mouth, a belly-mounted double hook, and a tail-mounted double with no tail hook metal insert. The 1931 catalog is the last to illustrate this plug. Size: 3 1/4", 3/4oz. Colors: natural shiner, scale finish; red side minnow, scale finish; white with red head, silver flash. **$75-$220**

Top 'N Pop (plastic) 1960-1967

This plastic lure "plunks, pops, short jerks, walks, jumps, frantic swimming with slow retrieve." It has a peculiarly shaped metal lip. First illustrated in the 1960 catalog, it was last illustrated in the 1967 edition. Colors: perch scale, white with red head, yellow spotted, silver flash frog. **$5-$10**

Open Mouth Shiner

Husky Musky 1919-1955

This is another early Creek Chub lure. A large plug for musky fishing, it has the reversible metal lip blade, a belly-mounted and a trailing treble hook. Prior to 1915 this hook hardware was the simple washer and screw eye. All after that have the cup and anchored hook hardware. Several 3T models have turned up. In 1936, the company offered the "Improved Husky Musky." Up until then they sported two line ties, one on top of the head and the one on the dive plane. The head-top line tie was eliminated and the Thru-body hook hangers and reinforced dive plane were added. They appeared continuously in catalogs until 1955. Size: 5", 1 1/2 oz. Colors: natural chub, scale finish; natural mullet, scale finish; natural perch, scale finish; white with red head; silver flash. **$50-$275**

Husky Muskys.

Mitie Mouse (Plastic) 1963-1978

This little fellow floats at rest, but runs deep upon retrieve. The metal dive lip is always equipped with a snap swivel. Its size was never listed, only its weight, 1/4 oz. Colors: field mouse, black, gray tiger, silver flash. **$5-$10**

The Famous Pikie Minnow

1920-1978 (Plastic, 1961-1978)

An undated pocket catalog of around 1919-1921 illustrates this plug with the reversible metal lip blade, slope nose, two belly mounted treble hooks and a trailing treble. Earliest models had no eyes, hand painted gill marks and two line ties. The plastic Pikie Minnow came along in 1961. The plastic model was also available with the Deep Diving lip from 1961 on. Size: 4 1/4", 3/4 oz. Colors

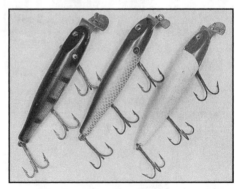

*Famous
Pikie
Minnows.*

(wood): Pikie Minnow, scale finish; white with blue head; black with white head; white with red head; natural perch, scale finish; golden shiner, silver shiner, mullet, rainbow, silver flash; orange and black spots; "new black scale," "rainbow fire," "fire plug." (Plastic): pike scale, perch scale, white with red head, silver shiner, silver flash, black, mullet, mackerel, fluorescent red, blue flash, chrome, amber. Wood: **$40-$85** (much more in some finishes), plastic: **$5-$10**

Deluxe Wag Tail Chub 1918-1953

This lure appears in a 1918 pocket catalog as available with the reversible metal lip blade, two belly-mounted double hooks (reversible to make the plug weedless), and a metal tail fin hinged to the lure so that it could flap on retrieve. Size: 2 3/4", 1/2 oz. Colors: natural creek chub, scale finish; natural perch, scale finish; red side minnow, scale finish; golden shiner, scale finish; white with red head; dace; silver flash. **$50-$150**

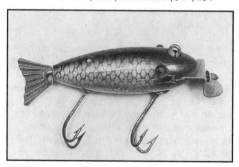

Deluxe Wag Tail Chub.

The Baby Pikie Minnow

1921-1963 (Plastic, 1963-1978)

This is a smaller version of the famous Pikie Minnow No. 700. The other basic difference is the elimination of one of the belly-mounted treble hooks. The plastic version was cataloged first in 1964 and was available to 1978. Size: 3 1/4", 1/2 oz. Colors (wood): natural Pikie finish, scale; white with red head, natural perch, scale; golden shiner, scale; silver shiner, scale; silver, rainbow; silver flash; orange and black spot, new black scale; rainbow fire; fire plug. (Plastic): pike scale, perch scale, white with red head, silver flash, fluorescent red, black scale, chrome. Wood: **$40-$60**, Plastic: **$5-$10**

Creek Bug Wigglers and The Big Creek Bug Wiggler

1000 Series	**1924-1947**
1100 Series	**1924-1947**
1400 Series	**1920-1932**

The Big Creek Bug Wiggler originally appeared around 1919-1920 in three finishes, weights and lengths. It was a bass plug, but apparently wasn't offered in the bait casting size from about 1932 on. Around 1924, the same design appeared in two smaller, lighter sizes for fly fishing (Creek Bug Wiggler Series No. 1000 & No. 1100), but these two disappeared from the catalogs around 1945. They were all of wood, had a reversible belly-mounted double hook and three tail-mounted strings or red cord. Sizes: No. 1000, 7/8"; No. 1100, 1 1/4"; No. 1400, 2 1/2", 1/2 oz. Colors: bug finish (yellow gold body, painted brown wings and legs, dash of red on the head); black; white and red. **$250-$500**

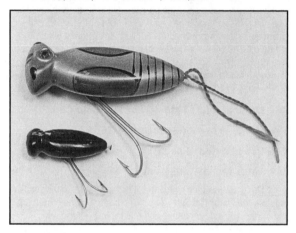

Big Creek Bug Wigglers.

Fly Rod Pikie 1924-1925

The earliest examples found have a cylindrical tapered tail and a scooped nose. Later the nose and tail grew more blunt. The nose was still scooped a bit, but the tail just became smaller in diameter as the body neared the tail and ended with a blunt rounding. The wire leader was consistent through the years. Sizes: No. 1200, 1 1/4"; No. 1300, 1 5/8". Colors: Natural Pikie scale finish, white with red head, red side scale finish, dace. **$150-$175** (add **$100-$200** for original box)

The Original Injured Minnow or Flat Side Chub

1924-1963, 1973-78 (Plastic, 1964-78)

The Baby Injured Minnow

1924-1963 (Plastic, 1964-78)

This plug was then called the "Flat Side Chub" and a smaller version, the "Baby Flat Side Chub." The larger one had three treble hooks, two side-mounted, and one trailing. The smaller is equipped with one side-mounted double hook and a trailing double, but the catalog states it could be ordered with treble hooks. The double hooks were reversible so as to make the plug weedless. Both sizes had nose- and tail-mounted propeller spinners. The design of the earliest models incorporated a flattened side so that the plugs swam on the side like an injured minnow. Much later models do not have this flat side. Sizes: No. 1500, 3 3/4", 3/4 oz.; No. 1500-P, 3 3/4", 5/8 oz.; No. 1600 (Baby), 2 3/4", 1/2 oz.; No. 1600-P (Baby) 2 3/4", 1/2 oz. Colors (wood): dark green, silver and red, scale finish; natural perch, scale finish;

golden shiner, scale finish; red side, scale finish; silver flash; white and red, "day-n-nite" (luminous); rainbow fire; fire plug; dace; yellow spotted, frog finish; red wing; white scale. (Plastic): pike scale, perch scale, white with red head, purple, golden shiner, dace scale, shad, silver flash, frog, black scale, black. Wood: **$45-$200**; Plastic: **$15-$20**

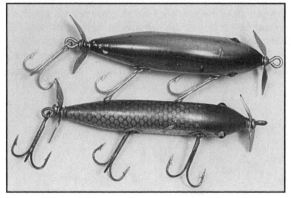

Baby Injured Minnows.

The Polly Wiggle 1923-1931

Introduced in 1923, this lure was gone from the catalogs by 1931. It is a weighted bait that would not float, but has the reversible metal lip blade to be used as a surface plug. It has a long wire leader at the nose that has a three-wire weed guard. The single hook is mounted near the tail. There is a provision for attaching a pork rind but it came with an artificial ribbon rind attached. They have been found with black and red eyes and often without the weed guard. This depresses the value considerably. These are fairly scarce. Size: 1 3/4", 1/2oz. Colors: natural polly-wog; white with red head. **$100-$200**

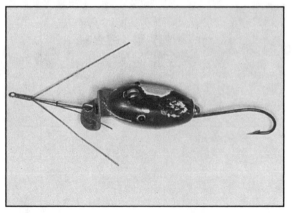

Polly Wiggle.

Silver Side 1957-1961

Although 1957 is the earliest catalog listing for this slim 4 3/4" lure, it may have been around a little longer. It has the sturdy thru-body construction making it quite strong. Size: 4 3/4", 7/8 oz. Colors: pike scale, perch scale, white with red head, silver flash, blue flash. **$50-$75**

Wiggle Diver, 1800 Series

1957-1962 (Plastic, 1963-1978)

Spinning Wiggle Diver, 5000 Series

1960-1962 (Plastic, 1963-?)

Sometime in the 1950s, Creek Chub acquired the rights to manufacture and sell Shakespeare's Wiggle Diver. Creek Chub modified it by making it a little longer. The earliest of these sport a tail-reinforcing metal cap. By 1960 this tail cap was gone. It has through-body wire construction for strength. The 1961 catalog is the first that lists the Spinning Wiggle Diver. The 1962 catalog lists it, but it is stamped "DISCONTINUED." This spinning model was never listed again, but they have been found in plastic. The small ones have a V-notch at the tail. Sizes: No. 1800, 5", 1 1/2 oz.; No. 1800-P, 5", 1 1/2 oz.; No. 5000, 2 1/4", 1/2 oz.; No. 5000-P, 2 1/4", 1/2 oz. Colors wood): white body with red head, silver flash, tiger stripe, yellow with red head, yellow with black head. (Plastic): white with red head, silver flash, tiger stripe. Wood: **$50-$100**, plastic: **$10-$20**

The Underwater Spinner Minnow

1800 Series 1924-1934

The Creek and River Fishing Lure

1900 Series 1924-1934

A 1924 catalog listing states this plug is weighted and both the larger and smaller versions are available in the same three-color designs. Both sizes have flattened sides, and propeller spinners at nose and tail. Early catalogs show round-body lures in illustrations. The larger version has two double hooks mounted on each side and one trailing double hook. The smaller one has the trailing double, but only one double hook on each side. It had disappeared from the catalog by 1935. Size: No. 1900, 2 3/4", 1/2 oz.; No. 1800, 3 3/4", 3/4 oz. Colors: red side, scale finish; green back, scale finish; rainbow; silver flash. **$700-$900**

Underwater Spinner Minnows

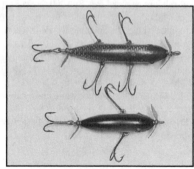

Striper Strike (Plastic)

Series 1900 1960-1978

Series 2100 1961-1978

Series 2200 1962-1978

Series 2400 1962-1978

Series 2500 1962-1978

Introduced in the 1960 catalog as the Striper Striker, it had become the Striper Strike in the next year's catalog. This plastic popper caught on fast as an explosively successful lure. Creek Chub quickly added four new models. All five had the very strong through-body hardware. Sizes: No. 1900-P, 5 1/4", 2 1/4 oz.; No. 2100-P, 4 1/2", 1 1/2 oz.; No. 2200-P, 4 1/2", 1 oz.; No. 2400-P, 2 1/2", 1/2 oz.; No. 2500-P, 3", 3/4 oz. Colors: silver flash, blue flash, gray, amber, chrome, silver shiner, red eye, mackerel, banana, fluorescent red (these last two appeared in the early 1970s, but didn't last long). **$10-$20**

Creek Darter

("The Two Thousand")

1924-1978 (Plastic, 1960-1978)

Appearing around 1924, this plug has two belly-mounted treble hooks and one trailing treble. Just about all the Darters are found with painted eyes, but a rare few have turned up with glass eyes. It continued in production in four sizes and a jointed model.

Some time between 1956 and 1960, the wood Saltwater Darter, Series 2000-SW appeared. It was gone by the time plastic Darters were on the scene. Sizes: No. 2000, 3 3/4", 5/8 oz.; No. 2000-P, 3 3/4", 5/8 oz.; No. 2000-SW, 4", 1 oz. Colors (wood): Frog, white with red head, yellow with black and red spots, silver flash, dace scale (red side), black with nite head (glows in the dark), pikie scale, perch scale, rainbow fire and fire plug, pearl, coach dog, shad. (Saltwater Darter): White body with red head, silver flash, blue flash, purple eel. (Plastic): Pike scale, perch scale, white with red head, shad, yellow spotted, silver flash, frog, black scale, coach dog, solid black. Wood: **$20-$75**, Plastic: **$5-$10**

Wooden reproduction of the Creek Darter.

The Jointed Darter, 4900 Series

1938-1964, 1970-1978

The Midget Darter, 8000 Series

1938-1978

The Jointed Darter is the same plug as the original Creek Darter, but is jointed. The Midget Darter is a smaller version and has one less treble hook. Sizes: No. 8000 (Midget), 3", 3/8 oz.; No. 4900 (Jointed), 3 3/4", 1/2 oz. Colors: Natural Pikie; white with redhead; yellow spotted; silver flash; frog finish; perch; rainbow fire (1950-52); fire plug (1950-52); black scale; pearl. **$20-$75**

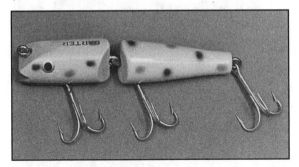

Jointed Darter.

The Number 8000-CB

Wood, 1946-1978

Plastic, 1961-1973

This lure is the same body design as the 8000 Series Darter, except the belly was made concave (C.B.). It sports two belly treble hooks instead of one. The plastic model came out in the 1961 catalog, listed along with the original wood model until 1973. Size: 3", 3/8 oz. Colors: (wood & plastic): pike scale, perch scale, white with red head, yellow spotted, silver flash, frog, coach dog, black scale, shad black. Wood: **$10-$35**, Plastic: **$5-$10**

No.
8000
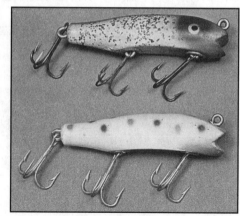

Spinnered Darter 1946-1978

This is the same plug as the No. 2000 Series Creek Darter with the addition of a tail-mounted propeller. It was introduced around 1946 continuing in production into the 1950s. Size: 3 3/4", 1/2 oz. Colors: Natural Pikie; white with red head; yellow spotted; silver flash; frog finish. **$20-$75**

Spinning Darter

1952-1961 (Plastic, 1962-1978)

This was introduced with a group of five Creek Chub classics to be made in spinning size. Sizes: No. 9000, 2 1/4", 1/4 oz.; No. 9000-P, 2 1/4", 1/4 oz.; 9000-P-UL, 1 5/8", 1/8 oz (ultralight). Colors (wood): yellow spotted, silver flash, frog, pike scale, perch scale, white with red head, solid black, pearl, black scale. (Plastic): pike scale, perch scale, white with red head, yellow spotted, silver flash, frog, black scale, shad, pearl. Wood: **$20-$60**, Plastic: **$5-$10**

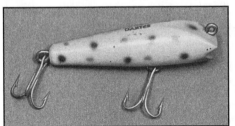

Spinning Darter.

Fin Tail Shiner 1924-1947

New in 1924, this lure underwent a few significant changes before it was eliminated from the line. First available with rubber fins, they had trouble with deterioration and/or hardening. They were then made with flexible fiber dorsal and tail fins. About 1930 another flexible fiber fin was added to each side of the head just under the eyes. Size: 4", 3/4 oz. Colors: red side shiner, scale finish; silver shiner, scale finish; golden shiner, scale finish; yellow perch, scale finish; white and red, silver flash. Metal fins: **$150-$300**; Fiber fins: **$150-$300**

Fin Tail Shiners.

Midget Pikie Minnow 1924-1960

This has the same body shape as the other "Pikies" but is considerably smaller at 2 3/4". This floating plug has two line ties on the older models, a belly treble hook, a trailing treble, and the reversible metal lip blade. The newer models lack the screw eye line tie on the head. Colors: Natural Pikie, scale finish; white with red head, scale finish; natural yellow perch, scale finish; golden shiner, scale finish; rainbow, solid black; white and red; silver shiner; silver flash; rainbow fire; fire plug. **$40-$85**

Spinning Pikie, 9300 Series

1952-1963 (Plastic, 1964-1978)

Spinning Jointed Pikie, 9400 Series

1952-1963 (Plastic, 1964-1978)

These two were among five classics that were released in a new 1/4-ounce spinning size in 1952. Sizes: No. 9300 wood, 2 1/4", 1/4 oz.; No. 9300 plastic, 2 1/4", 1/4 oz.; No. 9300 plastic, 1 5/8", 1/8 oz (ultralight). Colors (wood): pike scale, perch scale, white with red head, silver flash, black scale, solid black, frog, orange with black spots (added in 1957 for the jointed lure only), shad. (Plastic): pike scale, perch scale, white with red head, shad, silver flash, frog, orange with black spots, black scale. Wood: **$30-$50**, Plastic: **$5-$10**

Spinning Pikie.

Husky Pikie Minnow, 2300 Series

1924-1978

Jointed Husky Pikie Minnow, 3000 Series

1930-1978 (Plastic, 1964-78)

This plug is large and has two belly-mounted treble hooks, one trailing treble, and the reversible metal lip blade and the sloped nose typical of all the Creek Chub Pikie Minnow plugs. The 1931 catalog states that the Jointed Husky Pikie Minnow is a "new" lure. It is a 6" jointed version of the No. 2300 Series weighing 1 1/2 ounces. They redesigned the hook hardware in 1936 to utilize the rugged through-body rig making it considerably stronger. The available colors and finishes are the same. A plastic version of the Jointed Husky Pikie Minnow was introduced around 1962-64. Colors (wood): Natural Pikie, scale finish; natural perch, scale finish; golden shiner, scale finish; white with red head, rainbow; mullet, silver flash; orange and black spots; black scale finish; blue flash; purple eel; yellow flash; rainbow fire; fire plug. (Plastic 3000 Series): pike scale, perch scale, white with red head, rainbow, silver flash, black scale, blue flash, tiger stripe, solid black. No. 2300: **$40-$90**; No. 3000: **$40-$90** (**$100** plus with box); Plastic: **$20-$40**

Husky Pikie Minnow.

Giant Pikie Minnow (Straight Pike) 1960-1978

This large version of the Pikies is not widely known. It was apparently only illustrated once in the catalogs, in 1960. It lasted until the company sold in 1978. It was never made in plastic. Size: 8", 3 1/2 oz. Colors: pike scale, perch scale, white with red head, gray, silver flash, blue flash, gold scale, black. **$40-$90**

Giant Jointed Pikie Minnow 1956-1978

This is the biggest lure ever made by Creek Chub, measuring 14 inches. The first appearance of this monster was in the 1956 catalog. It was made of wood and remained in the line until the company was sold. Glass eyes indicate the earliest of these lures. Colors: pike scale, perch scale, white with red head, solid black, silver flash, orange with black spots, blue flash, purple eel. **$60-$90**

Three Jointed Pikie (Plastic) 1960-1978

The Three Jointed Pikie is more accurately called the Three Section Pikie, as it was called in catalogs later. Size: 6 1/2", 1 1/2 oz. Colors: pike scale, perch scale, silver shiner, white with red head, solid black, silver flash, black scale. **$20-$40**

Wiggle Fish 1925-1957

Appearing in 1925, this is a jointed plug with a fluted nickel tail, mounted to let it wag. Wiggle Fish has been found with a plain tail. That variation is thought to be the oldest. It has two line ties, two belly-mounted treble hooks and the reversible metal lip blade. Size: 3 1/2", 3/4 oz. Colors: natural perch, scale finish; silver shiner, scale finish; golden shiner, scale finish; red side, scale finish; white and red; Natural Pikie; dace; silver flash. **$80-$250**

Wiggle Fish.

Baby Wiggle Fish 1925-1933

This is essentially the same lure as the No. 2400 Wiggle Fish. It is a smaller version and has only one belly treble hook. Size: 2 1/2", 1/2 oz. Colors: natural perch, scale finish; silver shiner, scale finish; golden shiner, scale finish; red side, scale finish; white and red, silver flash. **$80-$250**

The Jointed Pikie Minnow

1926-1978 (Plastic, 1961-78)

New in 1926, the Jointed Pikie Minnow is a jointed version of the No. 700 Series Pikie Minnow. It was also available from 1950 with the Deep-Diving lip. Plastic versions of both models were first available in 1961. Size: 4 1/2", 3/4 oz. Color (wood): Natural Pikie, scale finish; natural perch, scale finish; silver shiner, scale finish; golden shiner, scale finish; white with red head, silver flash; rainbow, mullet, black scale; orange and black spots; rainbow fire; fire plug. (Plastic): pike scale, perch scale, white with red head, golden shiner, mullet, rainbow, silver flash, frog, orange with black spots, black scale. Wood: **$40-$80**, Plastic: **$20-$50**

The Baby Jointed Pikie Minnow

1926-1963 (Plastic 1964-78)

New in 1926, this plug is a jointed version of the Baby Pikie Minnow. Size: 3 1/2", 1/2 oz. Colors (wood): Natural Pikie, scale finish; natural perch, scale finish; golden shiner, scale finish; silver shiner, scale finish; white with red head, rainbow; silver flash; silver flash with red tail, silver flash with yellow tail, orange with black spots; black scale finish; rainbow fire and fire plug were available only from 1949 to 1953. (Plastic): Pike scale, perch scale, white with red head, silver shiner, golden shiner, rainbow, silver flash, frog, black scale. Wood: **$40-$80**, Plastic: **$5-$10**

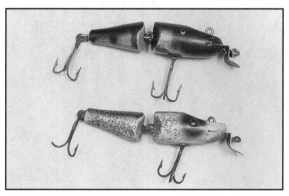

Baby Jointed Pikie Minnow

The Weed Bug 1927-1935

This lure was variously called the Weed Bug, Weed Frog, or Weed Chunk. It is a weedless floater with two single-point hooks and a pork rind attachment on its back. Size: 2", 3/4 oz. Colors: Weed Bug, yellow body with green wings; Weed Chunk, white body with red eyes; Weed Frog, Meadow Frog colors. **$400-$800**

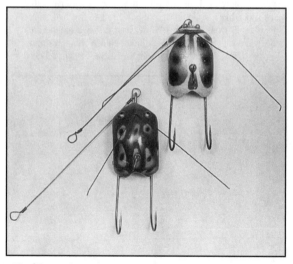

Weed Bug.

The Gar Underwater Minnow 1927-1946, 1950-1952

This lure has a slender body almost pointed at each end (gar shape). It sports a propeller spinner at nose and tail, two belly-mounted treble hooks, and a trailing treble. Size: 5 1/4", 3/4oz. Colors: natural gar with scale finish, green gar with scale finish. **$400-$600**

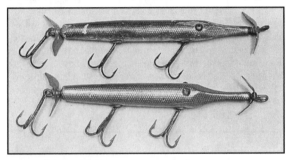

Gar Underwater Minnows.

The Castrola 1927-1942

The lure has two belly treble hooks and one trailing treble. There is a long wire leader extension attached at the top of the nose with a small spinner blade mounted toward the end of it. The lure is not considered complete without this rig. Size: 3 5/8", 3/4 oz. Colors: Natural Pikie, scale finish; natural perch, scale finish; golden shiner, scale finish; silver flash; white with red head; rainbow. **$140-$250**

The Plunker, 3200 Series

Wood, 1926-1978

Plastic, 1964-1978

Appearing around 1926, this plug continues in production. Around the late 1930s it underwent a slight body design change. The original design had a fatter body whereas the later bodies were slimmed a bit toward the tail. All had a trailing treble and a belly mounted treble hook. In 1964 a plastic model was added to the line. Size: 3", 5/8oz. Colors (wood): Natural Pikie with scale finish, natural perch with scale finish, golden shiner with scale finish, white with red head, rainbow, silver flash, solid black, frog, yellow spotted, red wing with white scale, rainbow fire, fire plug. (Plastic): Pikie scale, perch scale, white body with red head, black, silver flash, frog. **$25-$75**

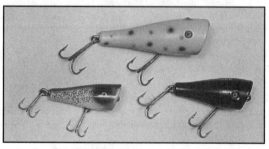

Plunker, top, Spinning Plunkers.

Spinning Plunker 1952-1964 (Plastic, 1965-78)

This was introduced in 1952 with four other classics, all in 1/4-ounce weight. The 1964 catalog was the last to list it in wood. All after that were plastic. Colors (wood): pike scale, perch scale, white with red head, silver flash, frog, pearl, solid black, golden shiner, black scale, shad. (Plastic): pike scale, perch scale, white with red head, solid black, silver flash, frog, black scale, yellow spotted. Wood **$20-$40**, Plastic: **$5-$10**

Snook Plunker 1953-1962

Over the years it was also called the Spinning Popper, Salt Spinning Popper and finally simply the Salt Popper in the 1962 catalog. This is probably a replacement for the "Seven Thousand." The Snook Plunker was available with or without the bucktail on the trailing treble hook. They originally had glass eyes, but these became painted eyes around 1959. Size: 5", 1 1/2 oz. Colors: Pikie scale, perch scale, white with red head, mullet, yellow spotted, silver flash, blue flash, eel, yellow flash. **$80-$125**

The "Sarasota" Minnow 1927-1934

This lure is rather slender, has a belly-mounted treble hook and a trailing treble. There is another model with a different hook configuration. After Creek Chub ceased manufacturing the lure in 1934, the Sarasota Special showed up. It has a treble hook on each side and a trailing treble. The line tie is located beneath the nose rather than on top. There is additional internal weight in the tail. Size: 4 1/2", 3/4 oz. Colors: Natural Pikie, scale finish; natural perch, scale finish; golden shiner, scale finish; rainbow; silver flash; white with red head. Sarasota: **$100-$175**, Sarasota Special: **$150-$350**

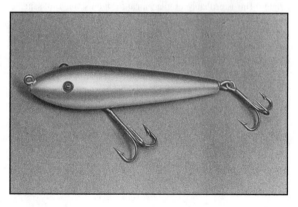

"Sarasota" Minnow.

The Snook Pike 1930-1978

This lure shows up in catalogs around 1930 and eventually came to be known as the "Straight Pikie." It was made exactly like the No. 700 Series Pikie Minnow except larger and much stronger. The belly hooks are swiveled and anchored entirely through the body. Size: 4 7/8", 1 1/8 oz. Colors: pike scale, perch scale, golden shiner, white with red head, rainbow, silver flash, silver shiner, mullet. **$60-$90**

Snook Pikie

The Husky Injured Minnow 1930-1960

This is the same lure as the No. 1500 Series Injured Minnow except made larger and stronger. Size: 5", 1 1/2 oz. Colors: natural perch, scale finish; golden shiner, scale finish; red side, scale finish; white with red head; silver flash; Pikie scale; dace. **$125-$225**

Lucky Mouse 1930-1946

This lure has aluminum ears, bead eyes, a flexible braided fabric tail, a belly treble and a trailing treble hook. Size: 2", 3/4 oz. Colors: natural gray mouse, black mouse, white mouse with red eyes. **$75-$150**

River Rustler 1931-1935

This lure has a sloped nose, protruding eyes, a lip, one belly treble hook and a trailing treble. Size: 2 5/8", 5/8 oz. Colors: natural pike, scale finish; natural perch, scale finish; golden shiner, scale finish; white with red head; rainbow; silver flash. **$75-$150**

River Rustlers.

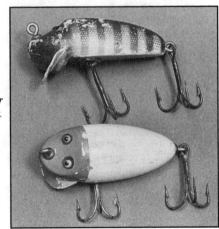

The Beetle 1931-1954

This plug appears in a 1931 catalog as "The New Creek Chub Beetle." It is a deep-running plug with a non-reversible metal lip plane. Its bead eyes protrude from the face plate portion of the lip plane. It has one belly treble and a trailing treble mounted on a wire extension which has two pearl-finished blade spinners attached. Size: 2 1/2", 3/4 oz. Colors: yellow beetle, green beetle, white and red beetle, orange beetle, gold beetle, black beetle, pike scale, white and green. **$100-$200**

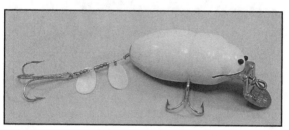

Beetle

The Midget Beetle 1939-1954

This is a small version of the 3800 Series Beetle. The major difference is there is but one pearl spinner on the rear whereas there were two of them on the larger version. Size: 2", 1/2 oz. Colors: yellow beetle, green beetle, white and red beetle, orange beetle, gold beetle, black beetle. **$100-$200**

Sucker Series 3900 1932-1933

Called new in 1932, it was listed again in 1933 but not in any subsequent catalogs. It is available in only two finishes: natural yellow or natural blue sucker scale. It has an unusual corrugated metal lip. The catalog lists the size as 3 1/2", but all those found so far measure 4 1/2". **$350-$600**

Sucker Series.

Tarpon Pikie 1933-1960

New around 1933, this lure is a large, strongly built lure made for heavy saltwater use. The metal lip is heavily reinforced and the hook hangers are extremely heavy-duty and anchored all the way through the body. It was available with either single or treble hooks. Size: 6 1/2", 3 oz. Colors: white with red head; natural mullet, scale finish; silver flash; Pikie scale; perch scale. **$100-$150**, the rarer single-hook version is **$375-$500**

The Creek Chub Jigger 1933-1946

This is Creek Chub's first and only "Water Sonic" plug. There is a hole with a metal scoop on the bottom to cause water to flow through the body on retrieve. It has a belly-mounted treble hook and a trailing treble. Size: 3 5/8", 3/4 oz. There is also a very rare Baby Jigger at 3 1/4". Colors: white with red head, red side, scale finish; yellow body, black and red spots; silver flash; frog finish; black body with luminous head. **$60-$90**, with Baby Jigger **$275-$550**

Midget Jointed Pikie 1934-1961

Why it took 10 years to come up with a jointed version of the No. 2200 is anybody's guess. In the beginning, the forward portion of the lure had the classic Pikie profile. Over the years the scoop grew more shallow and the head fatter with a more rounded nose. Size: 2 3/4", 1/4 oz. Colors: natural pike scale finish, natural perch scale finish, white with red head, golden shiner scale finish, rainbow, silver flash, silver shiner, solid black, fireplug, rainbow fire, black scale finish. **$40-$90**

The River Scamp 1933-1953

The earliest River Scamps had two line ties. After 1936, the name became The Scamp. They are easily confused with a Pikie, but this lure is a sinker with an internal weight. All Pikies are floaters at rest. The 1953 catalog lists a "Deep Diving Scamp" as the same as the River Scamp except with a "Deep diving mouth piece." All had a metal lip, a belly treble and a trailing treble hook. Size: 3 1/4", 5/8 oz. Colors: white body with red head, dace scale finish, silver flash, chub scale finish, natural perch scale finish, rainbow. **$40-$90**

Flip Flap 1935-1941

The first page of the 1935 catalog illustrates "Creek Chub's new FLIP FLAP! The Only Lure That Swims With an Up-and-Down Movement." This new "Startling Creation" must not have lived up to expectations for it was conspicuously absent from catalogs from 1942-43 on. It has a loose flapping spoon-like lip attached to the line tie at the nose. There was a belly treble hook and a trailing treble. The spoon was nickel-plated but could be ordered with a copper spoon if desired. Size: 3 1/4", 5/8oz. Colors: white body with red head; dace finish; silver flash; frog finish. **$80-$200**

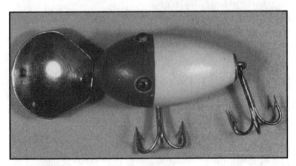

Flip Flap

Wiggle Wizard 1936-1938

This jointed plug had two line ties on the earliest models, the reversible metal lip, a belly treble, and a trailing treble hook. This lure replaced the Baby Wiggle Fish. Size: 2 1/2", 1/2 oz. Colors: natural perch, scale finish; silver shiner, scale finish; golden shiner, scale finish; red side, scale finish; silver flash; white with red head. **$125-$250**

Wiggle Wizard

The Skipper 1936-1947

This lure has a weighted tail, a belly treble hook, and a trailing treble. Size: 3", 5/8 oz. Colors: Pikie finish, perch finish, white with red head, natural frog, black with white head, solid black, silver flash. **$40-$80**

Fethi-Min 1936

This is probably the most elusive lure produced by Creek Chub. There is no known example in any collection. It was offered as new in a 1936 catalog, but never seen again in any subsequent catalogs. Size: 2 1/2", 5/8 oz. Colors: chub finish, perch finish, brown. No market data.

The Wee Dee, 4800 Series 1936-1946

The Wee Dee, Series 200-P 1962-1968

This lure has three single hooks rigged up with swinging pivots to be weedless. The Wee Dee shows up again in 1962 in a new design in spinning size and made of plastic. Sizes: No. 4800, 2 1/2", 5/8 oz.; 200-P, 1 1/2", 1/4 oz. Colors: bug finish, frog finish, white with red head, yellow frog, green frog. Wood: **$375-$650**, Plastic: **$5-$15**

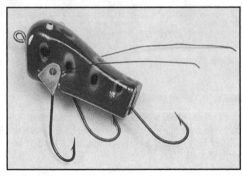

Wee Dee.

The Close-Pin 1937-1947

This lure was made in only one finish: white body with a red head and yellow and red tail fins. The lure has two gold-plated treble hooks and was made for saltwater fishing. Size: 3 1/4", 1 1/2 oz. **$250-$500**

The Dingbat, 5100 Series

Wood, 1937-1956

Plastic, 1956-1978

Midget Dingbat, 5200 Series 1938-1957

Husky Dingbat, 5300 Series 1938-1946

Fly Rod Dingbat, 1300 & 1400 Series 1938-1952

New in 1937, these plugs had fluttering hair legs protruding from each side, a metal blade lip, one belly-mounted treble and a trailing treble hook. A plastic Dingbat was first listed in the 1965 catalog. It sported a straight diving lip rather the classic Creek Chub lip. Size: No. 1300, 5/8"; No. 1400, 7/8", 1/2 oz.; No. 5100, 2", 5/8 oz.; No. 5200, 1 5/8", 1/2 oz.; No. 5300, 2 1/2", 1 1/8 oz.; No. 5300-P, 2", 1/4 oz. Colors (fly rod sizes): pike scale with brown legs, perch scale with green legs, golden shiner scale with yellow legs, white with red head and red legs, all black, silver flash with red legs, frog with green legs. (Wood): pike scale with brown legs, perch scale with green legs, golden shiner scale with yellow legs, white with red head with red legs, solid black, silver flash with red legs; frog with green legs. (Plastic, 5300 Series): pike scale with brown legs, perch scale with green legs, white with red head and red legs, black, silver flash with red legs, frog with green legs. Wood: **$35-$125**; Plastic: **$5-$10**; Midget: **$35-$125**; Husky: **$175-$275**; Fly Rod: **$150-$250**

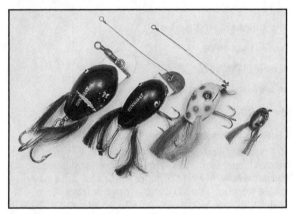

Dingbats.

The Surface Dingbat No. 5400 Series 1938-1955

This lure is quite similar to the other Dingbats, but is designed without the metal lip. It has two double hooks, one at the belly and one trailing. The lure was available in exactly the same finish designs as the others but around 1942-43 two more were added as available on the Surface Dingbat only, red wing and white scale. Size: 1 3/4", 5/8 oz. **$35-$125**

Jointed Snook Pikie Minnow 1939-1964, 1969-1978

The first catalog description said, "Shaped just like the regular Jointed Pikie, No. 2600." But it's a little larger and built strong to withstand heavy fishing for pike, muskies, lake trout and the varieties of lighter saltwater fish. Its metal, line to hook construction makes it amply strong for any fish except the heavier saltwater species. Size: 4 7/8", 1 1/8 oz. Colors: natural pike scale finish, natural perch scale finish, white with red head, golden shiner scale finish, rainbow, silver flash. **$40-$80**

The Creek Chub Dinger No. 5600 Series 1934-1954

The Midget Dinger No. 6100 Series 1940-1947

This Dinger (4", 1/2 oz.) has a metal lip, two ventrally located treble hooks, and a broom-like tail. A distinctive feature of this plug is a metal plate covering the top of the head although it is not always present. The Midget Dinger (3 1/2", 3/8 oz.) was just a smaller version available in the same colors. Colors: Natural Pikie, scale finish; natural perch, scale finish; natural dace, scale finish; golden shiner, scale finish; white body, red head, solid black; silver flash; natural frog finish. **$50-$150**

The Husky Dinger No. 5700 Series 1939-1946

Appearing at the same time as the Creek Chub Dinger, 5600 Series, this is a larger, stronger version. Size: 5 1/2", 1 oz. Colors: Natural Pikie, scale finish; natural perch, scale finish; natural dace, scale finish; golden shiner, scale finish; white body with red head, silver flash; natural frog finish. **$150-$300**

Husky Dinger.

The Plunking Dinger 1940-1952

This is the same design as the original Plunker but with the addition of the broom-like hair tail of the Dingers. It is equipped with two treble hooks. Size: 4", 5/8oz. Colors: Natural Pikie, scale finish; natural perch, scale finish; golden shiner, scale finish; natural dace, scale finish; white body with red head, solid black; silver flash; natural frog finish; red wing; white scale. **$50-$150**

The Pop'n Dunk 1941-1954

The Pop'n Dunk was essentially the same as the Plunker with a metal lip added. Size: 2 3/4", 5/8 oz. Colors: Natural Pikie scale; natural perch scale; natural frog finish; dace scale; white with red head, silver flash; red wing; white scale. **$40-$75**

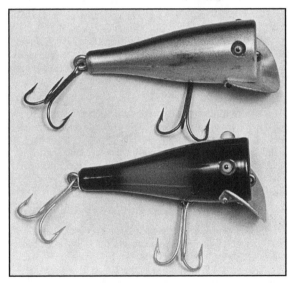

Pop'n Dunk

Mouse, 6380 Series

Mouse, 6577 Series

Mouse, 6580 Series

1950-1962 (Plastic, 1963-78)

Sometime in the 1950s, Creek Chub acquired the right to manufacture and sell Shakespeare's Swimming Mouse. It retained the Shakespeare numbers for the lures. It can be difficult telling the difference between the Shakespeare product and the one made by Creek Chub. One good way is to know that the pure Creek Chub Mouse was never made with internal belly weights, glass or tack eyes. They were always painted eyes.

Although the first catalog to list these lure was the 1957 edition, there is good reason to suspect they were around before that. Sizes: No. 6380, 2 1/4", 1/4 oz.; No. 6577, 2 1/2", 3/8 oz.; No. 6580, 2 3/4", 1/2 oz. Colors: (wood): Solid gray, solid black, white body with red head, tiger stripe, pearl, glo-pearl. (plastic): Solid gray, solid black, white with red head, tiger stripe, glo-pearl. Wood: **$15-$30**, Plastic: **$5-$10**

Tiny Tim 1942-1954, 1970-1974

This is a peculiarly shaped plug. It has a reversible metal lip, a belly-mounted treble hook, and a trailing treble. It was available with a deep-diving lip from 1950 through 1953. Size: 1 3/4", 1/2 oz. Colors: Natural Pikie scale, natural perch scale, white scale, white with red head, silver flash, red wing, white and red with wings, spot, gray. **$50-$80**

The Baby Bomber Series No. 6500 1942-1947

The Dive Bomber Series No. 6600 1942-1954

The Big Bomber Series No. 6700 1942-1947

The Bomber was new in 1942 and by 1950 the name had been changed to the "Kreeker," although most collectors refer to all of them as Bombers. The lure had two belly-mounted treble hooks and lip that is part of the lure, not attached with screws. The Baby Bomber had only one belly treble hook. Sizes: No. 6500, 2 1/4", 3/8 oz.; No. 6600, 2 7/8", 5/8 oz.; No. 6700, 3 3/4", 7/8 oz. Colors: Pikie scale; perch scale; golden shiner, silver flash; white with red head; yellow with red head. **$50-$75**

Big Bomber Series

Striper Pikie and Jointed Striper Pikie 1950-1978

This is an extra-strong, bigger and heavier version of the Pikie Minnow that was made for saltwater or very heavy fish. Size: 6 1/4", 3 1/4 oz. Colors: Pikie scale; perch scale; white with red head; mullet; rainbow; silver flash; fire plug; rainbow fire. **$50-$125**

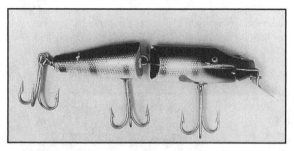

Jointed Striper Pikie.

The "Seven Thousand" 1950-1952

This plug is a very deep runner. It is a reverse running plug with a metal diving lip. It has legs attached to the belly similar to the ones on the No. 300 Series Crawdad, and two belly-mounted treble hooks. Size: 2 3/4", 3/4 oz. Colors: Pikie scale; perch scale; white with redhead, solid black; silver flash; rainbow fire; fire plug. **$100-$225**

Pocket Rocket 1957-1961

The lure is equipped with extra heavy hooks and the strong through-body wire construction. It was never made in plastic. Size: 4", 1 1/8 oz. Colors: silver flash, blue flash. **$5-$10**

Surfster, 7200 Series

Wood, 1953-1968

Plastic, 1964-1965

Surfster, 7300 Series 1953-1959

Salt Water Surfster, 7400 Series 1953-1959

The 7200 Series Surfster is the only one of the series to also be made in plastic. The colors offered on the plastic version were the same as on the wooden lure with the exception of Mullet. Sizes: No. 7200, 4 1/4", 3/4 oz.; No. 7300, 6", 1 7/8 oz.; No. 7400, 7 1/4", 2 1/2 oz. Colors: Pikie scale, perch scale, white with red head, silver flash, blue flash, purple eel, yellow flash, mullet, solid red. **$75-$125**

Surf Popper 1955-1959

This is a fairly difficult lure to find due to its short-lived production time. It was designed for surf casting from the beach. It is a very large version of the 7100 Series Snook Plunker/Salt Popper. Size: 7 1/8", 4 oz. Colors: white body with red head, silver flash, blue flash, purple eel, yellow flash. **$75-$200**

Surf Darter 1955-1959

The 1956 catalog calls this lure new. It is a very big plug designed for the surf caster, made strong with the through-body harness construction. Size: 7", 4 oz. Colors: white body with red head, mullet, silver flash, blue flash, purple eel, yellow flash. **$75-$175**

Salt Spin Darter 1955-1959

This is a longer, stronger version of the classic 2000 Series Darter made for salt water use. Size: 5 1/2", 2 1/4 oz. Colors: white with red head, mullet, silver flash, blue flash, purple eel, yellow flash. **$75-$175**

Viper (Plastic) 1965-1971

The last catalog it was illustrated in was the 1971 edition, but the lure remained in the price list until 1978. Size: 3 1/2", 1/4 oz. Colors: white with red head, silver shiner, silver flash, blue flash, chrome. **$20-$30**

Spoontail 1954-1956

There are two sizes of the Spoontail. For some reason this handsome wood-bodied lure wasn't around very long. The body is attached to a metal plate that serves as the lip, under-belly, and tail piece all in one. Sizes: No. 9100, 2 1/4", 1/4 oz.; No. 500, 3 1/2", 1/2 oz. Colors: Pikie, perch, white body with red head, silver flash. **$30-$40**

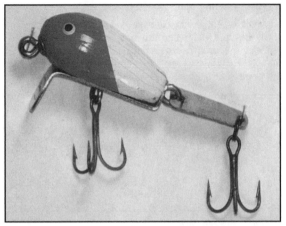

Spoontail

Spinning Deepster 1953-1955

This 2 1/4" bulbous head plug reminds one of Eger Bait Company's Bull Nose Frog. Unlike the Eger bait, however, this one has a longish metal deep-diving lip. It must not have been much of a seller because it lasted two years or less. The black sucker in the color list is a unique color design created for this lure alone. Colors: pike scale, perch scale, white with red head, silver flash, black sucker. **$20-$30**

Feather Casting Minnow 1924-1927

New in 1924, this lure disappears as a casting lure by 1928. It was then apparently redesigned for use with a fly rod. It has a propeller spinner at the nose and trails fancy feathers. Size: 1 5/8", 1/2 oz. Colors: white and red; creek chub, scale finish; yellow perch, scale finish; goldfish, scale finish. **$250-$400**

Feather Casting Minnow

Streeker (Plastic)

S Series 1971-1978

LS Series 1973-1978

This is a plastic underwater lure that "... casts like a bullet," equipped with two propeller spinners and two treble hooks. Sizes: S, 3", 3/8 oz.; LS, 4 1/2", 1 oz. Colors: pike scale, perch scale, white with red head, silver shiner, purple, silver flash, chrome. **$5-$10**

The "Wicked Wiggler" (S Series) 1926-1940

Cohokie 1968-1978

This 2 1/4" Wiggling Spoon (original name) was new in 1926. Initially the lure was offered in two hook styles, a feathered treble (S1) or a hook for pork rind (S2). In the 1935 catalog, a third option was offered, a single-pointed rigid hook (S3). In 1967, this lure was re-released more than 20 years after it was discontinued. The new version, now called the Cohokie, was listed in the catalogs in a larger and smaller size than the earlier model. The larger size, however, was actually the same size as the original. Size: S, 2 1/2", 3/4 oz.; No. 1000, 2 1/2", 1/2 oz.; No. 1100, 2", 1/4 oz. Old model: **$40-$60**, New model: **$10-$20**

Wicked Wiggler

Wiggle-Jig 1966-1967

This must not have been a hot seller. It was announced as "New for 1966," was listed and illustrated in the 1967 edition of the catalog, and was gone in the 1968 edition. An all-metal lure of two-piece construction, it had two holes, one as an eye and the other in the dorsal fin. The listing said to snap a swivel in the eye for casting or trolling and in the fin for ice jigging. Listed as the Jiggle-Jig in 1967, it was available in silver or gold sides. The lower metal belly plate was pink. The listings gave no length. **$30-$40**

Sinful Sal 1930-1940

This is a wobbling spoon with twin blade spinners, and a single treble hook attached to the trailing edge of the spoon. Size: 2 3/4", 3/4 oz. Colors: all nickel, nickel inside, white & red outside; copper inside, white & red outside; nickel inside, white & black outside; nickel inside, yellow spotted outside; nickel inside, frog finish outside. **$25-$50**

Sinful Sals.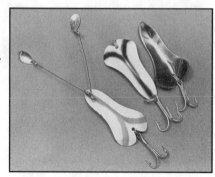

Creek Chub/Shur-Strike

Sometime in the late 1920s, the Creek Chub Bait Company initiated the Shur-Strike line to offer the fisherman a less expensive lure and to compete with other companies. In addition to retailing them as Shur-Strike, it sold them wholesale to other companies for distribution under their own brand. Some of them: W. Bingham Co. (Uncle Tom Lures); True Value (True Value); Montgomery Ward (Ward's, Hawthorn); Sears and Roebuck (Meadow Brook). They each had their own distinctive box. Creek Chub was not mentioned as the manufacturer.

The baits were not cheaply made. They have glass eyes or tack eyes and cup/screw eye hardware. It never used the signature Creek Chub dive lip. It didn't use the Creek Chub series numbering system, using only combinations of letters or letters and numbers. It made dozens of Shur-Strike baits and you can run into almost anything. **$10-$40**

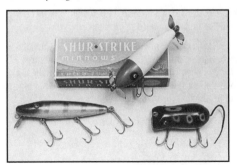

Shur-Strikes

Paw Paw Bait Company

Paw Paw, Michigan

Paw Paw was in business continuously beginning around 1909 as the Moonlight Bait Company into the 1960s. In 1970, the Shakespeare Company bought out all Paw Paw rights and equipment.

Catalog and all advertising studies have established that a transition of the Moonlight Bait Company to the Paw Paw Bait Company took place somewhere around 1927.

It is known that Paw Paw produced many fine plugs with glass eyes but most found so far have tacks or brads for eyes. They were installed before painting the body and the greatest majority of those found have had the paint knocked off through use.

To help recognize a Paw Paw lure, look for the one-piece combination diving lip and forward hook hanger.

Paw Paw's catalogs have proved to be unreliable in identifying what may have been available from year to year. Some lures seem never to have been cataloged at all and others sporadically. Still others only appear in one year. This makes it difficult to pin down years of production for many of their lures.

Paw Paw Fish Decoy

Found only in a 1929 catalog, this was actually called "The Greatest Spearing Minnow." It has glass eyes, two painted metal fins on each side, a metal dorsal and tail fin. It has three internal belly weights. The only color listed was perch, but there is at least one more called red horse. **$125-$225**

Bullhead Series

The Bullhead was new in the 1929 catalog at 4 1/4" and 3/4 oz. with glass eyes. Colors: silver perch, white with red head, pearl finish with red head, frog finish, dark brown (bullhead color), black with red spots. **$100-$150**

Bullheads

The Crab

Not found in any of the available catalogs, this lure has a wooden body and two braided feelers trailing, measuring 2 1/4". Dates and color finishes unknown. **$50-$75**

Crawdad

They were listed as "new" in the 1929 catalog. The lures both originally had two claws and six legs made of flexible rubber. Original models probably have glass eyes and occur only in a natural crawfish finish. Later models (c. 1931 and later) will have the tack painted eyes (TPE) and several other finishes. Size: 2 3/4", 3/4 oz. Colors: Yellow with black stripes, solid black, green with black stripes, solid red, brown with black stripes, brown with red stripes, black with yellow stripes. **$50-$75**

Crawdads. Photo courtesy Jim Muma

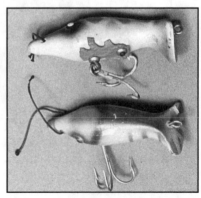

Crippled Minnow

Paw Paw Injured Minnow

3400 Series

Sometimes called the Crippled Minnow in Paw Paw catalogs, this is an unusual lure. It has glass eyes and two side-mounted trebles. It was first found listed in a 1928 mixed tackle catalog of the Shapleigh Hardware Company. Size: 4", 5/8 oz. Colors: green scale; white with red head, pearl with red head, silver scale; gold scale; frog finish. **$75-$100**

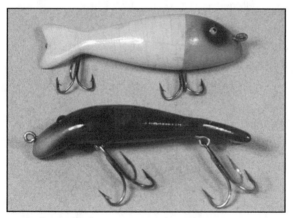

Injured Minnow

Lippy Joe Series 6300

Lippy Joe

Lippy Sue

The catalogs list only two sizes that were called Lippy Joe, the regular and the Baby Lippy Joe. They measure 3 1/8" and 2 3/4" respectively. There are actually a number of sizes as well as jointed versions of this lure. Some were listed with no name and others seem to have been named by size. They all share the same body style. The Lippy Sue seems to be no more than the standard lure with a feathered trailing treble, a "skirt" as it were.

Paw Paw introduced "a new iridescent scale finish" in 1940. A plastic version came out in 1942 called the Floater-Sinker. Even though it made plastic versions, it continued to produce them in wood into the 1960s. **$15-$25**

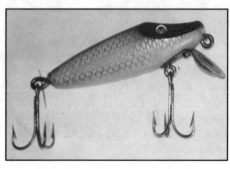

Lippy Sue.
Photo
courtesy
Ken
Bernoteit

Paw Paw Mouse Bait

The Paw Paw Mouse Bait dates from about 1931 to the 1950s. It has a flexible leather tail, one-piece combination diving lip and hook hanger. It was later called Minnie Mouse. Size: 2 1/2", 5/8 oz. Colors: mouse color (gray), black body with white head, white body with red head. **$100-$200**, Minnie Mouse: **$20-$40**

Paw Paw Mouse

Natural Hair Mouse

The earliest reference found was in a mixed tackle catalog of 1928 from the Shapleigh Hardware Company. It listed and pictured the No. 60 Hair Mouse at 3" and 1/2 oz. in Gray head or White head. A 1929 catalog introduced the larger size as new. It was offered as the Musky Mouse and Sea Mouse. Colors: gray head, yellow head, red head, white head. Sizes and values: Fly rod size, 1 1/4", **$100-$200**; No. 60, 2 1/2", 1/2 oz., **$75-$100**; No. 60, 3", 5/8 oz., **$75-$100**; No. 80 (Musky Mouse), 4 1/4", **$300-$400**; No. 90 (Sea Mouse), 4 1/4", **$300-$400**

Natural Hair Mouse

Old Flatside

Old Flatside Junior

(also called Wounded Minnow)

The earliest listing found was in a 1939 catalog, for a flat side floater, 3 1/2" long with only one side treble and a trailing treble (2T). A 1940 catalog listed a two side treble version (3T). In 1941, only the single side hook (2T) was offered and then in 1942 they were back to the 3T version. Earliest Flatsides have glass eyes mounted at the sides of the head, then came tack painted eyes (TPE) on the sides, then TPE on top. Colors: yellow perch, white with red head, shad, pike scale, frog, silver flitters, dace, black with silver flitters, gold shiner scale, green with gold dots, rainbow, perch scale. It was made available covered in real frog skin in 1940. **$20-$30**

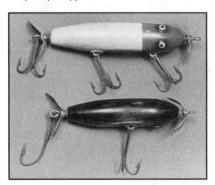

Old Flatsides

Darter, Series 2500

Paw Paw made a Darter like just about all the lure makers of the day. This is a 1930s glass-eyed lure that has a hollow in the face where the line tie is located. Size: 4", 3/4 oz. Colors: green scale, white with red head, rainbow, silver scale, frog, perch. **$20-$30**

Darter, Series 9200

This Paw Paw Darter is built in the more traditional body style, both straight and jointed. The straight Darter could be bought with a tail propeller spinner. It was new in 1940. Shakespeare continued the lure after 1970, calling it the Dragon Fly. Size: 3 3/4", 1/2 oz. Colors (Paw Paw): white with red head, pike scale, yellow with red and yellow spots, frog special, black with silver and red spots, silver flitters. (Shakespeare): silver flitter, shad, yellow with red on black spots, frog, black with red on gold spots, white with red head. **$10-$20**

Bass Seeker

First found in a 1928 mixed tackle catalog, this is a lure retained from the old Moonlight Bait Company line. It has a cupped head with a short heavy wire line tie attached to the screw eye and a projecting lower jaw. They were first available with glass eyes, then tack painted eyes. They came equipped with either two or three treble hooks and were made in two sizes. Sizes: No. 2600, 4", 3/4 oz.; No. 4600, 3 1/4", 3/4 oz. Colors: Green scale; white with red head, pearl finish with red head, gold scale; frog finish; perch; metallic glitters; red head, gold body, red head, green body, perch finish with green and silver metallic flitters; red head, silver body. **$20-$30**

Bass Seeker

Paw Paw River Type

There are two slightly different body designs for this plug. The more tapered body and relatively blunt nose plugs are likely the oldest. Size: 2 5/8", 1/2 oz. Colors: Perch scale; green scale; silver scale; pike scale; frog scale; white with red head; rainbow, silver flitters. **$15-$25**

Pike Minnow Lure

No. 1600 Series

Early versions were available with only two treble hooks. Later models have three trebles and a groove on each side of the nose. All lures have the typical Paw Paw tack painted eyes and combination one-piece diving plane and forward hook mount. Sizes and prices: Dreadnaught, 6 3/4", **$200-$300**; Musky, 6 1/4", 2 3/8 oz., **$40-$60**; Musky Jtd., 6 1/4", 2 3/8 oz., **$40-$50**, Regular, 4 1/2", 3/4 oz., **$20-$30**; Regular Jtd., 4 1/2", 3/4 oz., **$20-$30**; Baby, 3 1/4", 1/2 oz., **$10-$20**; Baby Jtd., 3 1/4", 1/2 oz., **$10-$20**. Colors: green scale; gold scale; white with red head, pearl finish; frog finish; yellow perch; pike scale; silver flitters; shad, dace; black with silver flitters; gold shiner scale. The 4 1/2" straight pike minnow was made available covered in real frog skin in 1940.

Pike Minnows

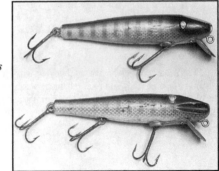

Paw Paw Wilson Wobbler

Carried over to Paw Paw from the old Moonlight line, this lure was last listed in catalogs of the early 1930s. The catalogs listed it as 4" and 3/4 oz. It comes with three trebles, two trebles, or two double hooks. Colors: white with red flutes, red, yellow, rainbow, fox fire. **$20-$40**

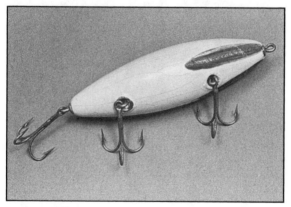

Wilson Wobbler

Bullfrog

A 1929 catalog listed and pictured this unusual tack-eyed lure. It was missing from catalogs by 1939. Size was not given, but colors listed were bullfrog finish, and white with red head. **$200-$300**

Bullfrogs

Fox Fire

This is the famous Moonlight Floating Bait retained by Paw Paw from the old Moonlight line. They changed the name and continued to offer it in their catalogs until 1939. They are 4" long with a belly treble and trailing treble hook (2T) and two color options: Fox Fire (luminous white) and white body with red head. **$25-$40**

Jug Head

This is a 1 3/4" fly rod version of the Fox Fire. It has a double hook hung on the belly and was available in at least four color finishes: white body with red head, green spotted, red spotted, rainbow. **$100-$200**

Spinning Pickerel and Bass Lure

Not much is known about this little 2" lure. The box stated that you needed to look for Paw Paw's "Bass Bugs and Feathered Lures." **$10-$20**, with box: **$30-$40**

Paw Paw Popper

This Popper dates from about the early 1930s and was missing from catalogs by 1949. Earliest examples will have glass eyes. Size: 3", 3/4 oz. Colors: yellow perch, rainbow, green with gold scale, pike scale, perch scale, white with red head, frog, silver flitters, genuine frog skin covering (1940). **$10-$20**

Plunker

First found in a 1929 catalog, this lure came in only one size: 2", 3/4 oz. Colors: yellow, white with red head, black with white head, silver, frog, perch. **$20-$35**

Casting Lure

The 1930s propeller spinner bait came only in white body and red head finish with no eyes. It had only one treble (belly mounted) and was 2" and 1/2 oz. **$25-$40**

Caster Bait Series

Paw Paw introduced these in 1940-41. All in the series, sometimes called "Nature Baits," are wood-bodied and all but the larger Saltwater/Muskie-size casters have the minnow tail. All also have the combination round diving lip/forward hook hanger. There are nine different lures in the series, each in small and/or large size with different hook configuration and some jointed version, making a total of 23 for the entire line. Most were available in a choice of 13 paint finish patterns.

Pike-Caster - Shape and action of a baby pike. Made in two sizes, 3 1/2" and 5 1/2", both straight and jointed. There were three treble hooks on the large size and two on the small ones.

Perch-Caster - Swimming and darting action. Made in two sizes, 3 1/2" and 5". Both in straight and jointed models. Hook configuration same as above.

Chub-Caster - Imitates a chub minnow. Iridescent finish. Made in two sizes, both straight and jointed, 3 1/2" and 5" with two treble hooks.

Shiner-Caster - "Shimmering silvery markings like the live shiner minnow." Two sizes, 3 1/2" and 5" with two treble hooks.

Dace-Caster - "Shimmering pearl finish." Made in two sizes, 3 1/2" straight and jointed and 5" straight only. Two treble hooks. Natural dace coloring only.

Trout-Caster - "True to nature shape and action." Made in two sizes, 3 1/2' and 5", both straight and jointed. Two treble hooks on small size and three on the large.

Bass-Caster - One size at 2 1/2". Two treble hooks. "Shimmering pearl finish."

Mud Minnow Caster - One size at 3 1/4". Two treble hooks.

Saltwater and Muskie-caster - Sometimes called the Dreadnought by collectors this lure was made in a 6 1/4" size, both straight and jointed. Three treble hooks.

Colors: yellow perch, green with gold scale, white with red head, silver scale with green back, natural pike, green back with silver flitters, yellow scale with black back and stripes, silver scale with red back and gray stripes, gold scale with red stripes, natural gold scale, silver scale with red head and stripes, iridescent silver scale with gray back, pike, perch, chub, shiner, dace, trout, bass, mud minnow. **$50-$200**

Jointed Chub-Caster.

Wounded Trout 7700-S Series

Measuring 3 1/2", the Wounded Trout has propeller spinners fore and aft and the hook on the side in the "injured minnow" style as well as a tail treble. It dates to about 1939. It is often confused with a Paw Paw lure that uses the same body. The color patterns are listed with the Caster-Bait Series. **$300-$400**

Underwater Minnow 3300 Series

Found only in a 1939 edition of the catalogs, it measures 2 1/2" and has three treble hooks, typical painted cup hardware and a nose-mounted spinner. Colors: yellow perch, green with gold dots, white with red head, rainbow, pike scale, perch scale, frog, silver flitters. Collector value range: **N/A**

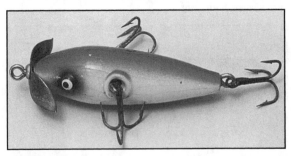

Underwater Minnow

Pumpkin Seed, No.1300 Series

First available sometime in the 1930s, these small lures have two propeller spinners, a trailing treble and belly-mount treble utilizing cup and screw eye hardware. Made only in a 1 7/8", 1/2 oz. size. Colors: yellow perch; green, gold dots; white, red head; rainbow; pike scale; perch scale; frog; silver flitters. **$20-$40**

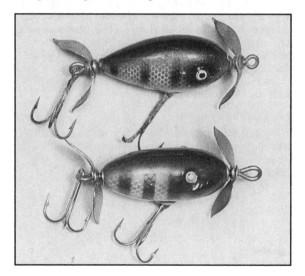

Pumpkin Seed lures.

Jig-a-Lure, No. 2700 Series

Little Jigger, No. 2600 Series

Described as new in the 1942 catalog, this lure underwent a metamorphosis by 1949 and was gone from the catalogs by the 1960s. Its first incarnation was as a handsome little plug with glass eyes. By 1949, they had been replaced by painted eyes. Both had a metal belly plate that was a dive or wobble plane at the nose and terminated at the tail as another plane. The Little Jigger is the same lure with a feathered treble. Size: 1 5/16", 5/8 oz. Colors: perch, red head with white body and silver metallic, pike, red stripe and scale with gold sides and white belly, silver body with white scale and blue stripe, yellow body with red head and gold metallic, black with silver flitters. **$15-$20**

Paw Paw Plenty Sparkle

Aptly named, this wooden lure came in two sizes, 4" and 3 1/4". The larger size has five rhinestones on the belly and the smaller has only three. Both have rhinestone eyes. Box marking identified the Series as No. 5500. **$20-$30**

Paw Paw Sucker

The No. 2400 Series was not found in catalogs. Size: 4 3/8".
$150-$200

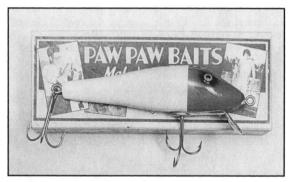

Paw Paw Sucker

Skippy Minnow

Not much is known beyond the illustrations in the catalogs.
$10-$15

The Shiner

The Little Shiner

First available in a 1942 catalog, the lures were made in weighted and non-weighted models and in a "Jr." size. In the 1949 catalog, The Shiner was featured in a box with the Torpedo headed "New Double-Strength Lures for Southern Fishing." It was made as a sinker and a floater. The Little Shiner was made only as a floater. Sizes: No. 8400 (Jr.), 2 3/4", 3/8 oz.; No. 8500, 4", 1/2 oz.; No. 8600, 4", 3/4 oz. Colors: Yellow belly with brown and silver back, yellow perch, green scale, white with red head, shad, pike scale, silver metallic, shad, frog, black with silver ribs. **$10-$20**

The Shiners.

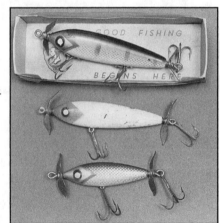

Slim Lindy or Torpedo

Midget Spinning Torpedo

In a 1929 catalog, this lure was called Slim Lindy, apparently in honor of Charles Lindbergh, who made his famous trans-Atlantic solo flight in May of 1927. It was the Torpedo by 1939 or so. They were made in a sinking model only until the late 1940s when a floating version was added. Oldest of the Slim Lindys will likely have glass eyes. The Midget Spinning Torpedo didn't show up in catalogs until much later. Sizes: No. 2400-S, 4", 5/8 oz.; No. 2400-F, 4", 1/2 oz.; No. 800, 1 7/8". Colors: green scale, gold scale, white with red head, pike scale, silver flitters, white with black serpentine stripe, white with green serpentine stripe, green with black serpentine stripe, white with vertical black stripe, yellow belly with brown and silver back, yellow perch, shad, frog, green with black serpentine stripe, black scale with yellow belly, coach dog (new in 1949). **$10-$20**

Weedless Wow

Called "new" in a 1941 catalog, there are two sizes. The larger measures 2 1/4" and the smaller, 1 3/4". They persisted in the line well into the 1960s. By the early 1960s, the body had been modified by inserting a double hook into the tail end and hanging rubber legs from screw eyes on each side. Be sure not to confuse this with another Paw Paw lure of the same name. Colors: perch scale, pike scale, red head, frog finish, silver flitters, fluorescent. **$125-$200**

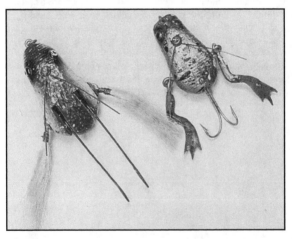

Weedless Wow

Weedless Wow No. 700 (Metal)

First found listed in a 1929 Paw Paw catalog, this spinner bait was listed at 5/8 oz. It is, however, reported to have been around as early as 1915. It was available with a red, white, or black bucktail. **$50-$90**

Metal Weedless Wow

Croaker

This frog plug was apparently new in 1940. It has a covering of genuine frog skin. It came in two sizes: 3" and fly rod size (1 1/4"), with a slightly different body design and only one integrated single hook. **$75-$125**, Fly rod size: **$150-$200**

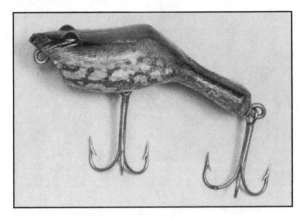

Croaker.

Wotta-Frog

Wotta-Frog Jr. (No. 74)

A catalog listing stated "New for 1941." They have hair or modified bucktails tied to each of the trailing treble hooks. To find them with the hair/trebles intact is fairly unusual. The junior size was new around 1948-49. The Wotta-Frog persisted into the 1960s when it was offered without the dive lip. **$40-$75**. Wotta-Frog fly rod lures measure 1/2" and 1/4" and feature rubber legs and cork bodies. **$30-$40**

Wotta- Frogs

Belly Spoon Wobbler

Belly Spoon

The Belly Spoon Wobbler measures 5 1/4" long and consists of the lure body attached to a polished metal belly plate. The metal serves as the belly hook holder and the dive plane. Colors are unknown except for white with gold scale, red head and stripe. Collector value range: **$100-$200**. The Belly Spoon is obviously a derivative of the metal portion of the other lure. It measures 3 3/4" and is white with red head and fins. Other colors are unknown. **$15-$25**

Centipede

These three measure 5", 3 1/4" and 1 1/2" respectively. They are made of metal. Colors: red with black splatter, yellow with the same splatter, and black with gold. **$30-$60**

Centipedes. Photo courtesy of Jim Muma

Mister 13 Junior, No. 1800

Mister 13 Senior, No. 1900

A 1963 catalog inferred this lure was new. It could be an older lure. Size: No. 1800, 2 3/4", 3/8 oz.; No. 1900, 4", 5/8 oz. Colors: perch scale, yellow perch, white with red head, frog scale with red head, shiner scale with red head, white coach dog, yellow coach dog. Wood: No data, Plastic: **$5-$15**

Paw Paw's "Economy" Lures

It appears that Paw Paw made a selection of lures that were not as expensive to make as their regular lures. These lines were sold at lower prices or, as the company says in some of its ad copy, "Designed to meet the popular demand for a good wood minnow at a moderate price."

The first of these to come along were the "Zipper" lures in the late 1920s into the early 1930s. Shortly after this, carded "Lucky Lures" were offered to tackle dealers. In January of 1939, it introduced a series of 10 "Silver Creek Lures." It also marketed many display cards of up to nine different lures to dealers for display in the early 1960s. These were called "Make 'em Strike" lures: "... Priced for Competitive Selling."

Pike

Found in its original box, this lure is typical Paw Paw all the way. It appears identical to the No. 1600 series Pike Minnow Lure. They were the same shape, length, and weight. They even shared some of the same color finishes. The only difference is that the No.

1600 series was available in paint patterns that were probably more expensive to render. Sizes: No. 1400, 3 1/4", 1/2 oz.; No. 1600, 4 1/2", 3/4 oz. Colors: green with gold dots, white with red head, rainbow, pike scale, perch scale, frog finish, silver flitters. **$20-$30**

Clothes Pin Bait (Make 'em Strike)

Almost all the major players in the lure business in the 1930s and 1940s had a clothes pin type lure. Paw Paw was no exception. It was listed as available in the 1939 and 1941 catalogs as part of the "Make 'em Strike" line. Sizes: No. 2300S, 1 1/2", 1/4 oz.; No. 2300M, 2 1/2", 1/2 oz.; No. 2300L, 3 5/8", 5/8 oz. Colors: yellow body with red head and silver flitters, white body with red head, rainbow, silver flitters, red head with spotted body, Christmas tree (metallic). **$15-$20**

McGinty (Make 'em Strike)

A tiny 1 1/8" wood body brass wing lure, its catalog listing said it was "A spinning Pickerel and Bass lure." Colors: copper with red head, white with red head and flitters, rainbow trout, silver flitters, gold spotted, green and white spotted. **$35-$45**

Wobbler (Silver Creek Lures)

Wobblers were first listed in a 1938 catalog, calling them new. There were three sizes with slightly different body designs. Each has the typical painted cup hardware. Sizes: 2 1/2", 3", 3 3/4". Colors: white body red head; perch scale; pike scale; silver flitters; yellow perch; rainbow; frog; white, red and green spots. **$5-$10**

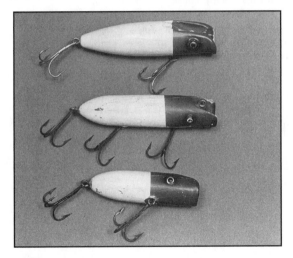

Wobblers

Groove Head Fly Rod Lure

This is a tiny fly rod version of the Wobbler. It was not part of the "Silver Creek Line," but it is a dead ringer for the Wobbler except for its size and the double hook at the belly. Colors: yellow perch, white with red head, rainbow, silver scale, natural pike, green scale, silver flitters. **$10-$15**

Paw Paw Plastic Lures

The company marketed its first plastic lure in 1941 with the Flap Jack and followed in 1942 with the Tenite Floater-Sinker. That was pretty much it until 1949 when it introduced 12 lures as being newly offered in plastic. Three of them, however, were two models of the Flap Jack and the Floater-Diver introduced seven to eight years earlier. At the same time it began offering a new finish on the plastics: Fireplug finishes. They are: neon red; fire orange; sodium yellow; saturn green; rainbow. It added one more plastic lure, the Woggle Bug, in 1963. It continued production of many of the wooden lures right up until the Shakespeare purchase in 1970.

Flap Jack, No. 3600 Series

Flap Jack Jr., No. 6500 Series

Midget Flap Jack, No. 6600 Series

Flap Jack Phantom, No. 3400 Series

Three Hook Flap Jack, No. 5300 Series

The "new improved" Flap Jack was introduced in the 1963 catalog. The first one, introduced in 1941, was the same shape, but it had complicated "ball bearing" hook hardware where four separate treble hooks hung from metal pieces located on each side fore and aft. The hooks dangled on wires attached to the inside of the metal piece. It had simple cup and screw eye hardware with one belly treble and a trailing treble. In 1949, when Paw Paw introduced the plastic lures, there was another called the Flap Jack Phantom that appeared to be fatter than the original. It had its own set of colors.

By the early 1960s, the lure had evolved and was available in a three hook version and two smaller sizes, the Flap Jack Jr. and the Midget Flap Jack.

The Flap Jack is one of a few Paw Paw lures Shakespeare continued to offer after it bought the company. Sizes: No. 3400, 3 1/2", 3/4 oz.; No. 3600, 3 1/2", 3/4 oz.; No. 5300, 3 1/2", 3/4 oz.; No. 6500, 2 1/2", 1/4 oz.; No. 6600, 1 1/4", 1/16 oz. Colors (Original Flap-Jack): perch scale, white with red head, pike scale, silver flitters, yellow and black with red spots, orange with red and black spots, light orange with red tip and black spots and top, white with red tip and top and spots, green frog, yellow with red tip and black top and spots, yellow with red and black spots, white with red and black spots, fluorescent, white with red head. (Flap Jack Phantom): yellow scale with silver ribs, green scale with silver ribs, white with red head and silver ribs, silver scale with black ribs, green with silver flash, orange scale with black ribs. **$20-$25**

Flap Jack

Floater-Sinker

Dapper Dan (Shakespeare)

This bait was introduced in 1942 and it was made in two models, a floater and a sinker. The Midget was a smaller model of this plastic lure. It was another of the Paw Paw lures that Shakespeare continued to offer. Sizes: No. 3700, 3", 5/8 oz.; No. 3800, 3", 5/8 oz.; No. 3900, 2 1/4", 3/8 oz. Colors: yellow perch, white with red head, red with white head, pike scale, black with white ribs, silver with white ribs, silver with black ribs, yellow with white ribs. **$5-$10**

Woggle Bug

"Sensational NEW!" was the heading over this lure in the 1963 catalog. Sizes: WB-700, 2 1/4", 1/4 oz.; WB-900, 3", 5/8 oz. Colors: Perch scale, white with red head, pike scale, frog, silver flitters, black scale with yellow belly. **$15-$20**

Plastic Lures Released in 1949

These are a group of lures that were illustrated on one page as newly released. There were no other details beyond size, weight and colors found.

Shore Minnow, No. 200 Series – 2 3/4", 1/2 oz. Colors: Yellow with belly scale and silver ribs, green with belly scale and silver ribs, dark red with silver metallic, white with red head and silver ribs and belly scale, black with silver metallic, orange with black ribs and belly scale, white with red ribs and belly scale, gold with gold metallic. **$5-$10**

Transparent Zigger, No. 300 Series. This is the same lure as the Zigger, in different color patterns. It has exactly the same color choices as the Shore Minnow. **$10-$15**

Zigger, No. 400 Series - 3", 1/2 oz. Colors: White body with black back and scale, perch scale, white body with red head, shad scale, dace scale, pike scale. **$10-$15**

Crazy Mike, No. 3300 Series – 3 1/2", 3/4 oz. Colors: Yellow scale with silver ribs, green scale with silver ribs, white with red head and silver ribs, silver scale with black ribs, green with silver flash, orange scale with black ribs, fireplug finishes. **$10-$20**

Platypuss, No. 3500 Series – 3 1/2", 5/8 oz. Colors: perch scale, white with red head, shad scale, pike scale, frog, dace scale, trout, orange with black spots, black with silver flash, yellow with black spots. **$10-$20**

Crazy Mike

Pflueger

The company was established in 1886 by Earnest F. Pflueger, a German immigrant, as the Enterprise Manufacturing Company. Pflueger has always used 1864 as the establishment date for the company and this has been confusing. The explanation lies in its purchase of the American Fish Hook Company, which was established in 1864. Over the years, it continued to exist in the Pflueger family hands as The Enterprise Manufacturing Company, and finally, Pflueger Fishing Tackle.

The company has almost always concentrated very heavily in reels and many types of metal spinner and spoon type artificial baits. These metal lures are numerous and most are not covered here. The following pages catalog the majority of the wooden plugs manufactured over the years to the early 1950s.

Pflueger patents include luminous paint on the fishing lures (first used on his lures in the mid-1880s). Another important Pflueger patent was for the Neverfail hook hanger granted in 1911.

Flying Hellgrammite

An 1885 catalog offers this very early, very rare wood body lure in four luminous models. The illustration with the entry clearly shows the 1883 Comstock patent date on the metal "wings." This is one of the earliest known wood body lures to be commercially produced. The only earlier one known is the 1876 Brush patent with a cork body. **$2,500-$4,000**

Breakless Devon

This all-metal lure was patented August 5, 1879. It was offered in the Pflueger catalog of 1897 in five sizes. By 1906, the Devon was available "Painted" in luminous and non-luminous or in "Brass, Nickel or Gilt." By 1919, the catalog entry was only "Polished Nickel Over All." In the 1920s, it was nickel and copper only. It gained the single blade spinner about this time as well. The lure was offered continuously in those two finishes and five sizes right on into the 1950s. Sizes were: 2", 2 1/4", 2 1/2", 2 3/4" and 3". **$15-$25**

Heart Shaped Spoon No. 661

Empire Spoon

These are very early, extremely rare old spinning spoons that date from around 1897 or before. The unusual seashell pattern on the Heart Shaped Spoon is illustrated in the 1897 catalog. **$650-$800**

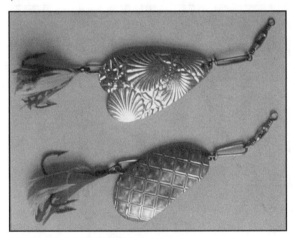

Spoon spinners. Photo courtesy Jim Muma

Tandem Spinner

This lure has been in the Pflueger catalogs from at least 1897. The older one was made in one size only, luminous or non-luminous. Look for the box swivel on the oldest. The newer style came along in the 1920s and have the beaded swivels from then on. **$15-$20**

Tandem Spinners

Colorado Spinner

This carded spinner is stamped "PFLUEGER COLORADO." The whole spoon is stamped with a star pattern. Pflueger bought the W.T.J. Lowe company in 1915 and carried the line for many years. The card states the lure won the highest award for fishing tackle at the Philadelphia Sesquicentennial in 1926. It measures 3 1/2" overall including the treble hook. **$15-$25**

Chum Spoon

Showing up around the mid-to-late 1930s, there were several versions of this metal lure. They were available in two weedless models with the traditional wire weed guard and in something called a "horse hair weed guard." There were five sizes of the spoon portion of the lure listed: 1 1/4" (fly rod size), 1 3/4", 2 11/64", 2 23/32" 3 3/8". **$5-$10**

Fish Decoys

The 1906 catalog lists several "Fish Spearing Decoy Minnow(s)." There were three models made of soft rubber in four sizes: 2", 2 1/2", 3" and 7". They also offered one made of cedar. It was available in two sizes, 3 1/2" and 5". There were two finishes available: "Decorated" and "Plain Silver." Either one could be had in luminous or non-luminous. **$250-$750**

Wizard Wooden Minnow

This glass-eyed plug is another of the earlier ones manufactured under the Enterprise name. It was made in four different sizes (2 1/2", 3", 3 1/2" and 5"). All but the 2 1/2" has five treble hooks (two mounted on each side and one trailing). The 2 1/2" size had only one treble mounted on each side and one trailing (3T). All four have nose- and tail-mounted propellers rotating on a common wire shaft running through the length of the wedge-shaped body. It has glass eyes and finishes available are. **$125-$200**

Wizard Wooden Minnow

Trory Minnow

This is probably among the earliest (c. 1900) wooden plugs in the Pflueger line (manufactured by Enterprise). It is shaped like a minnow with propellers fore and aft. It sports five treble hooks, one trailing and two mounted on each side. It has glass eyes and the body is about 4" long. Color finishes available were not very specific in the early catalogs. **$2,000-$4,000**

Conrad Frog

Mr. Frog first shows up in this model in 1905. It was available in a weedless version in the same style as the regular. Both were available in luminous and non-luminous finishes. The very first ones (pre-1905) were made of pressed ground cork, but subsequent to that they were made of rubber. **$80-$100**

Conrad Frog

Competitor (Wooden Minnow)

This is another early lure manufactured by Enterprise. It was produced in four sizes (2 1 / 2", 3", 3 1/2" and 5"). It has a round body with a wire shaft running through the length of the body connecting the line tie with the trailing hook link. It also has brass washer and tack eyes. It has a propeller mounted at the nose and the tail, one treble hook trailing, and one treble mounted on each side (3T). Colors: silver belly with green back and a solid silver color. It does not appear in catalogs from 1925 on. **$100-$175**

The "Monarch" Minnows (pre-1925)

Several types and sizes of plugs were called "Monarch." They were made as floating, underwater, and strong underwater especially for musky fishing. It is known that the regular underwater and the floating versions came packed in wooden slide-cover boxes. The collector will be fortunate indeed to find one in the very rare original packing box. None of these plugs are found in 1925 or later catalogs. **$200-$400**

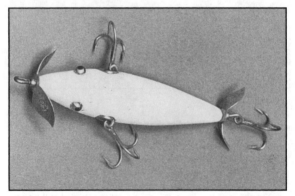

"Monarch" Minnows

Monarch Underwater Series 2100

The Monarch Underwater was made in two different sizes:
2 3/4" and 3 5/8". The smaller has a side-mounted treble hook
on each side and one trailing (3T) and the larger size has two on
each side and one trailing (5T). Both sizes had nose and tail propellers. Each size was available in 12 finishes: white belly, blended green back; white belly, blended slate back; yellow belly,
blended rainbow back; yellow belly, blended brown back; red
belly, blended brown back; silver belly, blended blue back; silver
belly, blended olive green back; solid white; solid red; solid silver.
$200-$400

Monarch Underwater Muskallonge

Series 2200

The Monarch Underwater Muskallonge (catalog spelling) was
made in two sizes: 3 5/8" and 5" for heavy game fish. Each size
has the through-body shaft on which was mounted the nose and
tail propellers. The lures have one treble hook on each side
(mounted to the shaft) and a trailing treble (3T). Colors: white
belly, blended green back; shite belly, blended slate back; shite
belly, blended rainbow back; yellow belly, blended brown back;
red belly, blended brown back. **$200-$400**

Monarch Floater Series 2300

The Monarch Floater was also available in two sizes: 2 3/4" and 4" with only the smaller being originally available with an optional buck tail trailing treble hook. The smaller has only a nose propeller, but the larger one also has a tail propeller. Both have a trailing and belly-mounted treble hook (2T). Colors: white belly, blended green back; white belly, blended slate back; white belly, blended rainbow back; yellow belly, blended brown back; red belly, blended brown back; silver belly, blended dark blue back. **$250-$400**

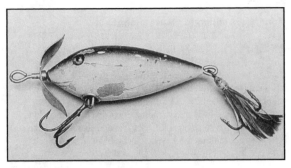

Monarch Floater

Simplex Minnow (pre-1925)

This is a beautiful little wooden minnow made in only a 1 3/4" size. They came in a small wooden box. These are sinkers, unless you use the accessory buoy to hold it close to the surface on retrieve. Earliest catalog was 1909. It was available in two qualities: The Premium with gold-plated hardware and The Favorite with nickel-plated hardware. They were made with one, two and three belly weights. The two-weight models are the oldest. They were not found in 1925 or subsequent catalogs. **$75-$150**

Red Devil

Pflueger brought this relatively hard-to-find lure into the line around 1920 and it disappeared from their catalogs in the 1940s. It was always available only in a red head, white body paint finish. The wood body measures 2 5/8". The spinner blade on it is marked "PFLUEGER" on one blade and "2" on the other. **$40-$50**

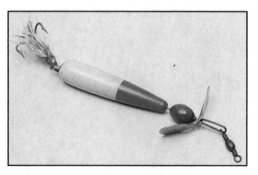

Red Devil

Neverfail

This name first appears in catalogs around the late 1920s, but the plug is remarkably similar, if not identical, to some of the older Monarch series plugs. It is known to have been produced by the Enterprise Manufacturing Company in the 1910s under the Four Brothers brand. The Neverfail was made into the 1950s (3" only in 1955) in two sizes, both being underwater baits. The smaller has two opposite side-mounted trebles and a trailing treble (3T) and the larger has two additional side trebles (5T). Both have fore and aft mounted propellers. Sizes: 3", 3/4 oz., and 3 5/8", 1 oz. Colors: luminous paint with gold spots, natural frog scale finish, natural perch scale finish, natural chub scale finish, white body with frog back, white body with green and red spots, yellow body with green and red back, rainbow, solid red, green cracked back, yellow perch, white body with red head, white body with red head and yellow and black spots. **$150-$250**, musky size: **$1,000-$1,500**

Neverfail

Electric Wooden Minnow

This bait was first produced around 1920-21 in two sizes: 2 3/4" and 3 5/8". It has glass eyes, propellers mounted fore and aft, and a through-body wire shaft. The smaller version has two opposite side mounted trebles and a trailing treble (3T). The larger one has two additional opposite side trebles (5T). These lures did not appear in the 1925 or subsequent catalogs. Colors: white belly, blended rainbow back; aluminum belly, blended olive green back; white belly, fancy (cracked) green back; white belly, blended rainbow back; white belly, blended olive green back; white belly, fancy (cracked) green back. **$500-$700**

Electric Wooden Minnow

Kent Frog

New for Pflueger around the late 1910s, the Pflueger Kent Frog had several changes over the years in eyes, hook types and arrangements, and body shapes. The last version has a non-tube floppy propeller. **$400-$900**

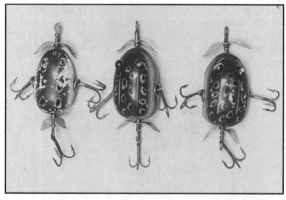

Kent Frogs

Kingfisher Wooden Minnow

This is the same as the Neverfail, made by Pflueger for the Edward K. Tryon company in Philadelphia to be sold under its Kingfisher brand. **$150-$250, with Kingfisher box: $200-$300**

Metalized Minnow

Patented around 1910-11, this plug doesn't appear in catalogs until the late 1920s. It was made in two sizes, the smaller with two opposite side mounted trebles and a trailing treble hook (3T). The larger has two additional side trebles (5T). Both sizes have fore and aft propellers. Color: metalized (polished nickel). **$150-$300**

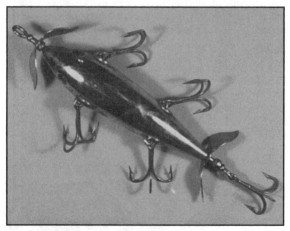

Metalized Minnow

Magnet or Merit 3600 Series

The oldest reference to the Magnet (first name) was a 1916 catalog entry with illustrations. The illustration is identical to a Shakespeare Surface Wonder except the forward hook hanger is extremely close to the collar. It looks as if Pflueger and Shakespeare were buying blank bodies from the same supplier at this time. The name remained Magnet until about 1935 when it was changed to Merit. Colors: white luminous, plain white, white with red head. By 1925, the all white non-luminous white body with red head was the only choice offered. **$40-$50**

Peerless

The Peerless minnow plugs were made as an inexpensive lure line with not quite the quality of the regular Pflueger line. All have opposite side trebles and a trailing treble hook (3T). They also have one nose-mounted propeller. They came along in the late 1920s and apparently didn't stay long. Size: 2 1/2", 1/2oz. Colors: white body, red head; white body, green back; white body, red back. **$30-$50**

Peerless

Peerless or Gem Minnow

This is a very inexpensively constructed critter that looks like another contender for competing with the Shakespeare Little Pirate. **$30-$40**

Globe

This entry must be from 1910 or later. The next reference was in a 1916 Pflueger catalog. It was called the Portage Reflex Bait and was available in two sizes, 2 3/4" and 3 5/8", and four finishes: Solid white, white with red head, yellow with gold spots, mouse color. A 1919 catalog offers only luminous white body and the yellow with gold spots. By 1925, the red head was back, making three choices. Colors in 1926: luminous with gold spots, yellow with gold spots, white with red head, natural perch scale finish with red head, natural chub scale finish with red head. Pike scale finish with red head was added in 1928 and in 1929 it added a larger size, 5 1/4". They were available into the 1950s. **$30-$80**

Pflueger Globe

All-in-One (pre-1925)

This interesting plug will probably be a very difficult item for the collector to find intact. It was furnished with four different interchangeable metal nose pieces. Each was different so that depending upon which you chose to use, the plug would rotate, dive shallow, deep dive or plane along the surface when retrieved. Because these metal planes were removable, it is not likely that you will find any but the one attached to the body unless you are lucky enough to acquire one new in the box. The plug has a belly-mount treble and a trailing treble hook. It was not found in catalogs of 1925 or after. Colors: Luminous paint, solid white; white belly, blended green cracked back; white belly, blended rainbow cracked back; white belly, blended frog back; white belly, green and red spots. **With all four planes: $1,000-$1,500, without extra planes: $250-$380**

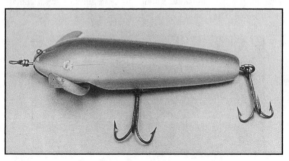

All-in-One

Bearcat

The Bearcat is almost identical to the Catalina (5500 series), except that it has a belly-mounted treble and a trailing treble hook. Patented in 1922, it appears in a 1925 catalog as available in natural mullet with scale finish, white with red throat, and white with a yellow and green back. It was missing from catalogs by 1930. **$75-$125**

Surprise

The patent for the Surprise was applied for in 1913 and granted in 1915. There was only a 4" size. It has two belly treble hooks and one trailing treble. By 1919, a 3" size two-hooker had been added and the 4" size had become a two-hook model also. The earliest models have empty eye sockets for eyes, just empty holes. By the early 1920s, they were sporting normal glass eyes. Colors: luminous paint with gold spots, golden shiner scale finish, natural mullet scale finish, natural frog scale finish, natural perch scale finish, white body with red head, rainbow, green cracked back. **$200-$400**

Surprise

Pal-O-Mine

First introduced about 1925, the Pal-O-Mine continued to be offered into the 1950s. It was first available in only two sizes: 3 1/2" and 4 1/4". In 1932 a smaller (2 3/4") size was added. The basic design of these plugs didn't change, but various color finishes were eliminated or added at particular year intervals. The larger (4 1/2") has always been offered with two belly trebles and one trailing (3T). The 3 1/2" and 2 3/4" sizes have always sported only one belly treble hook and the trailing treble (2T). All have a metal lip fitted into a cutout notch at the nose. Colors: golden shiner scale finish, red side scale finish, natural mullet scale finish, natural pike scale finish, natural frog with scale finish, natural perch scale finish, solid black with white head, rainbow, solid red, green cracked back, white with red head, white with red head and silver sparks, red, green and yellow scramble finish; solid white, red splash and gold specks; solid white, red and green spots; red head, pearl specks. **$15-$30**

Pal-O-Mine

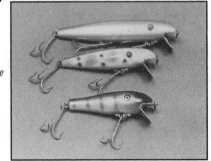

Jointed Pal-O-Mine

By 1936, the original Pal-O-Mine had become available in a jointed version. It was available in 3 1/4" and 4 1/4" and the body design was the same as the unjointed version. Colors: red side, scale finish; green mullet, scale finish; natural pike, scale finish; natural perch, scale finish; white with red head, silver sparks; rainbow blend. **$15-$30**

O-Boy

The O-Boy came along around the mid 1920s and by 1931 it was no longer found in catalogs as a plug (the name was reused on a spinner bait). It was made in two sizes and three weights. All have a metal lip, a belly treble and trailing treble hook. Size: No. 5400, 2 1/4", 1/2 oz., and 3 1/2", 3/4 oz. or 7/8 oz. Colors: golden shiner, scale finish; red side, scale finish; natural mullet, scale finish; natural frog, scale finish; natural chub, scale finish; black body, white head, white body, green and red spots; rainbow, green cracked back; white body, red head, red side, scale finish; natural chub, scale finish; silver color body, red head; rainbow. **$50-$150**

*O-Boy
plugs*

Wizard Wiggler

This lure was first found in a 1927 catalog and had disappeared from catalogs by 1936. It has a top tail-mounted metal flasher attached loosely so it would wiggle on retrieve. There is a pork rind attachment on the tail. Sizes: No. 4700, 1 1/2", 1/20 oz. (made with and without flasher); 1 3/4", 1/10 oz. (made with and without flasher); 2 1/4", 1/4 oz.; 3", 1/2 oz.; 3 1/2", 5/8 oz. Colors: luminous paint, gold spots; natural frog, scale finish; natural perch, scale finish; natural chub, scale finish; white body, green and red spots; rainbow, green cracked back; white body, red head. Note: The Wizard reappeared in a 1938 catalog in only the 3" size and in six finishes: natural perch, scale finish; black with silver lightning flash; luminous with red lightning flash; green cracked back; white body, red head; and gray mouse. **$50-$150**

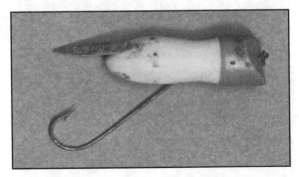

Wizard Wiggler

Wizard Mouse

Flocked Mouse

A thorough search through the Pflueger catalog collection turned up no mention of this lure. Collectors call it the Wizard Mouse or the Flocked Mouse. It is placed in here because of the presence of a metal flasher on its back just like the one on the Wizard Wiggler. The blade does have "PFLUEGER WIGGLER" stamped on it. The body measures 1 5/8" in length and the finish is fuzzy brown with a white belly. The eyes are large black beads. Belly hook hardware is a one-piece surface and the tail has a protective metal insert. **$150-$200**

Wizard Mouse

Catalina (pre-1925)

This plug was patented in 1910. It was in catalogs from 1925 to 1936 then disappeared. The bait is a 4 1/4" slim wooden type with a bronze wire shaft running through the length of the body. The shaft begins as a line tie at the nose and ends as a hook link for the trailing single hook. There is a propeller mounted on the shaft at the tail. Colors: natural mullet, scale finish; white with red throat, white with yellow and green back; solid red, metalized (polished nickel-plate all over). **$250-$400**

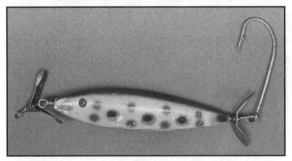

Catalina

Live Wire

Sometime around 1931, the Live Wire appeared in only four color designs and two sizes. It is made of celluloid and very slim. It has a nose and tail propeller spinner, two belly trebles and a trailing treble hook (3T) on the larger size and only one belly treble on the smaller (2T). There is a dorsal fin very realistic in shape and appearance. By 1932 a saltwater version was in the line. It has a 4 1/2" body, with only the tail propeller and one trailing single hook (1T). By the 1937 catalog, the plugs were still available in the saltwater version, but only one size of the regular lure was still being offered, 3 1/2". Colors: natural perch, scale finish; green gar, scale finish; silver sides, scale finish; white body, red head, gold sparks, green mullet, scale finish, silver sparks; solid red, pearl sparks all over; yellow body, red decorations; yellow body, black decorations; white body, red and green decorations. Older version: **$35-$65**; new version: **$20-$25**

Pakron

Appearing around 1931, this lure has a metal head with belly treble and a trailing treble. This trailing treble was hooked to a fastener that extended through the body to the metal head (2T). The lure was absent from catalogs by 1936. Size: 2 3/4", 1 oz. Colors: green mullet, scale finish; white body, red head, gold sparks; white body, red head. **$75-$150**

Frisky

Sometime in the mid 1930s, this bait appeared in catalogs. It has a very unusual nose shape, one belly and one trailing treble hook (2T). By 1952 the Frisky, as it was first designed, disappeared. The name was retained, but it applies to an entirely different lure. Size: 3", 1/2 oz. Colors: white body with green back and red splash, white body with red head, mouse finish. Older version: **$25-$40**; New version: **$35-$55**

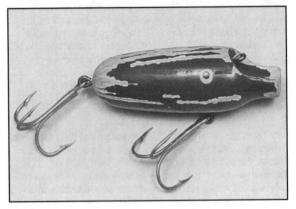

Frisky

Poprite

The Poprite first appears around 1935-36 and stays in catalogs into the 1950s. It was first available in one size only (4"), but around 1940 a smaller size (3") was added. The larger sported two belly trebles and a trailing treble (3T) and the smaller has only one belly treble (2T). The 1955 catalog shows only the 3" size and there has been a tail propeller added. Colors: red side, scale finish; natural pike, scale finish; natural perch, scale finish; meadow frog; white with silver sparks and red gills; white with green and red spots; green back, silver sparks; white with red head, silver sparks; yellow with red stripes; black with silver lightning flash. **$15-$30**

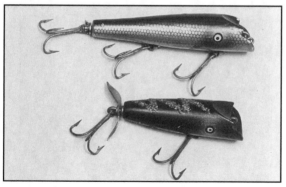

Poprite

Scoop

This is an unusual plug in that it has three-bladed propellers, fore and aft. Both sides of the body are slightly flattened and the body trebles are side mounted. New around 1937, it was first available in only one size (3 5/8"). By 1941, a second, smaller size (3") was available. The large size had two side trebles and a trailing treble (3T) and the smaller, only one side treble (2T). Both were removed from the line in the late 1940s or early 1950s. Colors: Rred side, scale finish; silver sparks, green back; meadow frog, natural perch, scale finish; white with black stripes. **$30-$60**

Scoop

TNT

This all-metal body plug was patented in 1929 and first observed in a 1931 catalog. It has a deep diving metal lip, a belly treble and a trailing treble. It had disappeared from catalogs by 1937. Size: 3 1/4", 1 1/10 oz. Colors: natural pike, scale blend; natural perch, scale finish; white with gold sparks, red head; spotlite finish with gold color lip; rainbow blend; polished nickel. **$50-$100**

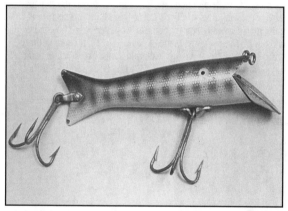

TNT

Miller's Reversible Minnow

This extremely rare lure was first made by the Union Springs Specialty Company. It can be found in two variations: the Union Springs model and the Pflueger model. The early (c. 1913) models have simple screw eye and washer hook hangers. It also has a slightly longer, much slimmer rear body section than the later version. The later one (c. 1916) utilizes the Pflueger type Neverfail hook hangers and a fatter rear body section. Examples of this latter model have been found new in a Pflueger box with the paper label identifying it as a Miller's Reversible Minnow. This lure is quite a wild-looking contraption. Its propellers were colored gold and silver. The body was made of cedar, 4 1/2". It came in three color schemes: No. 1, yellow with gold spots; No. 2, white belly, blended red and green spots; No. 3, white body, red head with gold spots. **$2,000-$2,500**

Miller's Reversible Minnow

THE SHAKESPEARE LURES

William Shakespeare

Kalamazoo, Michigan

William Shakespeare founded his tackle business in 1897. He invented and patented the first level-wind reel. It was so popular that he started the company to manufacture it. Shakespeare received the patent in 1896. The first lure he patented was for the wooden model of the Revolution in 1901.

By 1910, the Shakespeare Company had a large range of lures available. A 1910 catalog advertises a number of wooden minnows. The Shakespeare Company frequently included some of their competitors' lures in their catalogs.

By 1952, William Shakespeare had died (1950) and the company was sold to Creek Chub Bait Company. It must have been the tail wagging the dog, because Shakespeare still exists today. It bought out Pflueger in 1956 and Pflueger continued to operate as a separate entity.

Shakespeare "Revolution" Bait and

Shakespeare-Worden "Bucktail Spinner"

The first patent was for a wood-body Revolution. The lure was advertised in 1901, but apparently was quite brief in availability, for it and the Bucktail Spinner in hollow aluminum were offered the same year. The 1902 Shakespeare catalog offered both in aluminum only. The Revolution was offered in three sizes, 3", 4", and 6" and the Bucktail Spinner in 4" only. By 1907 they were offered in the original aluminum, but also in three colors: green body with gold spots, white body with red head, yellow body with red head. Both had acorn-style body sections. **Wood Revolution: $1,200-$1,500; other versions: $500-$800; Bucktail Spinner: $150-$250**

Wooden Revolution, lower, and Bucktail Spinner

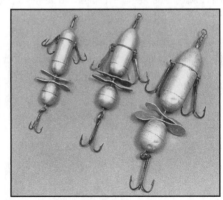

The "Sure Lure" Weedless

Appearing in the 1902 catalog, this bait was made with a pure rubber tube surrounding the hook. This supposedly gave it its weedless character. The rubber tube was at first of a solid aluminum color, but later (c. 1910), gold spots were added. Available in one size only. Not found in post-1924 catalogs. **$300-$400**

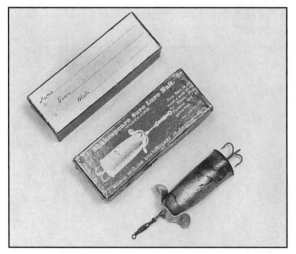

"Sure Cure" Weedless

The Shakespeare "Evolution Bait"

The fourth and last bait to appear in Shakespeare's 1902 catalog is the Evolution Bait. The body is in the shape of a minnow and made of soft rubber. It has propellers on both ends and has three treble hooks. It was available in three sizes. The Evolution Bait appears in a 1934 catalog and is essentially unchanged except that it was available only in the 2 5/8" body length. The earlier ones were also available in 2 1/8" and 4" lengths. It apparently was not available after 1936. The earliest models have "PAT PENDING" stamped on the propeller. **$100-$200**

Evolution Baits

Shakespeare Wooden Minnows

Sometime in 1905, Shakespeare acquired the rights to Fred D. Rhodes' patent for his wooden minnow. The hooks are attached to a device that is made by clipping a cotter key and giving it machine threads. It is screwed in or out of a bullet shaped, rimless brass cup imbedded in the lure body so that some of the rim extends beyond the body. Most Shakespeare Wooden Minnows use the Rhodes hardware. They are of the highest quality offered in their line. They were available in 5T (two on each side and one on the tail) and 3T (both belly and side mounts) at the time. They later added a 2T (single belly and one trailing). These were glass eyed and had the Gem-clip see-through hook hangers with brass cup hardware and Longhorn one-hump (or one notch) propeller spinners. The first sizes offered were 3", 3 1/2", and 4 1/2" bodies for each of the three hook styles. By 1910 they had added 1 3/4", 2 1/2", and 5 1/4" body sizes.

Colors: green back, white belly; red back, white belly; green back, yellow belly; red back, yellow belly; green back, aluminum belly; red back, aluminum belly; solid white; solid red; solid yellow; yellow perch, shaded. Later colors: fancy sienna back, yellow belly; fancy green back, white belly; solid bronze green; solid aluminum; metallized; solid copper; solid nickel; solid gold; white body, green and red spots; frog colors; rainbow; cracked gold. **Early versions: $200-$400, later versions: $150-$200**

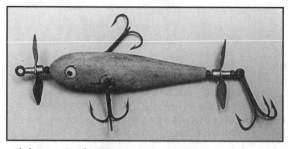

Shakespeare Wooden Minnow

Submarine Bait

For some reason, Shakespeare brought this lure out in 1925 as the Submarine Bait. It is essentially the same as their Wooden Minnow No. 42, underwater model. It appears as a separate offering sporadically throughout the years. It apparently was the last surviving member of the Wooden Minnows and it disappeared from the catalogs in the late 1930s. **$150-$200**

Krazy Kritter (plastic)

It looks like Shakespeare resurrected the old wooden minnow in plastic form. This lure has to be post-1967. These lures are marked "Shakespeare Spinning Krazy Kritter Hong Kong" on their bellies. They measure 2" and the spinners are unmarked. **$150-$200**

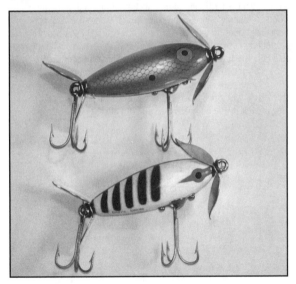

Krazy Kritters

"Rhodes" Wooden Minnows

Apparently Shakespeare was able to manufacture the Rhodes baits less expensively by utilizing a simpler round lure body. The earliest (c. 1907) Rhodes baits used a see-through type hook fastener and the 1910 catalogs depict this type in the lure illustrations. Those seen in the 1907 catalog are the early wired see-through type. There seem to be only three models of the Rhodes Wooden Minnow offered, and two sizes, 3" and 3 3/4". All versions have side-mounted trebles and one trailing. Each has two propellers, nose and tail and all were available with or without a bucktail. The lure had disappeared from Shakespeare catalogs by 1924. Colors: green back, white belly; red back, white belly; brown back, white belly; solid red; solid yellow; solid white; greenback, white belly, striped; red back, white belly, striped; brown back, white belly, striped. **$400-$600**

The Bass-A-Lure

This lure came available in 1923 and is one of the first plugs to utilize a fairly large metal lip to make a normally floating lure dive on retrieve. It was made at one time without the diving lip but the lip was standard equipment by 1925. The large size was made with two belly mounted treble hooks and one trailing, but there were some made with only one belly treble and a trailing hook. There are also some lipless versions of both sizes to be found. Sizes: No. 591, 2 3/4", No. 591 1/2, 1 3/4". Colors: (No. 591): black body, white head; green "fancy back", scale finish; green back, yellow belly, scale finish. (No. 591 1/2): rainbow, scale finish; white body, red head, yellow perch, scale finish. **$75-$150**

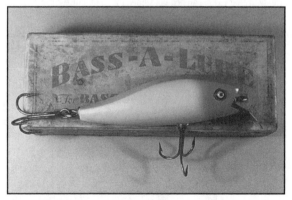

Bass-A-Lure

Shakespeare T. Robb Weedless Bass Fly

This feathered weedless spinner showed up first in a 1923 catalog. It appeared consistently until 1930 when it was gone from the catalog. The same four patterns were offered each year: Parmachene Belle, Black Prince, Scarlet Ibis and Yellow Sally. **$20-$40**

Shakespeare Bass-Kazoo

The 1924 catalog shows the Bass-Kazoo as being available in four colors and finish combinations and no eyes. This was reduced to two colors about 1935-36, which is the last year it was observed in catalogs. The plug has two belly-mounted treble hooks and one trailing treble (3T). The head is sloped to make it dive. Size: 3 7/8". Colors: green "fancy back," scale finish; rainbow, scale finish; white body, red head; yellow perch, scale finish. **$40-$80**

Shakespeare Bass-Kazoos

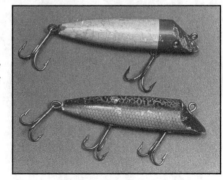

Shakespeare Buddy

This wooden plug was advertised as having an "invisible lip" made of clear plastic. This is the only occurrence of the clear plastic lip wooden lure in the Shakespeare catalogs. The Buddy has two belly-mounted treble hooks and one trailing treble. The lure is included in a 1934 and a 1937 catalog, but not from 1949 on. Size: 4 1/4", 3/5 oz. Colors: white body, red head, silver flitters; spotted, green perch, scale finish; natural pickerel, scale finish; silver flitter; green mullet, scale finish. **$200-$300**

The Darting Shrimp

This lure first appeared sometime around 1928-29. Looking sort of like a shrimp, it was jointed so that it would swim like one on retrieve. It has one belly-mounted treble hook and one trailing treble. It does not appear in catalogs from late 1930s on. Size: 1 1/4", 7/10 oz. Colors: natural frog, white body shaded red head, gold flitter; copper sides, dark back, silver belly, and a red flash at throat and tail. **$200-$300**

The Egyptian Wobblers

A 1934 catalog indicates that this plug had already been available for some time. The lure has a metal ventral fin, two belly treble hooks, a trailing treble, metal lip and has a gold-colored hook finish for saltwater use. An Egyptian Wobbler Junior was offered later as well as jointed versions of each. Sizes: No. 6636, 4 7/8", 1 oz.; No. 6635, 3 5/8", 1/2 oz. Colors: green "fancy back" with tangerine, green and white body; white body with red, black, and yellow spots and a black back stripe, silver flitters; yellow perch pattern; white body, red head, silver flitters; natural pickerel. **$75-$100**

Jointed Egyptian Wobblers

Sizes: No. 6677, 5 1/2", 9/10 oz.; No. 6676, 4 3/4", 1/2 oz. Colors: black back, scale finish and vertical stripes; white body with red, black, and yellow spots, silver flitters; white body, red head. **$75-$125**

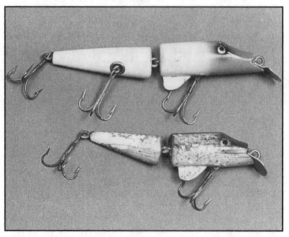

Jointed Egyptian Wobblers

The "00" Size Fancy Back and Metal Plate Minnows

This small bait is almost exactly the same design as the Shakespeare Punkin' Seed minnow, except made smaller. It was available in one body design and size only in the 1910 catalog, but several paint finishes were offered. The "Metal Plated" finish plugs were made by electroplating the body with copper, nickel, or gold, giving it a bright highly polished look. The Fancy Back Minnow has a crackle-like finish. These plugs have a propeller on the nose and only one treble hook (1T) trailing. Feathers were bound to the hook. The metallized versions are rare and can bring twice the price. This same lure is listed in a post 1934 catalog as "The Midget." Size: 1 3/4". Colors: "Fancy Back" in sienna, yellow belly; "Metal Plated" in copper, nickel, and gold. **$100-$150**

Rhodes "Mechanical Swimming Frog" No. 3GWF

This ingenious invention, offered in the 1910 catalog, was a rubber body frog that has flexible legs, which kicked back each time the fishing line was tugged. Each leg has single weedless hooks and the belly has a removable double hook to render it weedless. The body length is 2 1/4" with legs extended; the overall length is about 4". **$350-$500, with the original wood box: $2,000-$2,500**

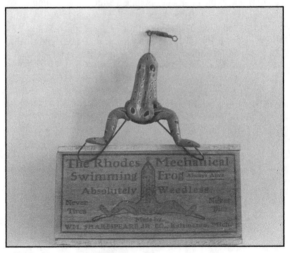

Rhodes "Mechanical Swimming Frog"

The "Pin Head" Bait

This appears in a 1934 catalog in one size, one weight. Heavily weighted in the head, it was made for saltwater pier fishing. It has a belly treble hook and a trailing treble. The line tie is on top of the head (screw-eye type). It was in production until the early 1950s. **$10-$15**

Rhodes Torpedo No. 6540

A 1934 catalog listing states that this "... two spinner underwater lure with side hooks was first put on the market by Shakespeare Company over 25 years ago ...." The collector should be aware of the possibility of the newer Torpedo being mistaken for the older one. Look at the hardware, size and body style closely. The propellers on the plug are marked with the Shakespeare name. Size: 3", 5/8 oz. Colors: greenback, white sides, silver flitters; spotted green frog; white body, red head. **$75-$150**

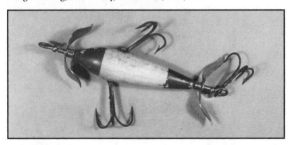

Rhodes Torpedo

"Kazoo" Wooden Minnow

Kazoo Wooden Minnows were inexpensively made, second line lures for Shakespeare. They appear in 1910 catalogs as available in several versions: floating or submerged; different hook numbers and positions, two sizes and several color designs. The body hooks (all treble) were attached by staples or a simple screw eye and now cup or cup hardware. All have a bow type tube propeller at the tail and nose and a trailing treble hook. Although this lure does not appear in catalogs from the early 1920s on, the name "Kazoo" is frequently used in connection with other Shakespeare lures. Versions: 31 GWK, 3", Floating style, 1 belly treble, 1 tail treble (2T), green back, white belly; 31 RWK, 3", Floating style, 1 belly treble, 1 tail treble (2T), red back, white belly; 33 GWK, 3", Submerged style, 2 side trebles, 1 tail treble (3T), green back,

Kazoo Wooden Minnow

white belly; 33 RWF, 3", Submerged style, trebles, 1 tail treble (3T), green back, white belly; 42 GWK, 3 3/4", Floating style, 2 side trebles, 1 tail treble (3T), red back, white belly; 42 RWK, 3 3/4", Floating style, 2 belly trebles, 1 tail treble (3T), red back, white belly; 43 GWK, 3 3/4", Submerged style, 2 side trebles, 1 tail treble (3T), green back, white belly; 43 RW, 3 3/4", Submerged style, 2 side trebles, 1 tail treble (3T), red back, white belly; 44 GWK 3 3/4", Submerged style, 4 side trebles, 1 tail treble (5T), green back, white belly; 44 RWK, 3 3/4", Submerged style, 4 side trebles, 1 tail treble (5T), red back, white belly. **$150-$200**

Kazoo Chub Minnow

This lure was first found listed in a 1932 catalog. It wasn't listed in any subsequent catalogs. The lure has glass eyes and measures 3 3/8". **$75-$125**

Muskie Trolling Minnow or

Kazoo Trolling Minnow

Called a "new type of lure" in the 1924 catalog, this plug has a reed body built around a treble hook. The three points of the hook protrude from the body. Another model has a single hook at the tail covered by a bucktail and moose hair tail, and fluted spoon forward of the body. The lure was available in three sizes, the smallest being the "Bass" with no trailing hook. By 1929, the "Bass" size had disappeared from catalogs and by the late 1930s, the lure disappeared from the catalogs. **$40-$100**

The Kazoo Wobbler

Called a "veteran bait" in the 1934 catalog, one would think it a later development of the Bass Kazoo or Pikie Kazoo. The plug has a metal lip, belly-mounted fin, one belly-mounted treble hook and a trailing treble attached by a regular screw eye or the Shakespeare "Ball Head Hook Retainer" used in the 1930s. Size: 4", 4/5 oz. Colors: black back, tan and gold sides with vertical stripes; black back, green and gold sides; green back, golden yellow sides, white belly, green back, salmon pink and silver sides; green back, white sides and silver flitters; white body, red head. **$75-$125**

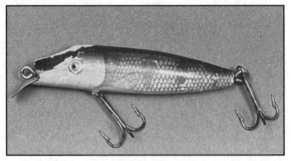

Kazoo Wobbler

Kazoo Wobble Tail No. 980

This lure was apparently short-lived for it appears only once in the catalog collection, a 1924 issue. It has a red body and highly colored scale finish, silk wound with a crude rubber flapper tail, one single tail hook, and a single blade propeller at the nose. **$75-$100**

Kazoo Flapper Wing No. 984

This lure is in the same category as the previous Kazoo Wobble Tail. It was first observed in the 1924 catalog and one other later one, a 1926. The 1924 catalog lists it as being available in the three color patterns, but the 1926 listing says nothing about the available colors. The Flapper Wing also has a reed body with a scale finish. It has two rubber wings, a single blade nose propeller and a long trailing buck tail hiding a single hook. There was no size or weight listed. **$75-$100**

The Pikie Kazoo

This lure, as depicted in a 1923 Shakespeare catalog, was available with two belly mounted treble hooks and a trailing treble. It is a long body pike lure with a metal lip that is "bendable" to vary the retrieve depth. Body length was 5 1/16" at first, but by 1924 it had shortened to 4 3/4". It was last observed in catalogs between 1934 and 1937. Colors: green "fancy back" with scale finish; green back with scale finish; rainbow with scale finish; white body, red head, yellow perch with scale finish. **$75-$125**

Pikie Kazoo

Baby Pikie Kazoo

This lure, a smaller version of the Pikie Kazoo, actually has a slightly different design in that there is no metal lip, rather the nose is designed to impart the same action. It has only one belly treble and a trailing treble (2T). It was available in exactly the same finishes as above. **$75-$100**

Shakespeare "Favorite" Floating Bait

This probably came out between 1910 and 1917. It was offered in only one size, 3 5/8". It has a double hook at the belly that is stabilized with a small pin. It is designed so that upon a fish striking, the hook can pull off the pin and swing away from the lure body. This lure is very much like the Heddon Zaragossa and the Creek Chub Sarasota. It had disappeared from catalogs by the late 1920s. Colors: Solid red, solid white, solid yellow, imitation frog color (later). **$250-$400**

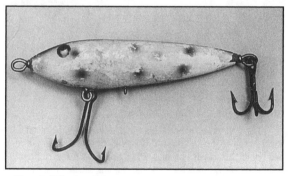

"Favorite" Floating Bait

Shakespeare "Albany" Floating Bait c. 1913 No. 64

The earliest listing for this lure was in a 1917 catalog. It was listed as available in a white body with a blue head. It is known to exist with a red head also. It has plate hook hanger hardware and is 5 1/2" long. **$1,500-$2,500**

"Albany" Floating Bait. Photo courtesy Jim Muma

Shakespeare Floating "Spinner"

The 1910 catalog shows this wooden lure could be obtained in three color schemes. It is a floating bait designed so the entire head of the bait rotated by an attached propeller. It sports three treble hooks (3T), one on each side and one trailing. The side hook fasteners are see-through plate type. The original was available only in a 3 1/8" size and three color designs, but in the early 1920s a 2 7/8" size was offered and a fourth color had been added. It is not offered after 1924. Colors: white body with red head, solid yellow with gold dots, solid white with gold dots, solid white and variegated dots. **$50-$90**

The Fisher Bait

This floating plug was called a new lure in a 1940s catalog. It has a metal lip to make it dive on retrieve and a single belly-mounted treble hook forward of a ventral fin and one trailing treble. There was a smaller version of this plug called the Junior Fisher Bait. Sizes: No. 6508, 2 7/8", 1/2 oz.; No. 6509, 3 3/4", 3/5 oz. Colors: black and green, vertical stripes, scale finish; green bronze back, silver sides, white belly, scale finish; white body, spotted red, green and black, narrow green back; white body, green head, white body, red head, yellow perch scale finish. **$60-$80**

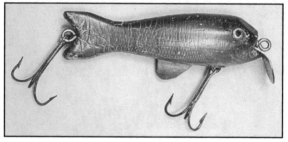

Fisher Bait

Frog Skin Bait

New sometime in the early 1930s, this was a wooden lure with actual frog skin stretched over the body. It is thought by some that this lure was actually made for Shakespeare by the Eger Bait Company. This is probably so, because Eger actually held the patent. The Shakespeare version has white iris glass eyes and the Eger products supposedly do not. The lure disappeared sometime in the late 1930s. Size: 3" and 3 3/4". Color: Natural frog skin stretched over the body. **$100-$150**

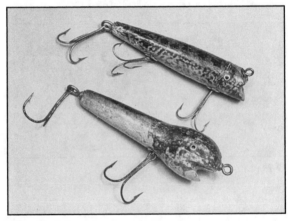

Frog Skin Bait

The Hydroplane

As shown in a 1920 catalog, this bait was available in only one size, but shortly thereafter it was offered in three sizes. It has two simple screw eye mounted belly treble hooks and one tail treble. It was packed with three sizes of metal planes, each designed to run the lure at a different depth. This bait was gone by the mid-1920s. Sizes: No. 709, 4 1/2"; No. 709 1/2, 3", fly rod size: 2 3/4". Colors: solid white, solid red, fancy green, frog back, spotted, rainbow, red and white, yellow perch. **$75-$175, fly rod size: $100-$200**

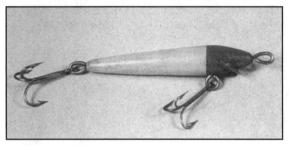

Hydroplane. Photo courtesy Jim Muma

Injun Joe

Little Joe

The Little Joe is a smaller version of the Injun Joe. They first showed up in a 1934 edition of the catalogs. Neither was found in subsequent catalogs. Both have metal diving lips and one trailing treble with or without fasteners. The larger has an additional treble on the belly. Both have a unique scissor-type tail hook hanger. Sizes: No. 6530, 3", 1/2 oz.; No. 6593, 2 1/8", 1/2 oz. Colors: rainbow with green back, green back with green and red sides, white body with red head, yellow perch, black body with yellow stripe, gray with tangerine striped belly, tangerine body with black back and black and yellow spots, black body with white head, lavender body with black spots. **$40-$75**

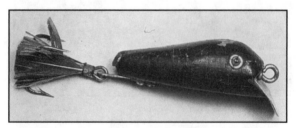

Little Joe

Jacksmith Lure

This is a heavy duty version of the Jack Jr. below. It has two belly trebles instead of one. The 1934 catalog illustration shows the Shakespeare "Ball Post Hook Retainer," but by the mid 1940s it was the simple screw eye once again. It has a metal ventral fin and was made in the same color patterns as the Jack Jr., but the white body, red head color combination does not have silver flitters. **$50-$100**

The Jack Jr.

A small version of the Jacksmith Lure, it was first offered sometime around the later 1920s. It is a top water bait with one belly treble hook and a trailing treble. It was probably discontinued in the 1940s. Size: 2 3/4", 1/2 oz. Colors: white body, red head, silver flitters; rainbow with green back; spotted, green and silver, scale finish; green "fancy back," scale finish; green perch, scale finish; white body, red head, black back, white belly, green and gold sides, scale finish; black back, tan and gold sides, with vertical stripes, scale finish. **$50-$75**

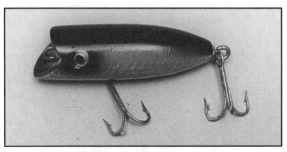

Jack Jr.

Jerkin Lure

The 1934 catalog shows only one version of the Jerkin Lure available. By 1949 there was a second one offered that had a tail propeller. It was a surface popping plug and the 1934 illustration shows two belly trebles and a trailing treble attached by the Shakespeare "Ball Head Hook Retainer." Size: 4", 3/5 oz. Colors: Frog; green and silver, scale finish; natural pickerel, scale finish; silver flitters; white body, red head; green back, red and white sides, scale finish. **$15-$20**

King Fish Wobbler

A 1934 catalog says it is the same body design as the Shakespeare Egyptian Wobbler. It disappeared by the end of the 1940s. This is a most unusual plug in that it has a chrome plated back plate and a gold-colored hook finish. It has a metal ventral fin, two belly-mounted treble hooks, a trailing treble hook and a metal blade lip. Sizes: No. 6535, 4 7/8", 1 1/4 oz.; No. 6601, 1 7/8", 1/2 oz.; No. 6510, 3 3/4", 5/8 oz. **$75-$125**

King
Fish
Wobbler

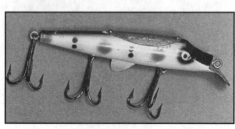

Luminous Floating Night Bait

In a 1929 catalog, this plug is advertised as being available in only one size. In a later one it is offered in two sizes, but doesn't list the sizes. All the plugs were coated with a white luminous paint. They have two belly-mounted treble hooks and a trailing treble (3T). All those illustrated after the 1920s have only one belly and the tail-mounted treble (2T). The early models have a red head and white body; later ones were solid white. **$50-$100**

Shakespeare Midget Spinner

Probably a newer design of the old Shakespeare Punkin Seed, this plug has a propeller at the nose and tail, a belly treble hook and a trailing treble. It appears in the 1934 catalog and was still present in the early 1950s catalogs. Size: 1 7/8", 1/2 oz. Colors: shiner finish; sienna fancy, back, silver flitters; white body, red head, pickerel finish; green back, green and red sides. **$10-$15**

Nu-Crip Minnow

This plug, called new in the 1934 catalog, is shown in a minnow shape with a propeller spinner at the nose and tail. It has a trailing treble hook and two side mounted trebles (3T). It does not appear in mid 1940s catalog. Size: 3 3/4", 5/8 oz. Colors: silver flitter; green frog; white body, red head, green back, red sides, scale finish; green back, golden yellow sides, scale finish; green back, tan and gold sides, dark vertical stripes, white belly, scale finish. **$50-$100**

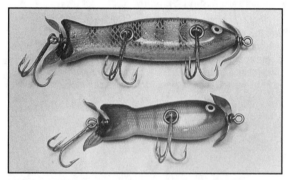

Nu-Crip Minnows

Oregon Midget

In the 1934 catalog this is described as a midget lure designed for use with a fly rod, but some fishermen trolled and cast with it by adding a lead weight to the leader. It has one belly-mounted double hook. Size: 1 3/4". Colors: white body, green head; green perch, scale finish; red, yellow and green spotted; green back, red and green sides, scale finish; yellow body, red head, white body, red head. No trade data

The Pad-Ler

A Shakespeare catalog of 1936 calls this a new lure. It was made in the shape of a mouse. The two small attached spoons were meant to impart the swimming action of the mouse's rear legs. The plug has a trailing double hook. Found in three sizes: No. 6678, 3 1/4", 1 oz.; No. 6679, 3 3/4", 1 1/2 oz. Colors: green spotted frog, gray body with white belly, white body with red head. No. 6680, 2 7/8", 7/10 oz. Colors: gray body with white belly, white body with black wavy stripe on sides, white body with red head. **$70-$100, musky size: $500-$700**

Pad-Ler

"Little Pirate" Minnow No. 23LP

This inexpensive lure appears in two pre-1920s catalogs at 15 cents and 17 cents respectively. It does not appear in later catalogs. The Little Pirate was available in white belly with either a green or red back. They are all 2 1/2" in length with one nose propeller spinner, two treble side hooks and one tail treble (3T). **$25-$75**

The Plopper No. 6511 or No. 7-11

This lure is also known as the Seven-Eleven. It came along about 1926-27 and has been found with the 1930s "Shakespeare Ball Head Hook Retainer." It has one belly mounted treble hook and a trailing treble. It was listed as available in only one size and color, 3/5 oz., white body with shaded red head. **$50-$100**

Shakespeare Sardinia Saltwater Minnow No. 721

Although the first and last time this plug appears in the catalog collection is in 1924 and 1925, there can be no doubt that it was around longer than two years. It was made in the shape of a minnow, complete with tail and cut-out mouth. It has one belly-mounted treble hook and one trailing treble (2T). Size: 3". Colors: solid white; Solid white with gold speckles. **$200-$300**

"Pop-Eye"

A 1949 catalog illustrates this as a top water plug. It is cone-shaped with two humps on the top of the larger and representing the Pop-Eyes, one belly treble and a trailing treble. Size: 3 1/2", 5/8 oz. Colors: green spotted frog, green back, white belly and silver flitters. **$20-$40**

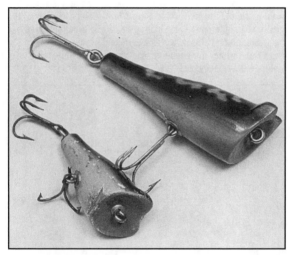

"Pop-Eye" lure

Shakespeare "Punkin Seed" Minnow

The 1910 catalog offers these lures in one size, six color styles and in a floating and underwater version. The plug probably didn't last much past 1920. It appears again as a No. 6601 in a 1937 catalog. The floating version has two treble hooks, one trailing with buck tail and one belly treble attached with the cup and screw eye hardware (CUP). The underwater version was available with or without the belly treble. Size: 2 5/8". Colors: (Sinker): green back, aluminum color belly; green back, white belly, red back, aluminum color belly. (Floater): solid white with red on head, solid white with green on head, green back, white belly, sienna yellow "fancy back" with brown head. **$250-$400**

Punkin Seed Minnows

Shakespeare's River Pup

This smaller lure is weighted for deep running. It has a metal blade lip, one belly treble hook and one trailing treble (2T). The metal lip is notched on the early models and the later ones have no notch and the lip is longer and more squared off. Size: 2 5/8", 1/2 oz. Colors: Rrainbow with green back; pearl, spotted, white body, red head, silver flitters; green perch with red head, scale finish; yellow body; frog, silver flitters. **$10-$20**

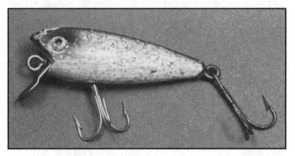

River Pup

Shakespeare Glo-Lite Pup (plastic)

In 1941, Shakespeare devoted a lot of space to its new luminous finishes on the River Pup. There was only one size listed, 2 3/4", 5/8 oz. Colors: frog with green spots, green perch with red head, mottled pearl finish, white body with red head, white body with red head and silver flitters. **$5-$15**

Shakespeare Saltwater Special Minnow No. 722

Essentially the same as the No. 721, the plug is only slightly different in body shape and has no mouth cutout. It was available in the same size and finishes. **$200-$300**

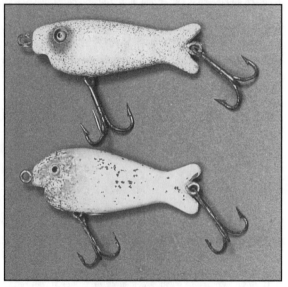

No. 721 Sardinia Saltwater Minnow, upper, and Saltwater Special No. 722

The Sea Witch No. 133 and No. 6533

As far as can be determined, this is an earlier version of the No. 6531 Sea Witch. The length of the No. 133 is more, but otherwise it appears to be essentially the same plug. The catalog states that the No. 6533 is the same lure as the No. 133 Sea Witch, with the major difference being the addition of another line tie " ... in top of head." It is thought to be of about 1928 vintage. Sizes: No. 133, 4", 3/4 oz.; No. 6533, 3/16", 1/2 oz. Colors: white body with red head, white body with red head and gold flitters. **$75-$125**

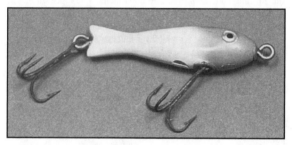

Sea Witch

The Sea Witch No. 6531

The Sea Witch Midget No. 6534

The 1934 catalog describes these plugs as weighted and having "... special plated hooks." They each have a belly treble and a trailing treble. Their differences are only in size, weight and color pattern availability, the body design being identical. Sizes: No. 6531, 3 3/4", 1 oz.; No. 6534, 2 3/4", 1/2 oz. Colors: solid white; solid white, red head, solid white, red head, silver flitters, solid white, red head, gold flitters; spotted pattern; pearl luster finish. **$25-$125**

Barnacle Bill

This very scarce saltwater lure is uniquely shaped in a curved body, with a wire that is both internal and external. It is continuous forming both the line tie and hook hangers. It appeared first in the 1931 catalog. Size: 3", 3/5 oz. Colors: white body, red head, gold flitters; white body, spotted red, yellow and black, gold flitters, black back, mud puppy (silver flitters); rainbow, blue, green, yellow, red, and white: white body, eyes and tail shaded black. **$100-$150**

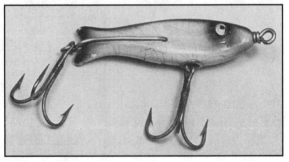

Barnacle Bill

Shakespeare "Shiner" Minnow

The crackle back Shiner measures 3 1/6" long, has white glass eyes, one internal belly weight and twisted through-body wire and see-through side hook hanger hardware. This lure was offered in two sizes (also 2 1/2") in the 1910 and subsequent catalogs, with or without a "fancy bucktail" on the trailing treble hook. It has two side treble hooks attached by the wire type "see through" hook hanger. Both sizes have three treble hooks (3T) and a propeller spinner on the nose. Colors: black back, white belly only. **$120-$250**

"Shiner" Minnow

Shakespeare "Slim Jim Minnow"

This plug is one of the earliest Shakespeare baits to have painted thin vertical stripes along the body sides. The 1910 catalog offers it in two sizes, 3" and 3 3/4". Smaller models have only one propeller spinner and larger models have two. Both have two side-mounted treble hooks and one tail-mounted treble hook. The side hooks utilize the "see through" fastener on the earlier plugs. By 1920, only the larger size seemed to be available. Colors: blue back, white belly, striped; green back, white belly, striped; red back, white belly, striped; brown back, white belly, striped and spotted; solid white; frog back, white belly, striped; solid red; solid yellow; solid aluminum color. **$50-$150**

"Slim Jim Minnows"

Shakespeare "Slim Jim Minnow" (Underwater)

A 1924 catalog first lists this plug, but a 1949 listing says they introduced the lure "... over 30 years ago." That dates the early ones around 1917-18 and they are very like the side hook No. 33 and No. 43. This newer one was offered in two sizes, the larger having two belly mounted treble hooks and a trailing treble. The smaller was the same except with only one belly treble. Both have nose and tail propellers. This plug continued in production until the 1950s with very little change. The bodies are weighted and finishes have varied considerably through the years. Sizes: No. 52 J or 6552, 4 1/2", 4/5 oz. Colors: blue back, white belly, scale finish. No. 41 J or 6541, 3 3/4", 3/5 oz. Colors: red back, white belly, scale finish; rainbow, scale finish; green back, yellow belly; green back, yellow belly, scale finish; yellow perch, scale finish; gold body, red head, white body, red head, green back, silver sides, scale finish; natural pickerel pattern; green back, red and green striped sides; dark crackle back, maroon and silver sides; green back, golden yellow sides. **$50-$150**

Strike-It No. 6666

New around 1930, the Strike-It is similar to the Tantalizer. It has no metal diving lip. There were only three colors available in the 1930 catalog. It is missing from catalogs after 1931. Size: 4", 4/5 oz. Colors: Herring; light grey back and sides, red at throat; white body, shaded red head; black body (white pickerel scale); bluish green body, spotted red and yellow, black back; mud puppy (light gray); white body, black head, white body, spotted red, black, and yellow, black back. **$125-$225**

Shakespeare Special

A surface lure with a tail-mounted propeller, it has a notched mouth below a forward sloping nose, one belly mounted treble hook and a trailing treble. Size: No. 6546, 3", 1/2 oz.; No. 6547, 4", 5/8 oz. Colors: frog finish, white belly; frog finish, yellow belly; natural pickerel with vertical stripes; solid yellow, black spots; green back, white belly, silver flitters; yellow body, green stripes. **$10-$20**

Shakespeare Special

The Mermaid

The Little Mermaid

New for Shakespeare sometime in the early 1920s, it actually dates back to at least 1917. The McCormick Mermaid was patented by John Thomas McCormick of Kalamazoo, Mich., in 1917. The Mermaid appears never to have been given eyes of any type. Sizes: 3 1/4", 3 5/8". Colors: rainbow, scale finish; yellow perch, scale finish; fancy green, scale finish; frog back, scale finish; green back, yellow belly, scale finish; white body, red head; black body, white head. **$50-$100**

Mermaid

The Sure-Lure Minnow

This familiar name was used for one of the first Shakespeare lures. This newer lure is made of molded rubber in the shape of a minnow. It is remarkably similar to the Evolution Minnow originally marketed around 1902. It appears in the 1931 catalog, but is gone from catalogs soon after. Size: 2 5/8", 1/2 oz. Colors: shiner pattern; yellow perch pattern. **$75-$100**

"Surface Wonder" No. 42 WW

This plug was initially available in only one color design, a white body with a red head. An undated catalog shows the Surface Wonder in a yellow body with red head and in "Imitation Frog Color" also. A 1936 catalog lists the same lure as #42F, 3 3/4" body length, as available in one finish only: white body with a red head. It is called "The Floater." This plug is substantially similar to the Luminous Floating Night Bait No. 680, but is not luminous. It has two belly mounted treble hooks and one trailing treble (3T). Size: 4". Colors: white body, red head; yellow body, red head; imitation frog color. **$50-$100**

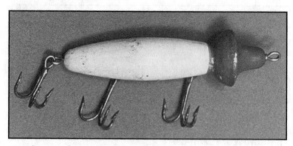

Surface Wonder

Shakespeare Swimming Mouse

This lure appears in a 1924 catalog and in various versions continues all the way into the 1950s. It has always been around 3 1/4" long with the exception of a 2 3/4" Junior Mouse, which appeared sometime in the early 1930s, and a 2 1/2" Baby Mouse, which is first found in a 1949 catalog. All have two belly-mounted treble hooks. The lure is frequently found missing the tail. Has been found with only one treble hook (1T) (post 1934). Size: No. 578, 3 1/4". Colors: solid black with white head, solid white with red head, yellow with white belly, black back and head; mouse gray with white belly, solid black. No. 6570, 2 3/4", 5/8 oz. Colors: gray body with white belly and black back, gray body with white belly, tiger stripe, solid white, white body with black head, white body with red head. All are luminous. No. 6577, 2 1/2", 1/2 oz. Colors: light gray, imitation frog colors, solid black, black body with white head, gray, tiger stripe, white body with red head, yellow body with red head. No. 6578, 3", 8/10 oz. Colors: black with shaded white belly. No. 6580, 2 3/4", 5/8 oz. Colors: white with shaded red head, mouse gray with white belly, yellow with white belly, black shaded back and head; tiger stripe, black over yellow; yellow body with red head, black body with yellow back stripe, black body with white head. **$25-$55**

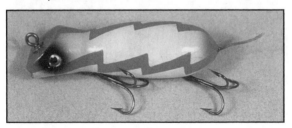

Swimming Mouse. Photo courtesy Jim Muma

Tantalizer

This is one of Shakespeare's first jointed baits. It appeared around 1927-29. It is also one of the earliest uses of the metal ventral fin. The plug has one belly-mounted treble hook and one trailing treble (2T). It was found with glass or painted eyes, in one size and weight, and only in two color patterns initially. In a 1934 catalog the trailing hook fastener has been changed to the "Ball Head Hook Retainer" from the original simple screw eye. By 1937, this fastener had disappeared and again the screw eye came into use. The 1937 catalog also shows a slightly smaller "Jr. Tantalizer" and both have gained a second belly treble (3T). Sizes: No. 638 or 6638, 4", 9/10 oz. Colors: white body with shaded red head, natural pickerel. No. 639 or 6639, 4", 3/4 oz. Colors: yellow perch with scale finish, shad finish, black back with tan and gold vertical side stripes, green back with silver and pink sides. **$50-$150**

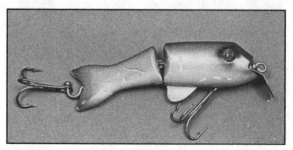

Tantalizer

The Tarpalunge

First observed in a 1930 catalog, this is another jointed plug. It has a sloped head, ventral fin, a belly-mounted single point hook and one trailing. It was absent from catalogs by the late 1930s to early 1940s. Sizes: 5", 2 3/4". Colors: shiner finish, mullet finish, red and white with silver flitters. **$250-$500**

Waukazoo Surface Spinner

The earliest reference to this lure found so far was in 1929, but it could date as early as 1924. It has a pear-shaped body, ventral fin, one nose-mounted propeller, a belly-mounted treble hook and trailing treble. "Shakespeare No. 1" is stamped on the propeller. It apparently wasn't too popular for it wasn't found in catalogs subsequent to 1931. Size: 2 5/8", 3/4 oz. Colors: white body with shaded red head, natural frog finish, gray body with white belly and a flash of red at the throat. **$100-$150**

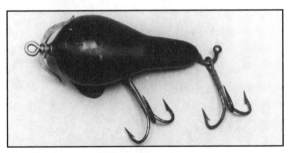

Waukazoo Surface Spinner

Shakespeare "Weedless Frog" No. 4 WF

As advertised in the 1910 catalog, this is a lure cast in soft rubber in the shape and markings of a frog. There are rubber guards protecting the single trailing treble hook (1T). It is 3 1/4" long and has a propeller on the nose. It apparently wasn't available long. **$400-$600**

Shakespeare "Whirlwind Spinner" No. 65 W

This interesting plug apparently went out of production early on. By 1920, it was absent from the catalogs. It was listed in the 1910 catalog in one size only, 4" length overall with the body measuring 1 1/4". The colors offered were solid red, white, or yellow. All had a "fancy feather buck tail" on the tail treble hook. The two side treble hooks were attached to the body with the see-through fastener (3T). There were two propellers, tail and nose. **$100-$150**

Whirlwind Spinner

Wiggle-Diver

The later lure (1940s), the Wiggle-Diver, was made of molded plastic (Tenite). It is probable that earlier ones have wooden bodies. Available in a 1940s catalog in three different sizes, each has one belly-mounted treble hook and a trailing treble. Sizes: No. 6357, 2 1/4", 1/2 oz. Colors: green bronze back with silver sides, white belly and scale finish. No. 6538, 3 1/2", 1 oz. Colors: silver flitter with narrow green back and white belly. No. 6539, 4 5/8", 1 1/4 oz. Colors: white body with redhead, yellow body with black head. **$10-$20**

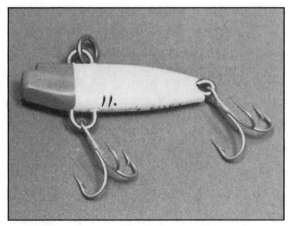

Wiggle Diver

Shakespeare Jim Dandy Lures

Around 1930, Shakespeare either bought or obtained the rights to the lure designs of the Wise Sportsman Supply of Chicago. Specific information regarding the inexpensive line of lures is sketchy due to incomplete catalog listings. They were called Jim Dandys in the 1931 catalog, but the name was seldom mentioned in subsequent catalogs. The lures were simply integrated into the standard line. In 1936 and 1937, the "Jim Dandy Casting Bait Assortment" was listed that consisted of three Floaters and three Spoon Bill Wobblers.

Jim Dandy Spoon Bill Wobbler

This glass-eyed Jim Dandy shows up first in a 1931 catalog and is never again listed. Size: 3 3/4", 3/4 oz. Colors: green back, red sides, white belly; gray back, shading down to white belly; red body, black head, black over yellow spots; white body, red head, yellow body, red over black spots, black back. **$100-$150**

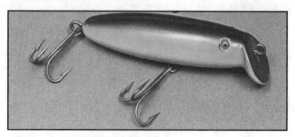

Jim Dandy Spoon Bill Wobblers

Jim Dandy Underwater

The Underwater is a glass eye 3T lure. Size: 3 3/4", 3/4 oz. Colors: red body, black head, rainbow, white body, red head, greenish yellow sides, perch stripes with pink lower stripe, white belly and dark back. **$75-$150**

Jim Dandy No. 6503

A 1931 catalog entry is the first place this darter-type lure was found. This lure was unnamed, but looks something like a fat, unshaped Bass-A-Lure without the metal diving lip. They have pressed, painted eyes, but might be found with glass eyes. Colors: red body with black head, white body with red head, green scale with silver sides and green back, yellow perch scale finish, black body with red head, orange and yellow body with red head. **$30-$50**

Jim Dandy Floaters

Jim Dandy floating lures have pressed, painted and zinc tack painted eyes. The colors match those listed with the Jim Dandy Underwater Minnow. They sport the late smooth edge, pointed Shakespeare propellers. **$25-$80**

South Bend Bait Company

South Bend, Indiana

In 1895, F.G. "Bucktail" Worden, inventor of the bucktail lure, started a small factory to manufacture fishing tackle in South Bend, Ind. He began manufacturing with only one particular lure, the Worden Bucktail. Because of the widespread interest in his lure, he began making others. By 1905 he was operating as the Worden Bucktail Manufacturing Company, Inc. He had three men working for him who acquired the business from Worden and attracted enough capital to organize and form the South Bend Bait Company in 1909. South Bend ceased to exist when Gladding bought them out in 1965.

At first the company specialized in the production of bucktail baits. One of the early catalogs offered various bucktail spinners, flies and spoons, etc., but there were also eight or so wooden casting and trolling plugs. Over the next few years several lures were added to the line and about the mid-1930s a new stronger hook-link hardware was introduced on the "Oreno" series plugs.

The listing of lures in this section is primarily of South Bend wooden lures from inception to the early 1950s. Some early plastics, however, are listed. The metal products are numerous and are not covered in any depth.

The Worden Wooden Minnow

One of the first lures made and marketed by Worden before his small company became South Bend, it can be tentatively identified by the shape of the propeller. The propellers almost always have the patent date of Dec. 29, 1903, stamped on the blade. Worden lures are rare. **$200-$400**

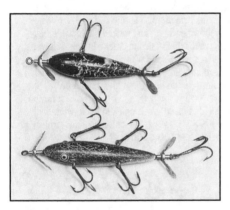

Worden Wooden Minnow, top, and Underwater Wooden Minnow

Midget Minnow No. 901

This is a very small version of the No. 902-906 Underwater Minnows. It first appears in the 1921 catalog, but may have come along a bit before. They were gone by 1940. The plug is 2 1/2" and 1/2 oz. The same colors were available. **$125-$300**

Underwater Minnows

Nos. 902, 903, 904, 905, 906

(c. 1912-1939)

The 1912 catalog illustrates several types of Underwater Minnows. The No. 903 and 904 both have three treble hooks, two propellers, and weight and length are the same. The only difference appears to be the type of finish applied. Size: 3", 3/4oz. Colors: rainbow, yellow perch; green cracked back, white belly 'red cracked back, yellow belly' sienna cracked back, yellow belly' white body, dark shade back; solid white; white body, red head, white body, red head and tail, solid aluminum color, solid red, black nose; scale finish; scale finish, red blend, gold finish, red-head. No. 902 (2T, weedless hooks), 3", 3/4 oz. Colors: rainbow, white body, dark shaded back, green cracked back, white belly. No. 905 and 906, 3 5/8", 1 1/4 oz. The colors are the same as No. 903 and 904 respectively. **$100-$200**

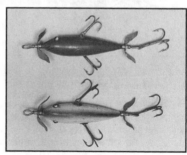

No. 905 Underwater Minnow

BeBop

Announced as new in the 1950 catalog, this wood lure was offered in two sizes. Sizes: No. 902, 3 3/8, 1/2 oz.; No. 903, 4 1/2", 5/8 oz. Colors: white body with red arrowhead; yellow body with black tiger stripes and red arrowhead; silver speckled yellow body with black shad-o-wave stripe; yellow perch scale; yellow body with red and black spots, green stripe on back and red arrowhead; scale finish, green with silver speckles; blue mullet scale; orange body with black and red spots; light green frog, dark green frog with yellow belly. **$5-$15**

Callmac Bugs

The earliest reference to the Callmac Bugs was in a 1923 South Bend advertisement. They are cork body, single hook floating fly rod baits. The 1923 ad said there were 12 colors available. By 1923, the list had grown to 24 for the bass size and 12 for the trout size. **$20-$30**, double with original box

Nip-I-Didee

Introduced in 1947, this 3" lure was available in a floating model with double or treble hooks and an underwater model with treble hooks only. The underwater model wasn't made available until 1951. Sizes: No. 910 (Floater), 3", 5/8 oz.; No. 911, 3", 3/4 oz. Colors: aluminum color, aluminum color body with red arrowhead, white body with red arrowhead, yellow body with red arrowhead, black body with white arrowhead, yellow perch scale; dark green frog finish with yellow and black marking, aluminum color body with red, green and black marking, silver speckled body with green stripe on back, rainbow, neon red, saturn green, fire orange. **$40-$60**

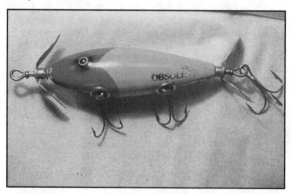

Nip-I-Didee

Spin-I-Didee, No. 916

Wee-Nipee, No. 912

Both of these lures came along about 1952. They are two small spinning versions of the Nip-I-Didee. They each have fore and aft propeller spinners. The Wee-Nipee was absent from catalogs by the 1954 edition, but the larger Spin-I-Didee remained along with its big brother. Sizes: No. 912, 2 3/8", 3/8 oz.; No. 916, 2 1/4", 1/4 oz. Colors: aluminum color, black with red gills; dark green frog finish with yellow and black decorations; white body with red arrowhead; yellow perch scale; yellow body with red gills; aluminum color body with red, green and black markings; silver speckled body with green back. **$5-$15**

Spin-I-Didee. Photo courtesy Ken Bernoteit

The Panatella Minnow (c. 1912-1942)

This plug first weighed about 9/10 ounce and body length was 4 1/4". The last ones available weighed a bit more (1 1/8 oz.), but the length remained the same. Earliest versions had either three or five treble hooks (one trailing and the others side or belly-mounted). Later catalogs made detachable single hooks an option. Colors: Green cracked back, white belly; rainbow, yellow perch; white body, dark shaded back; red body, dark shaded back; white body, red head and tail; scale finish; red head, aluminum color body; frog; scale finish with red blend, gold finish with red head; red head, white body. **$125-$200**

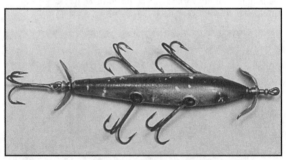

Panatella Minnow

Surface Minnow

This particular plug shows up first in a 1912 catalog. There were three versions: The 920W and 920F, 921RH, and 922L, all 3 1/2", 3/4 oz. All have two trebles and one nose-mounted propeller (notched until about 1914). The same numbers were used later for different lures. A 1939 catalog lists No. 920 as a "Wounded Minnow," No. 921 as a "Panetella Wobbler," and No. 922 as a "Darting Bait." All are completely different plugs. Colors: solid white; frog finish; white body, red head, luminous. **$100-$200**

Weedless Surface Minnow

This is the same as 920 and 921 except that it was offered with weedless hooks. Colors: white body with red head or frog finish. **$100-$200**

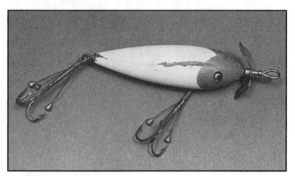

Weedless Surface Minnow

Explorer

Jointed Explorer

The 1922 catalog said these were "... brand new lures added to the South Bend line this year, designed for medium to deep traveling on a steady, fairly rapid retrieve." But neither appeared in catalogs after the next year. Sizes: No. 920, 3 3/4", 1/2 oz.; No. 2920 jtd., 3 7/8", 1/2 oz. Colors: white body with red arrowhead; yellow body with green back, red and green spots; red blend scale finish; fire orange body with black shad-o-wave stripe; neon red body with black shad-o-wave stripe; fire orange arrowhead; saturn green body with black shad-o-wave stripe. **$5-$15**

The Woodpecker

Found in a 1912 catalog, the only design was white with red head. It had a distinct collar around the head. By 1921 it was available with a frog finish and weedless hooks if desired. A "midget" size was also made available in the 1914 catalog. By the mid-1910s it was being offered with a luminous surface paint. It had disappeared from catalogs by the late 1930s. Sizes: No. 923, 4 1/2", 1 oz. Colors: red head with white body, frog finish; all white. No. 924, 4 1/2", 1 oz. Colors: luminous. No. 925 (midget), 3", 3/4 oz. Colors: red head, white body, all white. No. 926 (midget), 3", 3/4 oz. Color: luminous. **$75-$125**

Combination Minnows, No. 931-934

These baits, sometimes known as Worden Combination Minnows, appear in the 1912 catalog in two types. One has a single trailing treble and the other has the trailing treble and two more trebles, one mounted on each side. All types are in catalogs from then to the mid-1920s. Sizes: No. 931, 2 5/8", 1/2 oz. Colors: white body, red and green spots, natural bucktail; yellow body, red and green spots, natural bucktail, red body, black spots, natural bucktail, rainbow, natural buck tail, green cracked back, white belly, natural bucktail, yellow perch, natural bucktail; white body, dark shaded back, natural buck tail; red body, dark shaded back, natural bucktail, white body, red head, natural buck tail, luminous with white buck tail. No. 932, 2 5/8", 1/2 oz. Colors: White body, red and green spots, white buck tail, yellow body, red and green spots, white bucktail, red body, black spots, white bucktail. No. 933, 2 5/8", 1/2 oz.; No. 934, 2 5/8", 1 oz. Colors: white body red and green spots, natural bucktail; yellow body, red and green spots, natural bucktail, red body, black spots, natural bucktail. **$75-$150**

Combination Minnows

The Min-Buck, No. 943-955

The 1912 catalog first offered the Min-Buck in "All Standard Colors." Two versions were available in the listing: the No. 943 with three trebles and the No. 945 with five trebles. The belly trebles were opposite side mounted. Both had trailing bucktail trebles. About 1914 two more, the No. 944 and the No. 946, were offered. These sport the smooth edge (no-notch) propeller spinners and new colors were added. They are the so-called "Hex" colors. They were 3" long in 3T and 3 5/8" in 5T. The No. 955 was a musky size Min-Buck, 5T at 5 1/4". No Min-Bucks were listed in catalogs from 1921 on. **$90-$150; musky size $200-$300**

Muskie Casting Minnow, No. 953

This rare plug seems to have been offered for a very short time (c. 1914). Weighing in at 1 1/4 oz., this fighter is 3 5/8" long. This lure is essentially the same body style as the No. 943 Min-Buck, but it is bigger and heavier. It has the same hook configuration as well, but is not supplied with a buck tail on the trailing treble. **$1,500-$2,000**

Muskie Trolling Minnow, No. 956

This is the same lure as the No. 955 Min-Buck (5T) but does not have a buck tail on the treble and is bigger at 5 1/4" and 2 1/4 oz. It has five trebles and was available in the 1912 catalog in all the standard colors. It was around until about 1922. **$800-$1,500**

Ice Fishing Decoy, No. 258

This little known South Bend product showed up in only one of the catalogs, the 1923 edition. It is essentially the same body as the Muskie Casting Minnow, but is only the finished body with glass eyes and no hooks or hardware other than a screw hook/washer at the top with a swivel attached. It is 5" long. Colors: green scale and aluminum color body with red head. There are only four known. **$700-$1,000**

Surf-Oreno No. 963

First appearing around 1916, this lure continued to be available throughout the years, but the color design options dwindled from 13 choices (1921) to only six by 1953. It sports two propellers and the later versions were available with only three trebles. Early versions were available with either two or three. Body length is 3 3/4" and weight is 1 oz. The earliest No. 963 Surf-Orenos had more elongated (TSB) bodies almost pointed at both ends and the later models were more rounded at the head. Colors: red head with white body; frog design; rainbow; solid red, black nose; green cracked back with white belly; white body with green and red spotted decorations, blue head and aluminum color; scale finish with red blend; gold finish with red head. **$75-$150, blue head version and scale finish, $200-$250**

Midget Surf-Oreno

This plug appears around 1916 and is a smaller version of the No. 963 Surf-Oreno. It is 2 3/4" long and weighs 1/2 oz. The same general comments made about the No. 963 apply to this No. 962 Midget Surf-Oreno. **$75-$150**

Midget Surf-Orenos

Fly Rod Surf-Oreno No. 961

This is a tiny 1 1/2" version of the Surf-Oreno. It was around from the late 1920s until the early 1940s. Weight was cataloged as "1 pound per dozen." Colors listed in 1927 were: red head, white body; rainbow; imitation frog; white body with red and green decorations; green scale finish; scale finish with red blend. **$25-$40**

Muskie Surf-Oreno No. 964

Appearing first around 1925, this is a beefy version of the Surf-Oreno. It has nose- and tail-mounted propellers, two belly-mounted treble hooks and trailing treble, and 3 3/4" and 5 1/2" sizes. It had disappeared by the mid-1930s. Colors: red head, white body, rainbow, scale finish with green blend, frog; scale finish with red blend, yellow perch scale finish. **$200-$400**

Bass-Oreno No. 973

The most famous lure in the South Bend line appeared in 1915. South Bend didn't invent the lure but bought the patent rights from J.S. Olds, who had been making and selling his lure before 1915. It underwent many changes through the years, but the overall design remained much the same. They have gone from no eyes to glass eyes (until 1927) to tack eyes (c. 1935) to pressed eyes (c. 1951) and to painted eyes in the 1960s. In the 1934 model called the Better Bass-Oreno, the body was sawed out longitudinally, making a slot from the belly in. A die-cut aluminum plate was inserted, glued and riveted in. The result was that only the three hook hangers and line tie (integral with the plate) protruded from the body. This lasted until 1942. The standard cup rig continued to be available throughout this period also.

Sizes: No. 973, 3 1/2", 5/8 oz.; No. 473, 3 3/4", 3/4 oz.; No. 73, 3 3/4", 3/4 oz. Colors: red head, white body; yellow body, red and green spots; solid red, black nose; white body, red and green spots; rainbow; frog; red head, aluminum color body; luminous; scale; white body, blue head; scale with red blend; red head, gold color or body; solid black. **$40-$200**

Bass-Oreno. Photo courtesy Jim Muma

Saltwater Bass-Oreno No. 977

This is the same lure as the regular Bass-Oreno except it is built with much stronger hardware. It has only one belly treble and a trailing treble hook. Size: 3 1/2", 3/4 oz. Colors: red head, white body; red arrowhead, white body, rainbow, scale finish with green blend, scale finish with red blend; red head, aluminum color body, minnow scale finish; iridescent pearl, dace scale finish; yellow perch scale finish; pike scale finish; yellow body, red and brown decorations; luminous. **$25-$50**

Babe-Oreno No. 972

The birth date for this lure is believed to be 1916 and it was continuously available into the 1950s. At birth, it was 2 3/4" long, weighing 1/2 oz. It was available in at least 14 finishes by 1927. It is the same shape body as the Bass-Oreno and has one belly treble and a trailing treble. It was also available in the Better Babe-Oreno aluminum plate construction from 1934 through 1942. The oldest ones had no eyes and a more shallow cupped head than the later versions and the paint line on the head was a straight vertical line. Around 1926, eyes were added and a 1932 catalog illustrates it as available with detachable single hooks. By 1932-34, the paint design had changed to reflect an "arrow" or "arrowhead" design instead of the straight vertical paint line at the head. Colors: red head, white body, yellow body, red and green spots, red body, black nose; white body, red and green spots; rainbow, frog; red head, aluminum color body, scale finish; scale finish with red blend, gold finish with red head, white body, blue head, luminous. **$20-$75** (there is a rare red, white, and blue model that will bring much more)

Musk-Oreno No. 976

This is a large version of the Bass-Oreno, new about 1916. First found in a 1921 catalog supplement, it was offered with a "… 5-inch piano wire leader having a snap arrangement, permitting easy removal if preferred." The earliest models have no eyes, but by 1925-26, eyes were present and, sometime in 1934-35, the improved aluminum plate, hook-link was added. The plug has two belly-mounted trebles and one trailing. It was removed from the line sometime in the early 1940s. Size: 4 1/2", 1 1/8 oz. Colors: red head, white body, yellow body, red and green spots; white body, red and green spots; red body, black nose; rainbow, frog, red head, aluminum color body, scale finish; scale finish with red blend, gold finish with red head, white body, luminous. **$40-$200**

Troll-Oreno No. 978

Called the "newest and latest number of the 'Oreno' baits" in the 1921 catalog, it is made of light cedar, has two belly treble hooks and one trailing treble. Size: 6 1/2", 2 oz. Colors: green back, white belly; frog, scale finish with red blend, gold finish, red head, red head, white body, yellow body with red and green spots; white body with red and green spots; solid red with black nose; rainbow, red head with aluminum color body, white body, blue head. **$50-$75**

Trout-Oreno No. 971

The Trout-Oreno came along in 1920 and stayed in the line into the 1950s. It is the same shape as the Bass-Oreno, is 1 3/4" and has one belly-mounted double hook. **$15-$50**

Fly-Oreno No. 970

This little bit of a wooden lure was new about 1921 and continued to be available into the 1950s. It is 1" with one belly-mounted double hook. **$15-$50**

Wiz-Oreno No. 967

This is an unusual lure that used the Babe-Oreno body. There was a belly-mounted, long-shank, single-point hook with a special "swirling" propeller mounted on the hook shank and a gray hackle covering the point. There was a tail-mounted pork rind attachment also. New in 1925, this lure had disappeared from catalogs by 1930. Size: 2 3/4". Colors: red head, white body, yellow perch scale finish; rainbow, scale finish with green, blend, red body, black nose; red head, aluminum color body, copper finish. **$75-$125**

Wiz-Oreno

Tarp-Oreno No. 979

About 1921-22, this large plug appeared. It is the same body design as the other "Oreno" type baits. In 1922, this plug was fitted with a belly-mounted double hook and a trailing double, but by 1925 and from then on the hooks were single point. Size: 8", 5 oz. Colors: mullet scale finish; red head, white body, red head, aluminum color body, scale finish with green blend, scale finish with red blend, rainbow, iridescent pearl, minnow scale finish. **$75-$125**

King-Oreno No. 986

This is the same design as the Tarp-Oreno but smaller (6 1/2" body length) and has only one single hook (belly mount). It first appeared in the early 1920s and disappeared from the line in the 1940s. Colors: yellow perch scale finish; red head, white body, red arrowhead, white body, red head, aluminum color body, scale finish with green blend, scale finish with red blend, rainbow, minnow scale finish. **$75-$125**

Coast-Oreno No. 985

This bait is 4 1/2" in length and weighs 1 1/2 oz. All comments made about the King-Oreno apply to this plug as well. **$125-$175**

Ketch-Oreno No. 909

This small plug was first observed in a 1932 catalog. It has one belly-mounted double hook and was gone by 1940. Size: 1 1/2", 1 oz. Colors: red arrowhead, white body; red arrowhead, yellow body, scale finish with red blend, scale finish, green; pike scale finish; frog. **$75-$100**

Midge-Oreno No. 968

This plug was first found in a 1932 catalog and was included from that point on. It has one belly treble and one treble mounted just under the tail end of the plug body. Size: 2 1/4", 3/8 oz.

Colors: red head, white body; red arrowhead, white body, red arrowhead, yellow body; black arrowhead, white body; yellow perch, scale finish; green scale finish; pike; silver speckled, white body, green back stripe; rainbow; copper scale finish; white head, black body, minnow scale finish, silver, black and red, dace scale finish. **$15-$20**

Midge-Oreno

Dive-Oreno

New in 1941, the two sizes of this lure remained in production (except for the war years) through 1952. They were stubby tail versions of the Pike-Oreno. Size: No. 952, 3 1/4", 1 1/2 oz.; No. 954, 4", 5/8 oz. Colors: white body with red arrowhead, yellow perch scale, white body with silver speckles and green back, pike scale. **$15-$30**

Fish-Oreno No. 953

This interesting plug first appeared in South Bend catalogs in 1926, but there is evidence to suggest it was on the market earlier. The 1927 catalog states, "The Fish-Oreno is the first lure ever produced that is guaranteed by the manufacturer to catch fish." It is covered by an insurance policy attached to the bait. The lure is similar to the Bass-Oreno but has a polished metal head, a wire leader permanently attached to a screw eye at the top of the head, one belly-mounted treble hook and a trailing treble. The guarantee tag had disappeared by 1939, but the bait was produced on into the early 1950s. Size: 3 1/2", 5/8 oz. Colors: white body, red head,, pike finish; scale finish; yellow body, green and red spots; copper scale finish; silver body, frog; rainbow, pike scale finish; silver speckled white body, green stripe; minnow scale finish, silver, black and red, yellow perch scale finish. **$40-$75**

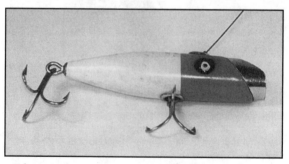

Fish-Oreno. Photo courtesy Ken Bernoteit

Vacuum Bait

This lure first occurs in a 1922 South Bend catalog but it was patented in 1909 by Francis O. Howe. Apparently South Bend obtained the rights to the patent. The earliest South Bend versions used the original Howe swivel hook hanger hardware. What probably happened is that upon purchasing the right to manufacture the lure, South Bend also acquired some of Howe's inventory. As this was exhausted, South Bend began using its own hardware. Hence the mixture of hardware and possible bodies. At first, South Bend only offered the larger size but soon after, a second, smaller size was added. Some of the earliest South Bend Vacuum Baits have glass eyes and tack-painted eyes. The lure remained in catalogs until discontinued in the 1940s. Sizes: No. 1, 2 3/8", 3/4 oz.;

No. 21, 2", 1/2 oz. Colors: white body, red stripes; yellow spotted with red and green; rainbow, dragon fly, frog; red spotted with yellow and black. **$100-$200**

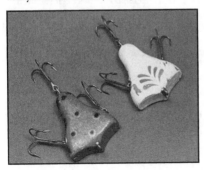

South Bend Vacuum Bait, left, and Howe's Vacuum Bait

Pike-Orenos

The first of the Pike-Orenos show up around 1922. They were nothing like the familiar two curved eye scoop model at first. They came in two models, the regular at 4 1/4" and the Midget at 3". The first body style was the same as the Bass-Oreno. They fitted a metal plate into the nose scoop that extended down, creating a lip. They have no eyes. The next model has the curved eye scoops, resulting in a fish-like face and nose. The body was slightly tapered but remained chunky. The company continued to refine the body to the more familiar shape (c. 1932). Two more sizes were added that year, the Baby Pike-Oreno (3 1/4") and the Big Pike-Oreno (5 3/8"). All three shared the same design. It had changed to a more pointed nose with eye depressions scooped out of each side of the nose. The metal lip no longer covers the nose but is mounted beneath the nose and bent downward to impart the deep diving action. It has a 1" wire leader permanently fastened to the plate. One of the treble hooks has been removed and the belly position of the two remaining trebles changed. By 1935 an even smaller one, the Midget Pike-Oreno (2 1/2"), was offered and the newer arrowhead paint design was utilized on the three smallest versions. A third treble hook reappeared on the two largest sizes about 1935. Colors: red head, white body; red arrowhead, white body; iridescent pearl; green scale finish; yellow perch scale finish; pike scale finish; rainbow, silver speckled white body, green stripe; scale finish with red blend, red head, aluminum color body, frog, red with black nose; white body, green and red spots. **$15-$40**

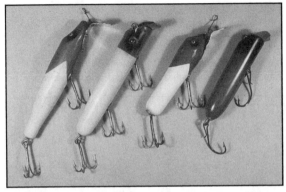

Pike-Orenos

Jointed Pike-Oreno No. 960

The jointed version of the Pike-Oreno shows up in the mid-1930s. It had undergone a design change by the 1950s and the number had changed to No. 2956. The old plug has a scoop taken out of the top of the head and was almost twice as long as the newer one, at 7". The newer version has two scoops in the head, one on either side making it more or less a pointed nose. The older one has two belly trebles and a trailer; new has the trailer but only one belly treble. Colors: red arrowhead, white body, scale finish, silver, black and red; green scale finish; red head, aluminum color body. **$20-$40**

Whirl-Oreno No. 935

New around the late 1920s, this unusual surface lure has feathers mounted on a trailing treble hook. The body is 3 1/2" overall, 3" wide, and weighs in at 5/8 oz. It was available in three finishes: red head with white body, frog finish and butterfly. The plug was available up to the early 1940s. **$75-$175**

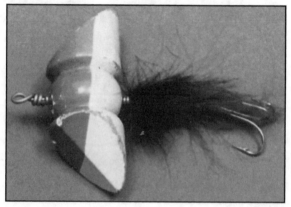

Whirl-Oreno

Li'l Rascal

This little 2 3/4" light tackle lure was announced as new in the 1950 catalog, going on to say: "Its Impudent Action Gets 'Em." It must have been a fairly successful lure for it stayed in the catalogs into the late 1950s. Colors: white body with red arrowhead, yellow perch scale finish, yellow body with silver speckles, black shad-o-wave stripe, rainbow with blue back, pike scale, white body with silver speckles and green back. **$5-$15**

Gulf-Oreno and Midget Gulf-Oreno

New around 1927, this plug is minnow shaped. It has a belly-mounted treble, a trailing treble, and a removable wire leader attached to the top, aft portion of the head. It had disappeared from catalogs by the early 1930s. Sizes: No. 983, 3 1/2", 7/8 oz.; No. 982 (Midget), 2 3/4", 1/2 oz. Colors: white body, red around eyes, red gills; white body, gold speckled, red head, white body, silver speckled, black around eyes. **$75-$150**

Minnow No. 999

This slender plug was first found in a 1930 catalog. It has a line tie eye on top of the nose, a belly treble and a trailing treble hook. There is a small metal fin protruding from beneath the head. Size: 4", 5/8 oz. Colors: red head, white body; green cracked back, scale finish; red head, black nose; yellow perch; musky finish. **$75-$125**

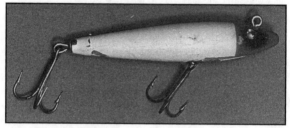

Minnow No. 999

Plunk-Oreno No. 929

This plug showed up in the late 1920s and stayed in catalogs until 1932. It disappeared for several years to reappear as an entirely different design around 1939. The early plug is a long tapered body with a scooped head, one belly-mounted treble hook, a trailing treble, and glass eyes. It is 3 3/4" and weighs 5/8 oz. Colors: red head with white body, green scale finish and yellow perch scale finish. The new design is a short wood body with a tail mounted weighted single hook covered with fancy feathers. It weighs 5/8 oz. and is 4" long overall (body less than 2"). It was available in red head/white body, red head/black body, yellow perch, rainbow and frog finish. **$30-$60**

Tease-Oreno No. 940

This plug was introduced prior to 1930. It has a chrome plated metal head plate, a trailing treble and a belly treble hook. It looks much like the Kautsky Lazy Ike of today. The Midget model came along about 1940. Sizes: No. 936 (Midget), 2 7/8", 1/2 oz.; No. 939 (Baby), 3 1/4", 1/2 oz.; No. 940, 4 1/8", 5/8 oz. Colors: red head, white body, rainbow, frog, green scale finish; yellow perch; minnow scale finish; iridescent pearl finish. **$40-$60**

Crippled Minnow

This plug first appeared in a 1930 catalog, but was gone by 1935. It has a belly-mounted treble and a trailing treble hook. There are two propeller spinners, one nose- and one tail-mounted. Size: 3 1/4", 5/8 oz. Colors: red head, white body, red head, black nose; luminous; green scale finish; silver speckled, musky scale. **$25-$50**

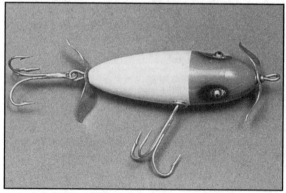

Crippled Minnow

Mouse-Oreno

New in the early 1930s, this 2 3/4", 5/8 oz. mouse-shaped plug has a flexible tail, a metal lip with wire leader attached and one belly-mount treble hook. The original finishes available were: gray mouse back with white belly, solid black, and white body with red blended eyes and gray stripes down the back. In 1934, a fuzzy gray mouse-like skin finish replaced the gray mouse back finish. There was a smaller fly rod version (No. 948) made as well. **$35-$50, fly rod size: $40-$60**

Mouse-Oreno

Plug-Oreno No. 959

This weedless surface plug was new in the 1930 catalog. It has two belly-mounted single hooks, a pork rind attachment on top of the body, and two wire weed guards. It was made into the 1940s. Size: 2", 5/8 oz. Colors: red head, white body, frog, yellow body, red and green decorations. **$300-$400**

Plug-Oreno

Min-Oreno

A new lure for 1932, the Min-Oreno is a departure from the usual shapes in the South Bend line. The lure was made in three different sizes, each available in six different finishes. It has an under-tail mounted treble, belly treble, painted eyes and a metal diving lip under the nose. It was made throughout the 1930s. Sizes: No. 926, 3", 3 1/2 oz.; No. 927, 4", 4 1/2 oz.; No. 928, 5 5/8", 6 oz. Colors: red arrowhead, white body, red arrowhead, yellow body, yellow perch, scale finish; pike, scale finish; green scale finish; scale finish with red blend. **$20-$30**

Lunge-Oreno

Midget Lunge-Oreno

This large plug was new around 1930. The first version of it has two belly-mounted trebles and a trailing treble. There are two extra-large aluminum propellers, one at tail and nose. By 1932, the tail propeller had been eliminated. The axis for the propeller was heavy wire passing through the length of the body with the line tie incorporated at the front and the trailing treble at the back making a direct connection. Size: No. 966, 6", 2 1/2 oz.; No. 965 (Midget), 3 3/4", 1 1/8 oz. Colors: red head, white body, pike scale finish; yellow body, red and brown decorations; scale finish with red blend. **$125-$200; midget: $175-$275**

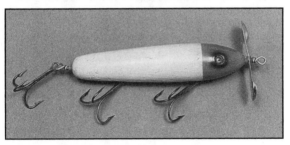

Midget Lunge-Oreno. Photo courtesy Jim Muma

Slim-Oreno No. 912

This was a new plug for 1932 that is very similar in design to the Panatella. It was offered through the 1930s. The plug has nose and tail propellers, a belly treble and trailing treble hook and painted eyes. Size: 3 3/4", 1/2 oz. Colors: red arrowhead, white body; green cracked back, white belly, rainbow, yellow perch, scale finish; scale finish with red blend, green scale finish. **$75-$100**

Truck-Oreno No. 936

This was new plug for 1938 and was produced until sometime in the 1940s. This lure has an unusual head, shaped so that it would turn like a propeller on retrieve. The body is a Surf-Oreno with one belly treble and a small trailing spinner forward of a trailing feathered treble hook. Size: 9", 5 oz. Colors: red head, white body, red and white feathers; frog, red and white feathers; yellow with black stripe, black and red dots, red and white feathers. **$300-$450**

Entice-Oreno No. 991

A new plug for 1938, it continued in production into the early 1940s. Apparently the Fish-Obite No. 1991 (Tenite body) was introduced in 1939 to replace the Entice-Oreno although the latter was still available. The Entice-Oreno has one belly-mount treble and a trailing treble hook. It has a metal lip and line tie under the nose. Size: 2 5/8", 1/2 oz. Colors: red arrowhead, white body; white arrowhead, black body; black arrowhead, white body; silver speckle, white body, green back stripe; yellow perch scale; dace scale; pike scale; white body, red and green decorations; pearl finish; rainbow, blue back, minnow scale finish; red body, black shaded eyes. **$800-$1,200**

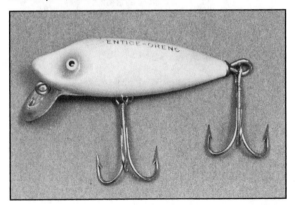

Entice-Oreno

Two-Oreno No. 975

Baby Two-Oreno No. 974

New in the mid- to late 1930s, this unique plug came in two sizes. Each has two belly trebles, four eyes (2 each end), two line ties and a metal lip. The line could be tied to either end. It had been eliminated from the line by the 1940s. Sizes: No. 975, 3 3/4", 3/4 oz.; No. 974, 3", 1/2 oz. Colors: red arrowhead, white body, rainbow with blue back; frog; yellow perch scale; pearl, green scale finish. **$30-$40**

Two-Oreno and Baby Two-Oreno

Two-Obite

Bass-Obite

These are the same plugs as the Two-Oreno and Bass-Oreno except that they are made of Tenite. These came out about 1938. **$20-$40**

Darting Bait

This is part of a series of Best-O-Luck low cost plugs marketed by South Bend in the 1930s and 1940s. The lure has a "V" shaped mouth notch, two belly trebles and one trailing treble hook. Size: 4", 1/2 oz. Colors: Splotch frog finish; red head, white body, silver speckled white body, green back stripe; pike scale; yellow perch scale finish; white head, black body. **$10-$20**

Goplunk

This lure appeared in catalogs between 1951 and 1954. It is a jointed popper-type that was recommended for night fishing. Size: 3", 3/8 oz. Colors: black with red around the eyes; green frog finish with yellow and black decorations; white body with red arrowhead, yellow body with red and brown decorations. **$10-$20**

Baby Pike Lure No. 907

Jointed Baby Pike Lure No. 908

Standard Pike Lure No. 930

Jointed Standard Pike Lure No. 931

These four baits are part of the low cost series called "Best-O-Luck" lures. All have a trailing treble, one belly-mounted treble, a slope nose, and metal lip with wire leader attached. Sizes: No. 907, 3 1/4", 1/2 oz.; No. 908, 3 1/2", 1/2 oz.; No. 930, 4 3/8", 5/8 oz.; No. 931, 4 1/2", 5/8 oz. Colors: red head, white body; pike finish; pike scale finish; green striped, silver speckled body, green back stripe; yellow perch, scale finish; rainbow, green scale finish. **$15-$20**

Select-Oreno No. 1950

This is an interesting 1 1/4" plastic fly rod lure. It came in four pieces. Each of the different heads and bodies came apart and were interchangeable. With that feature you could make 16 different combinations. **$10-$15 each; intact set with box: $75-$100**

Standard Wobbler No. 943

Baby Wobbler No. 942

These plugs are part of the South Bend low cost series called Best-O-Luck marketed through the 1930s and 1940s. They are the same design, the Baby Wobbler having one trailing treble and one belly treble hook and the larger having a second belly treble. Sizes: No. 942, 2 3/4", 1/2 oz.; No. 943, 3 3/4", 5/8 oz. Colors: red head, white body; green striped, pike finish; green scale finish; pike scale finish; yellow perch scale finish. **$15-$20**

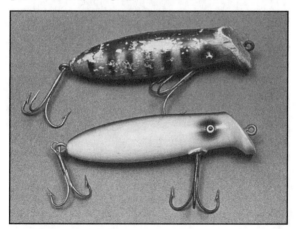

Wobbler

Weighted Wobbler No. 941

This lure is part of the "Best-O-Luck" series of low cost plugs. It has a metal lip belly-mounted treble, and trailing treble hook. Size: 2 5/8", 1/2 oz. Colors: red head, white body; green striped, iridescent pearl finish; white silver speckled, green back stripe; rainbow, blue back; red dace scale finish; pike scale finish; yellow perch scale finish. **$5-$10**

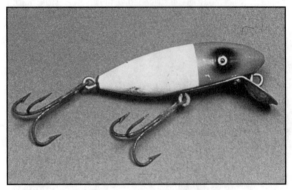

Weighted Wobbler

Baby Wounded Minnow No. 914

This plug is part of the low cost "Best-O-Luck" series. It has a nose and tail propeller, a trailing treble hook, and belly-mounted treble hook. Size: 2 3/4", 1/2 oz. Colors: red head, white body, silver speckled body, red and brown stripes; pike finish; yellow perch, scale finish. **$5-$10**

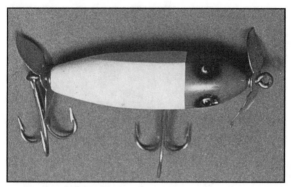

Baby Wounded Minnow

Surface Lure No. 916

This "Best-O-Luck" lure is an elongated egg shape plug with a propeller at the nose, a belly treble and trailing treble hook. Size: 2 3/4", 5/8 oz. Colors: red head, white body, frog finish. **$5-$10**

Surface Lure No. 950

One of the "Best-O-Luck" bait series, this plug has a front propeller, belly treble, and a trailing treble hook. Size: 3 1/4", 1/2 oz. Colors: red head, white body; green back blending to white belly; silver body, red throat; yellow body, red back stripe. **$20-$25**

Surface Lure No. 950

Weighted Underwater Lure No. 910 and 918

Part of the "Best-O-Luck" series, the No. 910 has one nose propeller spinner, one trailing treble hook and two side-mounted trebles, one on each side of the body. The No. 918 is the same except with one belly treble in place of the two side-mounted ones. Sizes: 3", 5/8 oz. Colors: red head, white body, greenback, white belly, yellow body, red back stripe; silver body, red throat; rainbow with blue back; pike finish. **$5-$15**

Wounded Minnow No. 920

Baby Wounded Minnow No. 914

One of the "Best-O-Luck" series, this lure has a nose and tail propeller, two belly-mounted trebles, and a trailing treble hook. The smaller model has only one treble on the belly. Sizes: No. 914, 2 3/4", 1/2 oz.; No. 920, 3 5/8", 3/4 oz. Colors: red head, white body; silver speckled body, red and brown stripes; pike finish; yellow perch, scale finish. **$10-$15**

Panatella Wobbler No. 921

This "Best-O-Luck" lure has a metal lip, belly-mounted treble, and trailing treble hook. Size: 4", 5/8 oz. Colors: red head, white body; red head, aluminum color body, green striped. **$15-$20**

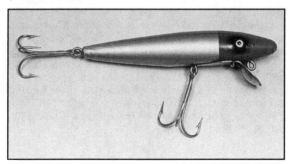

Panatella Wobbler

Trix-Oreno

Fly Rod Sizes, No. 593, 594

Bait Casting Sizes, No. 595, 596

Saltwater Sizes, No. 597, 598, 599

First found in the 1931 catalog, these lures lasted throughout the years. Careful reading of the entry leads one to believe that the fly rod sizes were released some time before and the two bait casting sizes were new in 1931. Then along came three saltwater sizes in 1932. **$5-$10**

Fin-Dingo

This funny rounded plastic South Bend lure did not originate with the company. The lure was advertised by the Ropher Tackle Company of West Los Angeles, Calif., in 1950. It was offered in sinking and floating models in nine different colors. It first showed up as a South Bend product in 1953 in a sinker only. It was gone from the catalog by 1955. Size: 1 5/8", 1/2 oz. Colors: (Ropher Tackle): red head, frog, white with black ribs, black with white ribs, orange with black ribs, spotted goldfish scale, green perch scale, yellow perch scale, yellow with black spots. (South Bend): frog, green perch scale, yellow with black spots, yellow perch scale, saturn green, white body with red arrowhead. Ropher: **$30-$40, South Bend: $10-$20**

A-B-C Minnow

George W. Bolton
Detroit, Michigan

There are two models of this clever lure. Each has interchangeable back pieces. The available colors were black, white, red, green, and silver. The lure has a carved mouth and a pointed nose, glass eyes and cup/screw eye hook hangers. There is a screw eye fastener for the removable backs. **$200-$350**, glass-eyed model: **$225-$375**

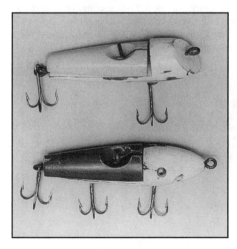

*A-B-C
Minnow*

Abbey and Imbrie Fishing Tackle

This famous New York company was founded in 1875 as the successors to Andrew Clerk and Company, purveyors of fishing tackle in New York since 1820. Abbey & Imbrie lasted until Horrocks-Ibbotson of Utica, N.Y., bought the company in 1930.

The Ghost

Measuring 6" overall, this lure dates back into the late 1800s to the early 1900s. The A&I logo on the box began use in 1893 and the lure looks much like the P&S Ball Bearing Company Lures of around 1900. In the box were an extra set of snelled hooks and an extra "Weedless Fly Gang." **$200-$300**. The box can easily be worth double that.

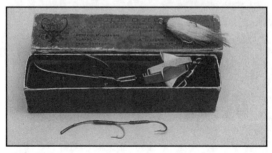

The Ghost

Abbey and Imbrie made by Heddon

Several lures are known to have been made by Heddon but marketed by A&I under its own brands and names. Almost all the Heddon manufactured A&I lures will have "Abbey & Imbrie" stenciled on the belly. When fitted with metal plates, propeller spinners or diving lips, they will have the same imprint in place of the "Heddon Dowagiac" imprint.

Here is an incomplete list of lures known to have been made for Abbey and Imbrie by Heddon: Lucky-13 and Lucky-13 Jr.; Basser; No. 175 Heavy Casting Minnow; Triple Tease; No. 700 Musky Minnow; Series No. 150 Flipper (side hook); Series No. 150 Injured Minnow style; Meadow Mouse (3T, no belly weights); Vamp (jointed); Series "O" Minnow; No. 1800 Crab Wiggler. **$65-$450**

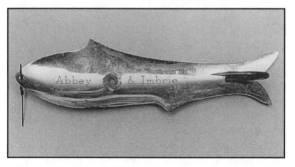

Abbey and Imbrie metal fish spoon

Mouse

This A&I mouse lure made by Heddon has a metal lip imprinted "Abbey & Imbrie." It has black bead eyes, leather ears and tail and sports an L-rig belly hook hanger and the Heddon one-piece short loop (Stolley patent) tail hanger. Size: 2 3/4" without the tail. Colors: gray mouse color, white body with red blush around eyes and chin. **$65-$150**

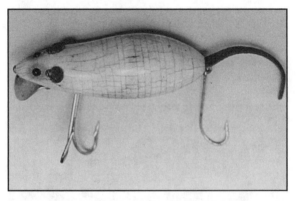

Mouse

The Griffiths Minnow

A 1923 Abbey & Imbrie catalog illustrated this lure. The only colors mentioned were copper, silver and brass. They were made in four sizes: 1", 2", 2 1/2", 3". **$275-$400**

The "Glowbody" Minnow

This dandy was introduced in 1920. It has nickel plated hardware made so that the changing of hooks is easy. The body is a glass tube with a smaller tube inside that is coated with a luminous material so that it could be fished at night. Length is about 3 1/2". **$75-$125**

Hiawatha Wooden Minnow

A 1914 Abbey and Imbrie catalog illustrates this plug as available in two sizes, 2 1/2" and 3 1/2", and hook configurations. Both sizes have nose and tail propeller. The smaller size has a side treble on each side of the body and a trailing treble (3T). The larger has two more side trebles (5T). These baits are remarkably similar to Heddon's No. 100 and No. 150 and may have been made by Heddon for A&I. Colors: fancy back; rainbow; solid white; solid red; blended green; yellow perch. **$400-$600**

The Octopus Wooden Minnows

These plugs were first observed in a 1911 catalog as available in two sizes: The No. 1 was 3 1/2" long and had a pair of trebles on each side and a trailing treble (5T); the No. 2 was 2 1/2" long and had only one treble on each side and a trailing treble (3T). Each sported nose and tail propeller spinners. **$500-$800**

Octopus Minnow

Crippled Minnow

Sometime in the 1920s, this plug became available. It is wood and shaped somewhat like a minnow with a realistic tail fin shape. It has one left-side-mounted treble and left mounted trailing tail treble (2T). Size: 4", 3/4 oz. Colors: white with red head, silver scale finish, frog finish. **$40-$85**

Bass-Catcher

This is a 1920s vintage plug with a slope nose and 1" wire leader attached. It has one belly treble and trailing treble hook (2T). It is the same as the Bass Seeker made by Moonlight Bait Company. Moonlight also made them for Abbey & Imbrie. Size: 3 1/2", 1 oz. Colors: white with red head, gold scale finish, silver with red head. **$150-$175**

Whippet

This lure first came along in 1929. It has nose- and tail-mounted propellers, a belly treble and trailing treble hook (2T). Size: 4", 5/8 oz. Colors: white with red head; gold scale finish; perch finish. **$65-$90**

Flash-Head Wobbler

This deep-water plug was first put in the line about 1929. It has a nickel-plated metal head, a wire leader, belly mounted and trailing treble hooks (2T). It was made for Abbey & Imbrie by the Moonlight Bait Company. Size: 3 1/2", 1 oz. Colors: gold scale finish; frog finish. **$65-$150**

Aeroplane Bait

H.G. Parker and Son

Battle Creek, Michigan

An ad from about 1910 reads: "The newest and most attractive bait on the market. It floats for casting. It sinks for trolling." Apparently, it came only in white. The spinners are brass. Only two are known to exist in private collections. **$1,000-$1,500**

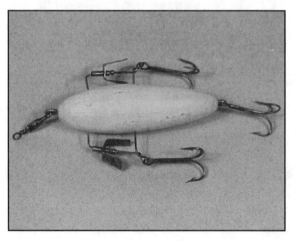

Aeroplane Bait.

Franklin A. Alger

(1862-1940)
Grand Rapids, Michigan

Franklin A. Alger was a sportsman and an extraordinary craftsman/inventor. He fashioned his lure bodies on a lathe he made from a foot-operated treadle-type sewing machine. His metal spinners were stamped out on a small homemade hand-operated apparatus. It is said that he designed and made more than 50 styles of lures. Few of these, however, were patented and marketed in any quantity.

He made most of his lures for his own and friends' use, but he did obtain patents on at least two of his lures. He marketed at least the Getsem, Tantalizer, and the Michigan Trout Spinner.
$500-$1,000

Getsem

All Star Bait Company

Chicago, Illinois
Gee Wiz Bait Company
Richland Center, Wisconsin
Gee Wiz

Gee Wiz Action Frog

Another of the many attempts at animated frogs, this lure has one single hook mounted on the belly with the barb portion pointed up and between the legs. The origins of the lure may a bit confusing. There were three advertisements found for the lure, by two different companies in two different states. The first was by the All Star Company in 1931, and the other was by the Gee Wiz Company in 1949 and 1950. The lures appear to be identical. Colors: red and white; musky size, natural green; natural green. **$50-$75 in green, in white with red head: $250-$350**

Gee Wiz Action Frog

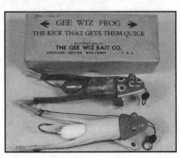

American Tackle Company/National Tackle Company

Tulsa, Oklahoma

This firm is known to have been doing business in the late 1930s. All the plugs were designed with a receptacle hole and pivoting cover in which you placed a special tablet that simulated the bleeding of a wounded bait fish when worked properly in the water. There were eight styles of lures and a hookless teaser. Some were available as a floater, diver or sinker making 16 different plug types, including the Teaser, for the collector to find. It would be a rare moment indeed to find a Bleedlure in the box with the vial of tablets. Each plug also came with detachable hook guards.

We know that there was also the existence of a Big State Bait Co., in Beaumont, Texas, that also made bleeding baits. It is very likely that this company was the forerunner of Bleeding Bait. The company apparently moved to Dallas toward the end of the 1930s, becoming the Bleeder Bait Manufacturing Co. The company moved to Tulsa, Okla., around 1939. At the same time the name of the company was changed to American Tackle Company and then to National Tackle Company. Bleeding Baits from Big State Bait Co: **$150-$290, all others: $20-$50**

The B.P.S. 100

Made in floating, sinking and diving models, this plug is 4" long and weighs 3/4 oz. It has two side-by-side belly trebles and a trailing treble. **$175-$275**

The B.P.S. 100

Broken Back

This is a jointed lure weighing 3/4 oz. and is 4" long. It has one belly treble mounted on the rear section and a trailing treble hook. **$125-$150**

Bubbler

Available in floating (1/2 oz.) and sinking (5/8 oz.) models, both plugs are 2 5/8". They each have one belly treble and a trailing treble hook. **$250-$350**

Chunker

This lure has a notched mouth with the line tie in the roof of the mouth. It is 2 1/4" long and weighs 5/8 oz. It has one belly treble and a trailing treble hook. There are unusual weedless features on the trailing treble hook. This is often found on Bleeding Baits. **$125-$175**

Dido

The Dido is a slow sinking plug weighing 1/2 oz. and 2 5/8" long. It was made with a belly treble and trailing treble hook only and a scooped out head where the line tie is located. **$125-$175**

Fish King

Made in diving, sinking or floating models, this lure is 2 7/8 oz. and 6 1/4" long. It sports three trebles, two belly-mounted and one trailing, and a metal lip blade. **$150-$250**

Mouse

This is a 2 5/8", 1/2-oz. mouse-shaped plug complete with flexible tail. It has one belly treble and a trailing treble hook. **$200-$375**

Apex Bait Company

Chicago, Illinois

Apex Bull Nose and Apex Bull Nose Jr.

The earliest advertisement found for the Bull Nose was in 1916. The ad noted the availability of a smaller one (Apex Jr.). Both have screw eye and washer type hook hangers. Sizes: 3", 4". Colors: white with red head, yellow with red head and red with yellow head. **$100-$200**

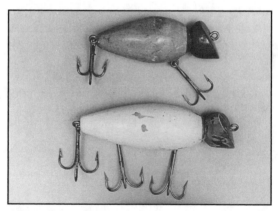

Apex Bull Nose

Fred Arbogast Baits

Akron, Ohio

The Arbogast Company was in business as early as 1926. He was a bait casting champion, winning competitions in 1922, 1923, and 1924.

His most important contributions to the development of the artificial lure are the invention of the rubber "Hula Skirt" and the famous "Jitterbug." The earliest Arbogast lures were mostly metal, with wood coming along in the 1930s. The original wood lures were made of aromatic cedar.

Fred Arbogast died in 1947, but the Fred Arbogast Company, Inc., is still going strong in Akron, Ohio, today.

Tin Liz

The earliest catalog listing for the Tin Liz was in a 1928 issue of a Shapliegh Hardware Company catalog. The entry illustrated the lure with a teardrop shaped spoon-type spinner attached to the hook with a swivel. It was then available in only two colors: natural chub finish and silver with a red head. In the first years of production, the lure sported glass eyes with the subsequent ones having painted eyes. All were made of metal and had a single hook with the trailing fin tail attached.

There were several versions made available after the initial plain Tin Liz: Tin Liz, c. 1924, 2 1/4", 5/8 oz. **$30-$40**; Tin Liz, glass eyes, 2 1/4", 5/8 oz., **$40-$70**; Tin Liz (3 fins), 2 1/4",

---

$50-$75; Tin Liz (3 fins) weedless, 2 1/4", **$100-$150**; Spin Tail Tin Liz, 2 1/4", **$125-$200**; Big Tin Liz, 2 3/4", 1 oz., **$200-$400**; Tin Liz, Weedless, 5/8 oz., **$60-$70**; Tin Liz Perch, 5/8 oz., **$60-$70**; Tin Liz Sunfish, 1 5/8", 5/8 oz., **$175-$225**; Tin Liz Sunfish (3 fins), 1 3/4", **$225-$250**; Tin Liz Walleye, 2 3/8", **$800-$1,000**; Tin Liz Muskie, 2 1/2", **$800-$1,000**; Tin Liz Snake (Baby Pike), 2 5/8", 5/8 oz., **$500-$750**; Tin Liz Hickory Shad, 2 1/4", 5/8 oz., **$20-$30**; Fly rod Tin Liz, 1 1/8", 1/64 oz.; 1 5/8", 1/32 oz.; 2", 1/16 oz., **$15-$25**; Tin Liz Twins, 5/8 oz., **$15-$25**; Tin Liz Minnow, 5/8 oz., **$15-$25**; Spin Tin Liz, 1", 1 1/2", 1 3/4", 2 1/4", **$15-$25**

Sunfish Tin Liz

Weedless Kicker

First called the Weedless Spin-Tail Kicker in ads, the lures were available in two sizes, 1/2 oz. and 5/8 oz., according to a 1926 ad. They have glass eyes, a single hook, fancy feathers, and a free-flipping tail fin attached to the hook. Colors: frog finish, silver finish. **$75-$125**

Weedless Kicker

Jitterbug

This is one of the most famous Arbogast lures. It was first introduced about 1937. The first Jitterbugs were made of cedar and had glass eyes. Some have a plastic nose blade because of the metal shortage during World War II. There are nine different models and sizes available including a jointed version. There were eight finishes listed in a 1941 catalog: black and silver scale, white and silver scale, perch, solid black, white body with red head, frog, yellow with herringbone stripes, pearl with herringbone stripes. By 1949 only one other had been added, a luminous finish with a blue head. In 1950, Arbogast announced three new "Fire Plug Daylight Fluorescent finishes." There are 25 or more different finishes to be found. Metal-lipped, wooden Jitterbugs: **$25-$75**, Plastic and metal-lipped plastic Jitterbugs: **$10-$65**

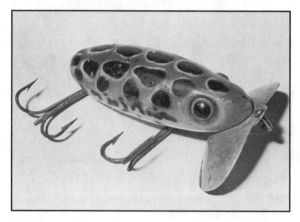

Jitterbug

Bait-Caster

Deluxe Mfg. Co., Inc.
Rome, Georgia

This is a clever contraption made, ostensibly, to enable the fisherman to cast a live minnow on a hook a long distance unharmed. It is red with an aluminum cylinder into which you place the hooked minnow and leader at the depth you wish to fish. When it lands it automatically turns over, dumping the minnow and leader out. It then becomes a bobber. It came in three sizes: 3/4" cylinder, 2 1/4"; 7/8" cylinder, 3"; 1" cylinder, 3 1/4". **$20-$30**

Bait-Caster

Bass Hog

T.J. Boulton
Detroit, Michigan

This lure was first found in a 1911 publication. The lure is 4 1/2" and painted white with a red head and red stripes and dots on the belly. It has cup and screw eye hardware with a reinforcing metal tail insert. There is a rare smaller size (2 1/4") that would bring a premium. $100-$200, smaller size: **$250-$350**

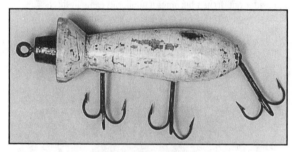

Bass Hog

Bass King

National Bait Company
Stillwater, Minnesota

This is thought to be the earliest version of the Bass King, with a flute on the body side that is slanted down from the nose. It utilizes the simple screw eye hardware. These 1927 lures came in two sizes, 3" and 3 1/2". They were white-bodied with red heads and are usually found with cup and screw eye hardware. **$50-$75**

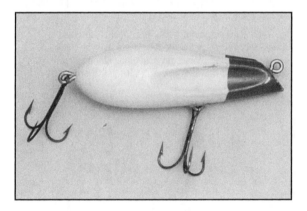

Bass King Jr.

Bidwell Bait

Clifford W. Bidwell
Kalamazoo, Michigan

The name "Bidwell Bait" is used by collectors to identify this lure. The patent was granted to Bidwell in 1915 and the lure is a match to the patent illustration. None of these lures have yet been found in a box, nor has any advertising or any other identifying literature been located. It has a brass plate on the bottom extending slightly up the tail, and a large brass washer-like hook preventer attached to the hooks. It measures 3 1/2" in length.

There has been another lure found that is attributed to Bidwell. It is 3" long and called the "Bottle Bait" by collectors because of its shape, almost identical to the old miniature cream containers served with coffee in the 1950s and 1960s. **$300-$500**

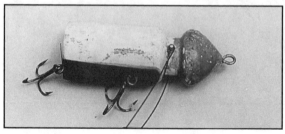

Bidwell Bait

Biek Manufacturing Company

Dowagiac, Michigan

This company was founded in 1930. A catalog dated 1941 illustrated eight wood lures and five fly rod bugs and flies. There were also a number of other items such as bobbers, landing nets, gaff hooks, etc. The lure entries gave no sizes, finishes or weights. One of the lures is The Agitator. It measures 2 5/8", has painted eyes, a recessed screw eye hook hanger (no cup), is marked "Biek," and is black with red scale finish. Other lures cataloged were a chunky surface popper named the Topper, a jointed Piker looking something like a Creek Chub Bait Co. jointed Pike Minnow, and a Biek Major that looks like a Heddon Basser. **$40-$60**

Agitator lure by Biek

Bing's Nemahbin Weedless Minnow

A.F. Bingenheimer
Milwaukee, Wisconsin

These plugs can be placed as early as 1905. Early versions show the weedless wires with loops at the end that attach to the hook points. Those hooks are single point and rigidly attached to the body. They have been found with nose- or tail-mounted propellers on both. Colors: gold, silver, metallic, crackle back and green back with red or white belly. Others have glass eyes and hand-painted gill marks. Their lengths vary from 3" to 6". The weedless treble hooks apparently were quite successful, as they are seen offered on lures in catalogs from other well-known companies. In the Nemahbin Minnow, the hooks are attached with the gem clip-type fasteners to the thru-body wire. **$500-$600**

Nemahbin Weedless Minnow

Bite-Em-Bate Company

Warsaw, Indiana (1917)
Ft. Wayne, Indiana (1920)

The dates with the two company locations represent the dates of periodicals in which their ads with the addresses appeared. The name is found two ways: "Bite-Em-Bate" and "Bite-Em-Bait." The earliest Bite-Em lure patent found was applied for in mid-1921.

Bite-Em-Bate

This wooden plug was shaped so that it would rotate on retrieve. The body pivoted on an exterior wire half-loop extending from the nose to the tail. The first (c. 1917) version had a treble hook attached to the wire loop and another attached directly to the tail end of the body. Later (c. 1920) the trailing treble was moved to the wire loop just beneath the tail. Size: 3 1/2". Colors: White body, red head and red tail; red body, white head; gold body, red head and red tail; aluminum body, red head and gold tail; black body, white head and gold tail; yellow body, red head and red tail; choc. green, red head and red tail. **$100-$200**

Bite-Em-Bate.

Lipped Wiggler

The diving lip on this plug is adjustable, enabling the fisherman to run it at the depth of his choice. The patent was granted in 1922. Hook hangers are a type of L-rig and the eyes are yellow glass. It was available with two or three treble hooks. Size: 3 3/4". Colors: unknown. **$100-$200**

The Bite-em Water-mole c. 1920

This 3" plug is shaped somewhat like a mole. It is found with a round head or with a flattened head and slightly chubbier body. A 1920 ad indicates the availability of this lure with a second line tie. It has a nickel plated metal piece attached along the belly extending in a spoon shape slightly past the tail end. A treble hook is attached just aft of the head on the bottom and there is a trailing treble. Colors: white body, red head; white body, red head and red tail; black body, white head and gold tail; black body, red head and gold tail; yellow body, red head and red tail; yellow body, green head and green tail; choc. green body, white and red head; gold body, white and red head and red tail; red body, white head; aluminum body, red head and red tail. **$100-$200**

Bite-em Wiggler c. 1920

This is a 3 7/8" plug with a sloping head. It has a treble mounted beneath the nose and another under the tail. It has the same metal plate/spoon attachment as the Bite-Em Water-mole. The colors available were the same also with the addition of cream white. **$100-$200**

Bite-em Floater Minnow

This classic two-propeller spinner floating lure was available in two sizes, 3" and 4", and has yellow glass eyes. Colors available are not known. **$100-$200**

Bite-em Bug

Only one illustrated reference to this lure was found. The catalog illustration shows a simple screw eye attachment of the trailing spoon. The body in the catalog is shaped a bit differently and its paint design is simpler. It utilizes the same L-rig type hook hanger, but it is mounted in the opposite direction. Colors: white body, red head; black body, red and white head; yellow body, red head; choc. green body, white head; Roman gold body, red and white head; red body, white head; aluminum body, red head. **$150-$250**

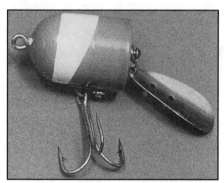

Bite-em Bug

Bonafide Aluminum Minnow

Bonafide Manufacturing Company
Plymouth, Michigan

Patented in 1907 by Hiram H. Passage, this little gem was available in two sizes: a 3 3/4" 5-hooker and a 3 1/4" 3-hooker. It was made in two halves of cast aluminum held together by a screw about mid-body. It is not solid but hollow, allowing the fisherman to make it a floater or adjust buoyancy by adding water or other interior weight. Note that there is a hole through the dorsal fin to allow the lure to be used as an ice fishing decoy. The lures are rare. **3-hooker $1,500-$3,000, 5-hooker $2,500-$4,000**

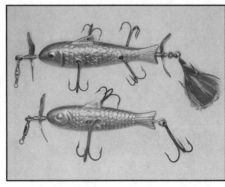

Bonafide Aluminum Minnow. Photo courtesy Clarence Zahn

Bonner Casting Minnow

Leo Albert Bonner
Okeechobee, Florida

This c. 1931 Florida lure looks very much like the South Coast Minnow. This lure is extremely well built and strong, for saltwater use. It has glass eyes, four internal belly weights and a twisted, through-body line tie/tail hook hanger. It measures 4" long. There are probably few to be found as it was the product of one man. It is thought that they were sold only by Bonner and through a bait shop in the town of Okeechobee. **$200-$275**

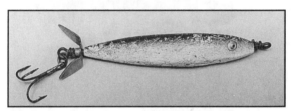

Bonner Casting Minnow

Bright-Eye-Lure

Bright-Eye-Lure Products
Detroit, Michigan

These lures are unique and are also difficult to find. They are made of an aluminum shell around a wooden core. There are holes in the outer shell to accommodate the glass eyes so that they may be mounted in the wood portion of the body. Sizes: 2 3/4", 3 1/4", 4 1/4". They are thought to date around 1933. **$125-$200**

Bright-Eye-Lures

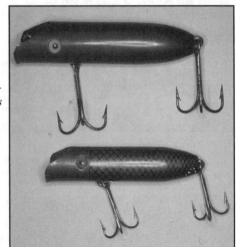

Brook Shiner Bait Company

Milwaukee, Wisconsin

One 1926 advertisement was found, inferring these were the only two lures the company made. Called new, they were available in two sizes, "Large" and "Small," 3 1/2" and 4". They have aluminum-colored bodies and red heads. **$175-$250**

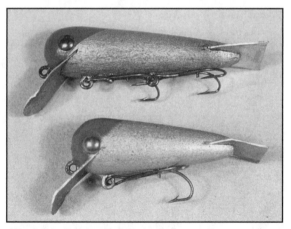

Brook Shiners. Photo courtesy Jim Muma

Paul Bunyan Bait Company

Minneapolis, Minnesota

This company made lures in the 1930s, 1940s and 1950s. The last ad found in fishing magazines was in 1952. Little else is known. It manufactured and marketed several collectible plastic plugs, some wooden lures, and some metal spoon or spinner types. It purchased the patents from Bates Baits when that company ceased operations in 1938.

Double Action Twirl Bug

This bait has a white body with nickel or copper wings which revolve on machine screw bearings. It has a red head with a scoop "... which causes the bait to wobble and dive and the wings to spin ... practically weedless," a 1940 catalog said. The wings were available in either nickel or copper. The lure measures 3" without the bucktail. **$35-$50**

Double Action Twirl Bug. Photo courtesy Jim Muma

Twirl Bug Wiggler

This lure is very similar in appearance to the Double Action Twirlbug. The body is white and the head red, but the wings are made of celluloid. The wings are finished in either red, gold or silver. It has a spinner at the head. It also has the split ring hook attachment and measures 3" without the bucktail. **$40-$80**

Albyler Basgeter Surface c. 1935

Al Byler
Seattle, Washington

Al Byler made and sold his lures under the name Albyler Basgeters in the 1930s. So far only three different lures have turned up. Those plugs that have so far been found all have a paint job that includes the use of glitter. Various types of hardware may be found on the lures. The three lures: Basgeter Straightail, 4 5/8", Basgeter Surface, 5 1/2", and Basgeter Underwater, 3 1/2". **$100-$150**

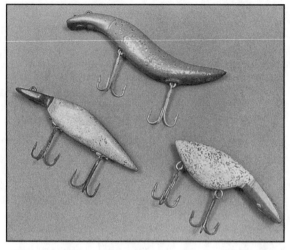

Three Basgeters

Carter's Bestever Bait Co.

Indianapolis, Indiana
Dunk's
American Display Company
Dayton, Ohio

In the beginning, these two companies were independent of each other. Patent application dates indicate Thomas J. Carter was in, or at least preparing to go into, business as early as the late 1910s. Milton S. Dunkelberger was apparently the owner of the American Display Company of Dayton, Ohio, which was in the tackle business in the early 1920s. It was either manufacturing and/or distributing lures under the name "Stubby Brand Fishing Tackle" in advertising that also carried the American Display Company name. Dunkelberger either bought Carter's company or obtained his lure patents around 1932.

Bestever

There were several sizes and hook configurations available in this plug type. It has a very distinctive nose design that looks much like a bird's beak. Most had treble or single hooks, but one ad clearly states the three basic sizes were available in a double hook configuration too. The location of the aft hook seems to be on the belly or at the tail end.

Sizes: Muskie, 5 1/2", 1 1/2 oz., 2T, **$200-$300**; Pike, 4 1/2", 3/4 oz., 2T or 3T, **$200-$300**; Big Boy, 4 1/2", 1 3/4 oz., 2T, **$200-$300**; Large, 3 5/8", 1 1/2 oz., 2T or 2D, **$75-$125**; Medium, 3", 3/8 oz., 2T or 2D, **$50-$60**; Midget, 2 3/4", 1/2 oz.,

1T or 1D, **$40-$60**; Baby, 1 3/4", 1/8 oz., 2T, **$40-$60**; Fly rod, 1 1/4", 1/16 oz., 1D, **$200-$300**. Colors: white with red head, red with black head, silver color with red head, gold with red head, yellow with red head, solid red, solid black, half black and half white.

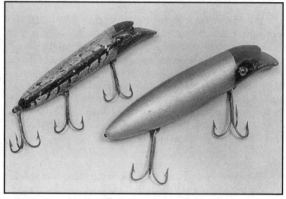

Pike and Muskie Bestevers

Carter's Double Header

This was cataloged as a 3", 3/4 oz. lure in 1933. It has a flat head with a rotating metal plate made so that it could be rendered a top-water or an underwater lure. Colors: white body with red head, silver body with red head, yellow body with red head, all black. **$90-$150**

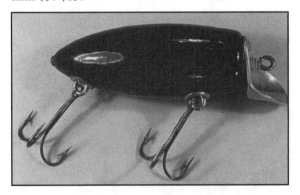

Carter's Double Header

Dunk's Double Header

You can do almost exactly the same thing with the head of this 3 1/4" lure as the Carter above. On this one the head is a sloped wooden affair that could be rotated to accomplish the same effect. Colors: white body with red head, yellow body with red head, green body with red head, all black. **$100-$200**

Cedar Propeller

Malcolm A. Shipley
Philadelphia, Pennsylvania
And Pocono Minnow
J.L. Boorse
Allentown & Easton, Pennsylvania

The Cedar Propeller surface plug was made in the late 1890s by Malcolm Shipley. An article said: "It was a plain uncolored cedar wood ... equipped with two very light-weight metal propellers, one fore and one aft, connected by a copper wire that extended laterally through the conical body. It bore three treble hooks." They were off the market by 1920. **$200-$300**

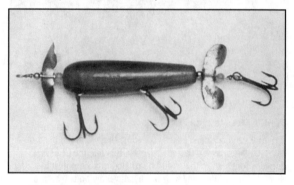

Cedar Propeller

Pocono Minnows

Pocono Minnows are 3 1/8" long. A reference attributed the lures to a J.L. Boorse and stated that they were manufactured in Easton and Allentown, Pa. Some collectors attribute the Poconos to Shipley because of the similarity of the rigging and propeller spinners. The body styles are significantly different. **$50-$90**

Chase-A-Bug

Leon Tackle Company
Detroit, Michigan

This is a cute little plastic action lure. The lower jaw is articulated and when the plastic propeller at the nose rotates on retrieve, the mouth opens and closes. It was patented in 1956 by Leo Krozaleski of Detroit. The only color seen is black and white. It measures 3 15/16" overall including the propeller. **$75-$125**

Chase-A-Bug

Charmer Minnow Company

Springfield, Missouri

These early wooden plugs have a nose-mounted propeller and a tail propeller mounted to rotate the rear section of the lure body. The lures are usually found with eyes, have two opposite see-through mount side trebles and a trailing treble. The rear rotating body section was painted with barber-pole style stripes. Sizes: 2 5/8", 3 3/8" and 5". There was also a surface model that has no nose-mounted propeller spinner. Colors: Gold body, green stripes; gold body, red stripes; white body, red stripes; white body, green stripes; brass body, green stripes; brass body, green stripes; brass body, red stripes; red body, white stripes; green body, white stripes. Some have been found with air-brushed stripes and a rare few have only air-brushed dots instead of the stripes on one or both sections. **$400-$800**

Charmer Minnows

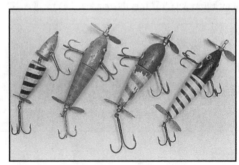

Clark's Make 'Em Bite Bait

Clark Brothers
La Porte, Indiana

A box and enclosed flyer identifies this lure. The lure is believed to date from the mid-1920s. The lure body measures 2 3/4". Colors: white body with red head, green body with red head, black body with red head, red body with black head. **$300-$600**

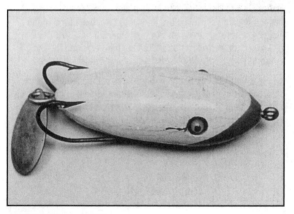

Clark's Make 'Em Bite Bait

Robert L. Clewell Mfg.

Canton, Ohio
The Snakerbait

The Frogerbait

This one-man company existed from 1926-1934, mostly in Clewell's home. Clewell's output included several fly rod lures and a couple of other, unusual lures that interest collectors. The Snakerbait and the Frogerbait were made of molded rubber and then spray painted. The colors known to have been used on the Snakerbait are red, green and brown. One can only surmise that the Frogerbait was offered in at least a green version. The Big Mouth Mins were made of brass with a silver finish.

It is unlikely that many of these lures will be found outside Ohio, Michigan or Wisconsin as he was not known to have actively promoted them anywhere else. The Snakerbait is the only one of the three that any trade data was found for. **$350-$450**

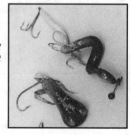

Snakerbait, Frogerbait and Big Mouth Min, from left

Coldwater Bait Company

Willis E. Phinney
Coldwater, Michigan

Also, Eureka Bait Company
Samuel O. Larrabee
Coldwater, Michigan

It is not yet known what the nature of the relationship between these two men and their companies was, but research proves that they were connected in some way in their early days.

The Eureka Wiggler is the earliest patented lure and granted only to Larrabee (Eureka Bait Company), but about two years later we find the Coldwater Weedless being patented with the rights being granted to both men.

Identifying which lure was made by which company is not always an easy task. Coldwater products will often have a washer-like tail protector device and most will have cup and screw eye belly hook hardware. The Eureka products are also found with simple screw eye hook hangers. Coldwater colors: fancy spotted, frog back with white belly, white with red throat, white luminous, white with sprayed red head, red back with white belly. Eureka colors: green crackle back with white belly and red painted mouth, red crackle back with white belly and red painted mouth, orange crackle back with white belly and red painted mouth.

Coldwater King

The patent for this plug was granted in 1917. The metal plate is installed at an angle so that the lure is erratic on retrieve. There is the typical Coldwater use of the slightly cupped washer at the tail hook attachment. **$200-$400**

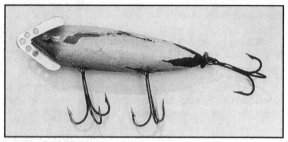

Coldwater King

Coldwater Hell Diver

This lure, about 4 1/4" long, was patented in 1918. The major feature of the Hell Diver is the adjustable diving lip. It is adjusted by loosening a screw under the nose and sliding the lip back and forth. This plug is similar to the Shakespeare Hydroplane. The Coldwater Hell Diver has been found with glass eyes (rare) but usually has no eyes. **$200-$350**

Coldwater Weedless

This 4 1/2" weedless lure is the rarest of the Coldwater lures and at least one actual lure has been found. It is somewhat slimmer than the one in the patent drawing and has a trailing double hook. **$300-$400**

Coldwater Wiggler and Eureka Wiggler

The Eureka Wiggler was the original name for this lure. It was the first of the Coldwater/Eureka products to be patented in 1914. It is designed with a "Y" shaped water passageway so that as the lure is retrieved water passes through, making the lure wiggle. The mouth (usually painted red) is larger than the two exit holes on the sides. The lure measures 3 7/8". The Coldwater Wiggler has typical Coldwater cup and screw eye hardware. **$200-$350**

Coldwater Wigglers

Coldwater Ghost

This lure is merely a curious version of the Wigglers. It is identical in all respects but instead of the passageway splitting into a "Y" and exiting the sides, it gets smaller like the "Y," but it remains a single passage way and turns up to exit out at the back. **$300-$400**

Comstock Chunk

Aptly named, this lure is a "chunk" of wood with two trailing single hooks that can pivot downward through slots in the body. It has two wire weed guards originating at the nose. The lure measures 2 1/2" and is available in white with red head or solid white. The Moonlight Bait Company obtained the rights to this lure around 1928. **$100-$150**

Croaker

Croaker Bass Bait Company
C.A. Wiford and Son
Jackson, Michigan

This jointed 4 1/2" plug was new in 1910. There are at least three slightly different body styles and sizes to be found. Colors were not listed. Difficult to find. **$300-$400**

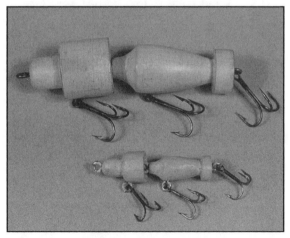

The Croaker

Crutch's Lizard

William O. Crutchfield
Elizabethton, Tennessee

This is a unique triple-joint wooden lure, 5" and finished in a burnished natural wood. The eyes appear to be ceramic beads. Crutchfield made these lures by hand over a period of years from the late 1940s or early 1950s until the 1960s. A design patent was granted in 1958. The lure was offered in three finishes: burnished wood, black with white stripes, white with sparkles. **$75-$100**

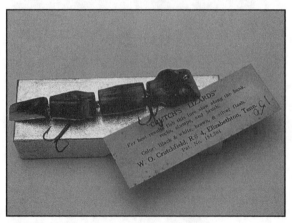

Crutch's Lizard

Darby Weedless
Spin Head Weedles(s)

T & M Darby or M. L. Darby
Whiting, Indiana

This lure dates from around 1934-1937. There were two ads found, one from each year. The lure is wood-bodied with one single hook protruding from each side. It is rigged so the shanks could be attached to the body so they would spring out upon a fish striking the lure. It has a spinner head with metal fins inlet into the wood. Colors: white body with a half white, half red head or green back body with a half white, half green spinner head. **$250-$400**

Darby Weedless

Decker Lures

Anson B. (Ans) Decker
Lake Hopatcong, New Jersey

Decker was in business from the early 1900s and died in
1940. His plugs are found in advertising and catalogs as early as
1907. Decker lures are fairly rare and there are many look-a-likes
and copies. It is known that three body styles were produced by
Decker because of illustrations in ads. The first examples showed
a blunt nose version. As the years went by, the nose became more
tapered. About the only sure way to identify a real Decker is to
find his name stamped somewhere on the propeller blade. Some
Deckers sport a weedless single hook made of one piece of metal
for ease of installation and removal.

Topwater Casting Bait

Found advertised in catalogs and sporting magazines from
about 1908 on, this plug was shaped a bit differently from the
Decker Plug Bait. It was available with three single or double hooks.
The hooks with screw eyes alone are oldest and those with "cups"
around the screw eye mounts are newer. Sizes: 2 3/4", 3 1/2".
Colors: white; yellow, mouse color, red, blue; green; yellow mottled,
white with red head, white with red painted blades; sienna gray.
$100-$200

Decker Underwater

This is a little known Decker lure, 3 1/8" in body length. It
sports two propeller spinners made of heavy-gauge metal, a trailing treble hook and two opposite side trebles that are offset.
Available colors are unknown. **$90-$225**

The "Decker Plug" Bait

This wooden lure was first found illustrated in a 1907 Abercrombie and Fitch Co. catalog as available in two sizes either in white or yellow. The propeller blades were aluminum and the buyer had the option of three single or three treble hooks. In a 1909 catalog there was an additional size option and a new color option: gray. We know that the lure was being actively used as early as 1882. Sizes: No. 1, 2 3/4"; No. 2, 3 1/2"; No. 3, 3 3/4". Colors: white; gray; yellow, white with red head, unfinished wood. **$60-$125**

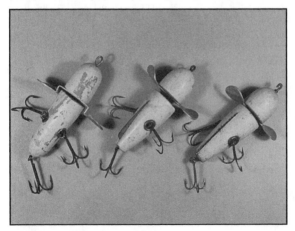

Decker Baits

Delevan or North Channel Minnow

Detroit Bait Co.
Detroit, Michigan

Very little is known about this lure. It is said to be made and/or distributed by the Detroit Bait Company around 1903-04. They are found in a three treble and a five treble version. The 3T model is usually around 3" and 3 1/2" for the 5T. They have unusual large glass eyes with gold flecks in the glass. The line tie and hook hardware is through-body twisted wire. Most are found with bow tie type tube propeller spinners although some will be found with the cruder prop. DELEVAN or NORTH COAST is occasionally found stamped or stenciled on the side of the 5T model though not as yet on the smaller one. **$275-$400**

Delevan Minnow

Detroit Glass Minnow Tube Co.

Detroit, Michigan

The earliest ad for this lure was in 1914. It illustrates a glass lure. With a magnifying glass, clearly visible are the words DETROIT MINNOW on the metal plug at the forward end of the lure. This was a hollow glass lure with four treble hooks side-mounted in opposite pairs. The angler was to place a live minnow in the 3 1/4" tube and it was supposedly magnified to twice its actual size by the glass tube and water inside. There were holes in the front and rear so that the "minnow will remain alive all day." A second style of this lure has been found. **$600-$900**

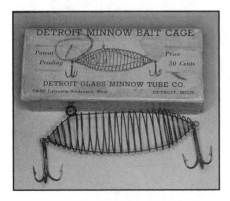

Detroit Glass Minnow Tube

Diamond Wiggler

Bignall and Schaaf
Grand Rapids, Michigan

This is another "Water Sonic" type lure that seems to be a close cousin to the lures of the Eureka Bait Company and the Coldwater Bait Company. This one measures 3 5/8" and has holes and flutes through which water may pass upon retrieve. It has cup and screw eye hook hardware. The lure dates about 1912-14.
$100-$200

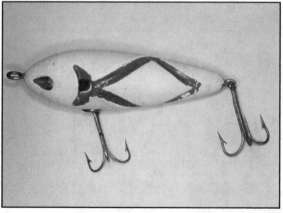

Diamond Wiggler

The Dickens Bait Co.

John W. Dickens
Fort Wayne, Indiana

This company was started around the time of the granting of Dickens' first patent in 1916. It was for a lure with a head that could be turned up or down by means of a spring-loaded apparatus, making it a surface or diving lure. It has not been named in any printed material found so far. It may have been a forerunner to the Liar Convertible Minnow. **$50-$90 for patent lure**

The Liar Convertible Minnow

Dickens' Duplex Darter

Patented in 1919, this plug has a sloped nose, a trailing treble and another, removable treble, that could be attached to the back or belly thereby causing the slope to be down or up. This made it either a surface or underwater wobbler. It measures 3 1/2" and this one has a red body with white head. The company apparently had two names for the lure and the box labels this one as a Dickens' Duplex Darter. **$75-$100**

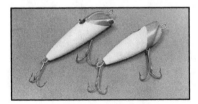

The Liar Convertible Minnows

Jim Donaly Baits

James L. Donaly
Newark & Bloomfield, New Jersey

Donaly was active as early as 1908. He marketed his lures under the Redfin brand. One of Donaly's lures, the Wow, is the forerunner of Heddon's Crazy Crawler. The original patent was granted to Donaly in 1928. It is known that Heddon acquired the rights prior to 1940 when it first appeared in their catalogs. Donaly died in the mid-1930s. His wife and daughter continued to paint and sell already assembled lures for a while after his death. They began selling the rights to some of his patents to others.

Redfin No. 27

This lure was around as early as 1911. It is a 3 1/4", 3/4 oz. lure that was made with three flasher blades and available in single-hook or treble-hook models. Colors: No. 27, white with red band; No. 37, green back with white belly; and No. 47, white with red stripes. **$1,200-$1,800**

Redfin lure

The Donaly Mouse Bait

The Mouse Bait is about as elusive as its namesake. They were very early Donaly lures that have not been found in catalogs or advertising. They were available in a gray or white finish, with and without the large propeller spinner and in various hook rigs. The example measures 2 3/4" and has the three-point New Jersey hook rig to comply with that states law of the time. No trade data

Donaly Wow and Jersey Wow

This lure was patented in 1928. Both the Wow and the Jersey Wow used the same body with the difference being in hook and line tie arrangement. The Jersey model has only a treble hook or sometimes three single hooks and was rigged for reverse running. The aluminum flapper blades are marked with Donaly's name and the Bloomfield, N.J., location. The regular Wow was made in two sizes, 2 3/4" and 3". The Jersey Wow was made in 3" only. Colors: red back, white belly; yellow body, white belly. **$225-$325**

Donaly Wow, left, and Jersey Wow

Redfin Floater

Advertised in 1916 is the "New Redfin No. 77." The illustration in the ad shows the side hooks are attached to the screw eyes with a safety pin or paper clip type affair and there is a small triangular flapper blade hung just beneath the tail of the lure. The Redfin Floater was made in two sizes, 2 1/4" and 2 7/8". It has two opposite-mounted side treble or single hooks and a large nose-mounted propeller spinner, usually marked with the Donaly name. Colors: red, yellow, gray, white or black. The white was luminous. **$225-$325**

Catchumbig Bait No. 57

The earliest reference to this lure was in a 1912 ad. It is a floating lure painted with a red collar normally. It was available in a 4" and a 3" size. The lure has simple screw eye hardware and an early brass box swivel. Another example has a brass wire line tie/rear hook hanger and staple-type hardware. Both of them have white bodies with red collars. The small one measures 3", is solid white with red gill marks and has a belly hook hanger that appears to have been fashioned out of brass wire. This rare small version is the only one known and a realistic value cannot be assigned to it. The 4" models: **$1,200-$1,500**

The Weedless Redfin Bait No. 67

The application for the patent was filed in 1913. The lure measures 3 1/8". It has heavy staple type hardware and the characteristic Donaly flapper blades as well as typical painted red gill marks. Some early models had more gill marks and a painted red eye. This is a rare, early Donaly lure. **$1,200-$1,500**

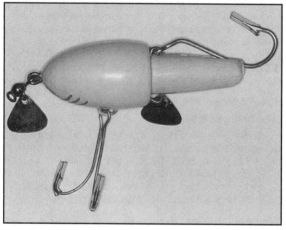

Weedless Redfin Bait No. 67

Eger Bait Manufacturing Co.

Bartow, Florida
c. 1930-1950s

William F. Eger retired in Florida and sometime in the early 1930s began offering fishing lures commercially. His company wasn't formally organized until 1936. Eger ran the business until 1945-46. He sold the company to his grandson Leroy Eger who ran it for a very short time. The Eger company continued in business with a succession of owners. Although all that is covered here are the wooden lures, it is known that Eger produced metal lures also.

Junior Dillinger 200 Series

Baby Dillinger 0 Series

These are smaller versions of the Master Dillinger and each has only one belly treble and trailing treble hook. Sizes: No. 200, 3 3/8", 5/8 oz.; No. 0, 2 1/2", 1/2 oz. Colors: white with black stripes, canary yellow with red stripes, white with red stripes, chrome yellow with black stripes, opalescent pearl, green scale, gray scale, silver flash, rainbow, Christmas tree. **$10-$25**

Weedless Dillinger 100 Series

This is a 2 1/8", 5/8 oz. plug with a single black spinner mounted on a wire leader. There is a hook-protecting steel wire from the nose down over the point of the rigid, single-point tail hook. The colors available were the same as the 200 Series Master Dillinger with the addition of pearl and vamp spot. **$15-$25**

Master Dillinger 300 Series

A slim wooden plug with two belly trebles and trailing treble, it had nose- and tail-mounted propeller spinners. Originally called the John Dillinger, it could be that the first finish, white with black stripes, reminded someone of the prison uniform of the day and named it after the bank robber. Size: 3 7/8", 3/4 oz. Colors: white with black stripes, red with red stripes, canary yellow with red stripes, chrome yellow with black stripes, green with black stripes, green scale, silver flash, gray scale, gray mullet scale, rainbow, Christmas tree, yellow with polka dots. **$20-$30**

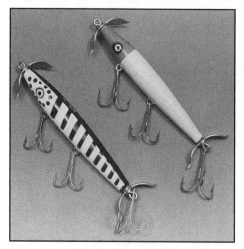

Master Dillingers

The Electric Luminous Submarine Bait Co.

Milwaukee, Wisconsin

The Glow Worm C. 1915

This has to be one of the earliest of the many attempts at the battery-operated lighted fishing lure. The battery/light unit in this one was reversible. One way it throws the light forward and reversed it shines through little port holes in the tail. It has nose and tail propeller spinners, a belly and trailing treble hooks.
$1,400-$1,800

Lou Eppinger

Dearborn, Michigan

Eppinger made his first Daredevle spoon in 1906. He called it the Osprey at the time. It stayed that way until he changed it in 1918. Over the years a few other lures were added to the line, the most desirable of these being the Klinker. It consists of a metal plate rounded at the head, side edges turned down slightly, a rigid-mount single hook points up and two small metal minnows trailing at the back corners. The most sought after Daredevles are those with three cartoon likenesses of the Axis leaders, Emperor Hirohito, Hitler and Mussolini. Sizes: Daredevle's Imp, 2 1/8", 2/5 oz.; Daredevlet, 2 7/8", 3/5 oz.; Daredevle, 3 1/2", 1 oz.; Huskie Devle, Jr., 4 1/2", 2 oz.; Huskie Devle, 5 1/2", 2 oz. Colors: black with white V, nickel on reverse side; black with white stripe, nickel on reverse side; red with white V, copper on reverse side; red with white V, nickel on reverse side; red with white stripe, copper on reverse side; red with white stripe, nickel on reverse side; green with white stripe, nickel on reverse side; yellow with black spots and red V, nickel on reverse side; frog coloration, nickel on reverse side; polished nickel on both sides; polished copper on both sides; pearl; mouse. No trading data

The "Expert" Wooden Minnows

F. (Franklin) C. Woods and Company
Charles C. Shaffer, Alliance, Ohio
J.L. Clark Manufacturing Company
Fred C. Keeling, Rockford, Illinois

The four names above represent the transition of Experts from 1901 to the 1930s. The 1901 date comes from the advertising of Experts in Outers Book magazine that year. The patent was granted in 1903 to Shaffer. There is a variation of the Expert that has "HOLZWARTH" imprinted on the side. J.C. Holzwarth of Alliance apparently sold them, buying from Woods and marketing them under his own name.

The Keeling company remained in operation until the 1930s when the company was sold to Horrocks-Ibboston. **Keeling Experts: $300-$500, Holzwarth Experts: $300-$500, Woods Experts: $1,000-$2,000**

Shaffer's original Expert Minnow

Fisheretto

c. 1918-1945
Brown's Fisheretto Co.
Alexandria, Minnesota
Osakis, Minnesota

This company was formed in the 1910s. In 1910, six brothers opened a general store in Osakis, Minn., and began making and selling lures. Sam Brown applied for a lure patent in 1918. They continued actively making and selling lures until 1945.

They fashioned four basic styles of lures and two of ice fishing or spearing decoys.

The original Fisheretto is most commonly found in a white body with red head finish, but has been found in other colors. The usual hardware is a screw eye and washer and the eyes are painted. **$75-$150**

The company also made ice fishing or spearing decoys. **$25-$50**

Fisheretto

Flood Minnow

Frederick L.B. Flood
Frostproof, Florida

Flood never went into commercial production with his lure although he obtained a patent on it. They all appear to be hand-made and painted. Consequently they are each unique and all are fairly difficult to obtain. He began fashioning them about 1922 and had perfected his design by 1925. The earliest of his "shinners" had leather tails, but sometime between 1925 and 1928 the leather was eliminated and the tails became wooden, carved integral with the body. The dorsal and ventral fins are made of metal and are imbedded into the body, and the pectoral fins are painted on. Two odd characteristics that are unique to Flood's lures are the rigid-mount belly hooks and the side-mounted line tie. About 1932 Flood made a deal with a man named Achter to produce bodies for him. These were essentially the same as the ones Flood produced except that the Flood bodies had a more blunt, flat-topped nose. **$500-$1,500**

Flood Minnow

Florida Artificial Bait Company

St. Augustine, Florida

The only catalog reference to this unique lure was found in a 1940 catalog. It is an articulated celluloid lure with eight sections. The catalog said it was available in two choices of color, "White body with red head or green and white body with red head." They have black bead eyes and are 5" long. The fisherman could get it either in a "light casting" version and two treble hooks or mounted with a "... single Tarpon hook." **$225-$325**

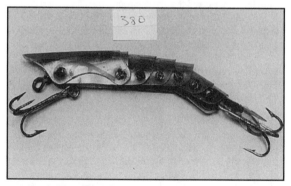

Florida Artificial Bait

Florida Casting Bait Company

Uz. C. Pemberton & Sons
Seffner, Florida
Tampa, Florida

This company began doing business in the mid- to late-1920s under the name Uz. C. Pemberton & Sons. Pemberton had been hand-making lures and was encouraged to start making them commercially. A friend joined him and founded the Florida Casting Bait Company in 1930. Over the years there was much experimentation, but it is believed that the company only actively marketed five lures: the Bug Bait, the Underwater Bait, the Florida Flapper, the Busy Bait and the Rat Bait. All but the Rat Bait were originally equipped with a unique tail hook patented by Pemberton. They were either single, double or treble and fitted with a pork rind device. It was soldered to the hook shank. Many have been found without this feature. The company went out of business in the mid-1930s. The lures are rare and not likely found outside of Florida.

The Underwater Bait

It is thought that the Underwater Bait is the first bait Pemberton offered. At about 2 1/2" the bodies are painted gold primarily with a stripe down the middle of the back and three stripes on each side. The stripes can be found in black, green or red. There has also been a yellow body found with a design similar to the Bug Bait. **$150-$300**

The Bug Bait

Two types of Bug Baits can be found. There are flat bellies. The metal lip is placed in a slot cut into the body. They utilize cup and screw eye hook hardware and the aft hook is sometimes found at the tail rather than on the belly. The later version has the lip held to the nose by the screw eye line tie. Colors found are gold body or yellow and white. They have a wing design on the back and legs painted on the bottom. **$150-$300**

Florida Flapper

There were two different lips in the patent, neither of them the same as the more simple lip they patented and used on the Florida Flapper. The Florida Flapper measures just under 3" in length and is found in two different body styles in diameter. The patent design is sometimes dubbed the "fat body" with a diameter of just over 1" and the more narrow style is under 1". The bodies for the slim- and fat-body versions of the Florida Flapper and the Busy Bait are virtually the same. The only difference is that glitter was never used on the Florida Flapper while it was always applied to the Busy Bait. The Florida Flappers have simple screw eye hook hangers. They sport two treble hooks and have unpainted tack eyes. Colors: white body with red head; white body with pink head and red band between the colors; green body with red head; green body with pink head; green body with gold head; deep green body with red head; deep green body with pink head; deep green body with pink head and silver band between the colors; gold body with red head; gold body with pink head; gold body with bronze head; dark gold body with light gold head and red band between the col-

ors; silver body with pink head; silver body with pink head and
red band between the colors; bronze body with red head; maroon
body with pink head; yellow body with red head; yellow body with
pink head; yellow body with pink head and silver band between
the colors. **$50-$90**

Florida Flapper

Al Foss

**Cleveland, Ohio and
American Fork and Hoe Co. (True Temper)
Cleveland, Ohio and Geneva, Ohio**

Al Foss began making his famous pork rind lures first, then
was bought out by the American Fork and Hoe Company, now
known as True Temper. Al Foss started in 1915 or earlier. There is
an ad in 1916 for the "Little Egypt Wiggler" and the "Skidder,"
both all-metal pork rind type lures. The patent to the Oriental
Wiggler was granted in 1918.

Early Foss spinner blades were unmarked and then he began
stamping them "AL FOSS." Later, when True Temper took over, the
patent date 1918 was added. This is true of all Foss regular or
"four" blades regardless of the type of lure on which they are
used.

Oriental Wigglers are found with unmarked regular, the
"AL FOSS," the "AL FOSS" with 1918 patent date and the "Adam"
type blades.

The **Shimmy Wiggler** came out about 1919 and has been
found with five blade types: The unmarked regular, the "AL FOSS"
regular, the "AL FOSS" with 1918 patent date, The "Adam," and
the "Ponca 1928." The Ponca blades have a 1928 patent date on
them.

The **Jersey Wiggler** was new around 1923 and has so far
been found with the "AL FOSS" 1918 patent date blades only.

Frog Wigglers became available in 1926 and as with the Jersey Wigglers, have been found with the "AL FOSS" 1918 patent date blades only.

Dixie Wigglers, new around 1928, can be found with the regular "AL FOSS," the "AL FOSS" 1918 patent date, the Ponca and a unique spinner that appears to be an unbalanced, two-blade Ponca spinner.

The **New Egypt**, also out in 1928, has so far been found with the "AL FOSS" 1918 and the Ponca blades.

The **Sheik** has shown up with the "AL FOSS" 1918 and another unique spinner, this one appeared somewhat like a modified Ponca blade but with a single blade only.

The **Hell Cat** has been found only with this latter spinner. **$30-$80**

Frog Wigglers

Four Tees Bait Company

1935-1953
William Robinson "Bob" Bales
Tampa, Florida

W.R. (Bob) Bales founded Four Tees, standing for his company name and logo "The Topper That's Tops." Starting with a scroll saw, sanding and painting supplies and equipment, Bales, with help from his wife, son, and daughter-in-law, began making his first lures for sale to the public in 1935.

The first models made were the Dolphin and the Cuke (short for cucumber). Then came the Torp (short for torpedo), the Frog, Shrimp, and the Mini Dolphin. Also made were single-jointed and double-jointed Dolphins.

The values of these lures are affected by age. **Dolphin: $25-$150, Mini-Dolphin: $25-$150, Cuke: $25-$150, Torp: $15-$45, Frog (rare): $275-$500, Shrimp (rare): $900-$1,200**

Four
Tees
Dolphin

Garland Baits

Plant City, Florida

The Garland Cork Head Minnow measures 3 5/8" long. The body is made of wood and the head of cork. The line tie has a long shank screw eye passing through a small diameter armature around which the cork head is secured and into the main part of the wood body. Garland lures were made from 1934 to 1940. A lure box pamphlet listed the available finishes as "Light Green Frog Finish, Dark Green Frog Finish, Green Silver Splash, and Red Silver Splash." There were believed to be 11 other lures in the Garland line. **$150-$300**

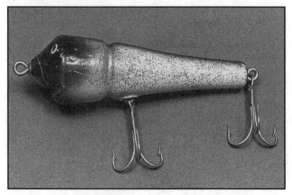

Garland Cork Head Minnow

Glowurm

Oliver and Gruber
Alfred Oliver
James Gruber
Medical Lake, Washington

Ads for this 4 1/4" lure began to appear in the early 1920s. One ad contained a 1920 patent date. It was made in red and white stripes or yellow and green stripes. The lure is double jointed with three body sections. The head has a metal plate protruding slightly below, forming a diving lip. The original box was a long block of wood drilled out and cut in half longitudinally to accommodate the lure. It had slots in the bottom section to make room for the protruding third hook of trebles. The lures were only made for a short time, until 1923. **$200-$250**

Glowurm

Goble Bait

Bert G. Goble
Tulsa, Oklahoma

Very little is known about this lure or its maker. A search turned up patents for two lures by Bert Goble, neither of which bears any resemblance to this one. The Goble Bait is handsome and well made. It is very sturdily built and measures 5 1/2" long. It has cup and screw eye hardware and clear glass eyes with yellow irises. The yellow scale finish is nicely done. The remaining paint has been careful sprayed and the pectoral fins are brush painted. The metal diving lip is somewhat bell shaped, held in place by a screw and the screw eye line tie. **$300-$600**

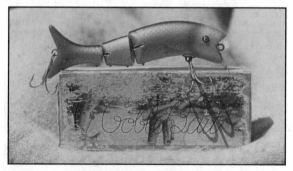

Goble Bait. Photo courtesy John W. Thomas

Go-Getter

Hayes Bait Company
Indianapolis, Indiana
John J. Hildebrandt Company
Logansport, Indiana

Sometimes known as the Hildebrant Wood Bait, this lure was manufactured by The Hayes Bait Company and distributed by Hildebrandt, a company known for its metal spinners. The lures date to 1927-30. There is a provision for easily removing and replacing hooks at will. It measures 2 5/8" and has painted eyes. All so far found have been painted white. **$100-$200**

Go-Getter

Earl Parker Gresh

1896-1977
St. Petersburg, Florida

All Earl Parker Gresh's lures were hand-made by him. He is a legendary figure around the St. Petersburg area. There is no accurate estimate as to how many he might have made. The lures are the highest quality, professional products. They were usually put up in sets in beautiful wooden boxes. He gave a few to friends and sold the rest. He stamped each one with his name on the underside of the lure. The six lures available are medium deep, deep sinking, slow sinking, top water, bright day, and late evening lure. A large wooden box full of his lures sold for **$450** at auction a few years ago. **$125-$150 each**

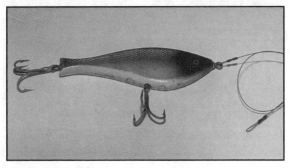

Earl Parker Gresh lure

Haas Tackle Company

Sapulpa, Oklahoma

Haas' Liv-Minnow

The patent was granted to Harry R. Haas in 1935. A 1930s ad illustrates a lure substantially similar except that the one in the ad is double-jointed. The protrusions at the lower edge of the lips are weights. The ad stated they were available in a 4" single-joint and a 5" double-jointed model. No colors were given. Glass eyes and painted-eye types have been found. **$250-$325**

Haas' Liv-Minnow

Jacob Hansen

1866-1945
Muskegon, Michigan

Jacob Hansen's name, along with others, was associated with a generic group of similar lures under the name Myers and Spellman. Hansen was granted a patent in 1908 for the Michigan Life-Like. The smaller one is 2 3/4" long and has three treble hooks and the larger one comes in 3 3/4" with five trebles. Both sport glass eyes and three-blade tail spinners. The articulated bodies are extraordinarily well-made. The side hook hangers on these two lures are of the style more commonly found and are thought to represent the oldest style. The second style protrudes further and the design is somewhat different. Colors: light green with speckled back and white belly, dark green with speckled back and white belly, aluminum color with dark back, brook trout, dark back with yellow belly, solid aluminum color, perch, green back with yellow sides and red belly, natural wood finish. **$600-$900**

Muskegon Spoon Jack Minnow

Hansen was known to be an inveterate tinker and it appears he couldn't keep from changing things about the lure. The majority are configured with either three or five hooks. They have a round body tapered to a nose and tail, a two-blade propeller spinner at the tail, a single-blade spoon-type spinner at the nose, and a through-body twisted wire line tie and tail hook hanger. The three-hooker is found either in an opposite side mount or a two belly-mount configuration. There also exist, although fairly rare, two-hook and four-hook models. Sizes vary from 3 1/4" to 4 1/2" usually, but there is one known unusual 5" version that has flat sides. They are found with no eyes, yellow or amber glass eyes and painted eyes. **$300-$600**

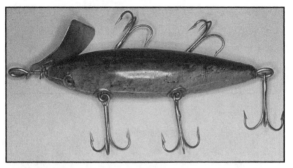

Muskegon Spoon Jack Minnow

Pull Me Slow

Hansen made fat and fatter versions of this lure in sizes varying from 2 3/4" to more than 4 1/2". There are at least three versions of the large nose-mounted spinners. They vary with the manner of mounting them on the armature, line tie. All the lures are cup and screw eye belly-hook rigged and have a white body, red head paint job. They are found with three treble hooks, two treble hooks and a third version with only a trailing treble hook (rare). **$100-$150**

Hanson's Irresistible Minnow

Wm. B. Hanson and Company
Pittsburgh, Pennsylvania

This c. 1919 odd-looking wooden lure was available with two treble hooks or two double hooks. It has a raised cup and screw hook hardware. Colors: Brown mottled back with red painted mouth; green; red and green. **$300-$400**

Hanson's Irresistible Minnow

Harkauf Minnows

Harry C. Kaufman and Company
Philadelphia, Pennsylvania
Pequea Works
Strasburg, Pennsylvania

The earliest ad was a 1903 H.C. Kaufman & Company ad for the "Harkauf Wooden Minnow." A series of papers show the evolution of the company names. The earliest lures had a square-end, three-blade propeller spinner, painted eyes and through-body hook hangers. They were available in three finishes with a "glistening silver belly," with or without a buck tail. Those with the buck tail have them attached to the body, not tied to the hook. They have been found with glass eyes and later versions will be found with a tube-type simple two-blade propeller spinner. Some are found with red painted gill marks and most have "THE HARKAUF" printed on the side. **$250-$400**

Harkauf Minnow

Harkauf Bass Minnow

The lure is obviously a high quality product. It measures 2 1/2", has glass eyes and very well made propeller spinner aft. It has a beautiful feather fly mounted forward of the nose. The lure was introduced in 1913. **$300-$600**

Charles R. Harris

1848-1922
Mackinaw City, Michigan
Niles, Michigan
Manistee, Michigan

For years collectors have known Harris to be the inventor and maker of the Harris Floating Cork Frog. He was granted a patent for it in 1897. He was also responsible for the Manistee Minnow. During the 1880s or early 1890s, he was in the sporting goods business in Mackinaw City, Mich. He also offered a Phantom or Devon type lure he called the Featherbone Minnow. Harris Floating Cork Frog: **$200-$300**

Manistee Minnow

This very rare lure has the words "The Manistee" on one side of the body. There is brass wire extending along the belly to the trailing treble hook and over the top of the tail where it is attached. There are metal hook restraining cups at the belly and tail. The spinner revolves on the armature connecting the head and body. This head does not rotate, only the spinner. It has zinc-painted eyes. **$900-$1,500**

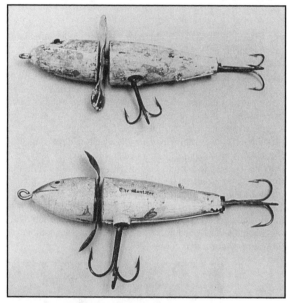

Manistee Minnows

Haskell Minnow

Riley Haskell
Painesville, Ohio

The Haskell Minnow is probably the most famous lure in the antique tackle collecting world. An example sold for $22,000 at an auction several years ago. That extraordinarily high price was an aberration, however, because it was so very rare then. About 30 or so have been found since. What makes this lure important, is the 1859 patent is the first American patent to mention wood as a possible material. It does use wood for the inner core over which the copper halves are soldered. The lure is finely made with much detail given to the scales. There are two slightly different designs to be found. The smaller one is 3 3/4" long (nose to tail). It appears slimmer than the larger one, but is about the same shape proportionally. It has no ventral fin as does its big brother. It sports a trailing treble hook. The larger (patent model) measures 4 9/16" (nose to tail) and 5 5/8" overall. It is rigged with two rigid-mount single hooks, effectively becoming a double hook. It has a ventral fin. About the back one third of both models rotates around an armature upon retrieve. **$5,000-$7,000**

Haskell Minnow

Hastings Sporting Goods Company

Hastings, Michigan

Wilson Wobblers

The company has its origins in the early 1900s. The first of its patents was for the Wilson Fluted Wobbler in 1913, granted to Richard T. Wilson and Aben E. Johnson. Around 1927-28 Hastings Company advertising disappeared from catalogs and periodicals and about the same time the Wilson Wobblers and Cupped Wobblers showed up in Moonlight Bait Company (Paw Paw) catalogs and ads. Apparently Hastings merged with or sold its rights to Moonlight.

Wilson's Fluted Wobblers

(Good Luck Wobblers)

Four different bodies were introduced. All had the distinctive four grooves or "flutes" in the forward portion of the body. They were available mostly in two- and three-treble hook configurations and differing hook hanger hardware. There were floating and sinking models.

Wilson's Wobbler, 5", 2T, Colors: White with red flutes, Yellow with red flutes, White with black flutes. **$125-$150**

Musky Wobbler, 4 3/4", 3T, Colors: Unknown. **$125-$150**

Wilson's Wobbler, 4", 3T, Colors: White with red flutes, Black with white flutes, Rainbow, Red and green spots, Solid red, Green with red stripes, Brown scale, Yellow with red flutes. **$40-$60**

Super Wobbler, 3 1/2", 2D, Colors: Luminous with red flutes, Rainbow, Brown scale finish. **$50-$70**

Luminous Wobbler, 4", 3T, Colors: Luminous with red flutes. **$40-$60**

Fly rod Wobbler, 2", 2T, Colors: White with red flutes. **$200-$300**

Fly rod Wobbler, 2 1/2", 2T, Colors: White with red flutes. **$200-$300**

Trout Wobbler, 1 3/4", 2T, Colors: White with red flutes. **$200-$300**

There have been Wobblers found with gold- and copper-painted flutes but it is not known if they were produced that way or were repainted by others later. Additional colors are green and silver, both with red flutes.

*Fly rod
Wobblers*

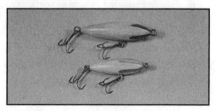

Wilson's Grass Widow

This 2 1/2" plug has an oddly shaped belly. It has one double hook. Colors: Red body, mottled spots; solid red; solid white; luminous; solid green; fancy green back, white belly; rainbow, brown scale. These colors are common to most of Wilson's lures. **$80-$135**

Wilson's Cupped Wobbler or Bass Seeker

The three sizes are 4 1/2", 3 1/2" and 3 1/8". The lure is called the Wilson Bass Seeker in a 1921 ad. The ad stated the lure was available in white luminous only. The top of the cupped head end is sliced off at the top. It is also found without the cut-off. They were new around 1915. **$60-$90**

Wilson Six-in-one Wobbler

This lure was patented in 1917 and has a unique six-position adjustable diving lip at its head. It was available in white with red head, light green crackle back, or red stripes on a green back. **$250-$300**

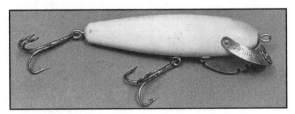

Wilson Six-in-one Wobbler

Wilson's Flange Wobbler or

Wilson's Winged Wobbler

This plug, patented in 1914, has a metal wing or flange piece fitted onto the bottom of the nose. The metal protrudes from each side creating the "wings." It has two belly trebles and a trailing treble hook. The flanges were sometimes painted red and the lure was made in all the same colors as the Fluted Wobblers. $80-$120, with box: **$300-$400**

Wilson's Bassmerizer

This is a 3 5/8" double-ended lure with a metal plane on each end. The angler may choose either end to render the plug action diving or surface. It has two belly mounted treble hooks. **$300-$400**

The Stagger Bug

This lure has a metal plane on the head similar to the one on the Six-in-one Wobbler. The head is much smaller. It has one belly and one trailing hook and can be found in almost any of the colors listed with Wilson's Grass Widow. **$900-$1,200**

The Stagger Bug

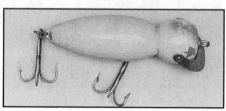

Hookzem

Hookzem Bait Company
Chicago, Illinois

When fished, the treble hook shank and hanger hardware of this 3" lure is pushed up into the lure with the barbs against the body. This renders the lure weedless. When the fish bites down on the lure hitting the metal trigger on the belly, the hook snaps out. The lure was patented by Henry L. Gottschalk in 1919. **$250-$400**

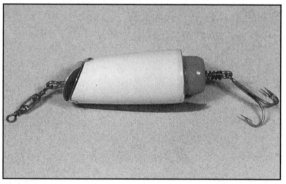

Hookzem

Hosmer Mechanical Froggie

J.D. Hosmer Company
Dearborn, Michigan

John D. Hosmer of Dearborn began making these lures in the late 1920s. They went into commercial production in the early to mid-1930s. He crafted and painted them all himself. He made only about 200 of them in the two years he was in business. The wood components were carved from balsa, about 5 1/4" in length when assembled, and had three weedless hooks, one at the feet and two on the belly. The colors available were yellow, green, silver and black, with green being the most common. The frog spots were painted with a contrasting outer edge. **$1,800-$2,800**

Hungry-Jack

Lloyd and Company
Chicago, Illinois

This most unusual, hard to find lure was available at least through the 1930s. A 1939 mixed tackle catalog listed it as available in "Natural scale finish only." The finish seems to apply to the "eater" and not the "eaten." Both red and amber glass eyes occur. The two are articulated. So, on retrieval, it looks as if the big fish is trying to gulp the little one down. They are cataloged at 4 3/4", 3/4 oz. **$200-$350**

Hungry-Jack

Lighted Pirate Lure

Although little is known about the Lloyd Company, it is known that it produced some other lures. Mentioned in a 1939 ad was a Lloyd "Lighted Pirate Lure." It was made of transparent plastic with an illuminated red head. It contained a small light bulb and a replaceable pen light battery. There was no size listed. **$15-$40**

Immell Bait Company

Blair, Wisconsin

The Immell Bait Company has a short history and its products are highly sought. The most well known are the Chippewa and the Chippewa Skipper (made by C.J. Frost). The Chippewa was invented by Omer F. Immell and he patented it in 1910.

The Immell Chippewa Bait was available in several sizes, floaters and sinkers. Sinkers are 3", 3 1/2", 4" and 5". Floaters were available in 4 1/2" and 5" sizes. It appears that all came with belly-mounted detachable double hooks and a trailing treble. All found so far have glass eyes except the 5" Floater. Colors: red and yellow, yellow perch, fancy sienna, rainbow, fancy green back, green back white belly, fancy green back with spotted sides. **$400-$800**

The Chippewa Skipper

In 1914 Immell arranged with the C.J. Frost Company to make the Chippewa Skipper. It has reversible double hooks, two belly-mounted and one trailing (3D). The lure was 4 1/2" long. Colors available were fancy spotted or green and white. All advertisements by the C.J. Frost Company disappeared by 1919. **$200-$400**

The Chippewa

Edward Lee Jacobs

Vicksburg, Michigan

Jacob's specialty was fly rod lures, but he made a couple of highly sought wooden lures, the Hoss Fly and the Polly-Frog. He patented both, in 1932 and 1941 respectively.

Jacob's Hoss Fly

The 2 1/4" Hoss Fly was somewhat complicated. The lure has a moveable metal collar to which the wings are attached. As you pulled the bait through the water the thin wings would flap. The thin metal wings were fragile and easily bent or broken when cast at a stump or rock. Colors: bug; all black; all green; gold body with red head; white body with red head; yellow body with red head; yellow body with black head. **$350-$600**

Hoss Fly.
Photo
courtesy
Jim Muma

W.J. Jamison Company

Chicago, Illinois

Perhaps the most famous lure produced by Jamison is the Coaxer (patented in 1905), but there were several others manufactured. The company was established in 1904 and, other than for the Coaxer, it was heavy into metal spinner and spoon-type baits. Jamison continued into the 1940s and manufactured some of the early plastic lures.

No. 1 Convertible Coaxer

Most of the Coaxers had red felt wings but some are found with leather. The body is 1 7/8" long and made of cork. It has a single hook mounted in the tail and a second single hook attached to the first single hook. There was a removable belly-mounted double hook also. It was also available with a buck tail. **$15-$32**

Coaxers

No. 1 Weedless Coaxer

This is the same as the No. 1 Convertible Coaxer, but does not have the detachable belly double hook. **$10-$20**

No. 1 Weedless Bookstall Coaxer

Same as above but with a bookstall. **$15-$30**

No. 2 Weedless Coaxer

Essentially the same as the Weedless Coaxer, but with a smaller (1 1/8") body and a slightly different shape. **$15-$30**

Luminous Bookstall Coaxer

The same as the No. 1 Weedless Coaxer but with luminous paint. **$20-$40**

No. 2 Convertible Coaxer

The same as the No. 2 Weedless Coaxer with the addition of the detachable double hook on the belly. **$15-$30**

No. 3 Weedless Coaxer

Made exactly the same as the No. 1 Weedless Coaxer only smaller. **$15-$30**

No. 3 Convertible Coaxer

Exactly the same as above, but with the addition of a detachable belly-mounted double hook. **$75-$125**

The Muskie Coaxer

Another of the Coaxer types, this larger one is made for surface trolling. It has a 2 5/8" body length, a tail-mounted single hook (optional trailing single) and a belly-mounted double hook. **$75-$125**

Fly Rod Wiggler

This plug came along about 1918 in three sizes and two hook type options. The sizes were 1 1/4", 1 3/4" and 2 1/2". They were available with double or single hooks and in eight colors. Colors: silver shiner, golden shiner, red side minnow, red head, white body, yellow perch, solid white, solid red, solid yellow. **$40-$70**

Fly Rod Wiggler

Mascot

In 1916-17, Jamison introduced several versions of a new lure called the Mascot. Value range of all: **$80-$160**

Chicago Wobbler

Advertised as new in 1916, it is very similar in body style to the Mascot series plugs. It has only one line tie (top of nose).

Colors: solid red, yellow or white; white body with red head.
$100-$200

Humdinger

New in 1916, this lure has a tear drop shape with the fat portion to the rear. It has two line ties, two metal up-swept wings on the head, a belly treble, and trailing treble hook. **$50-$150**

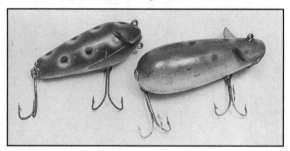

Humdinger

The "Nemo" Bass Bait

This 2 3/8" lure was introduced in 1910 as an underwater or surface plug. Made of wood, it has a revolving head, detachable belly-mounted double hook, trailing single hook with weed guard and a moveable weight. Colors: white, red, yellow, blue or green in any combination. **$500-$700**

The "Nemo" Muskie Bait

This is a larger version of the "Nemo" Bass Bait. It has a trailing double hook, and a double hook mounted on each side of the body. The colors and combinations are the same. **$600-$850**

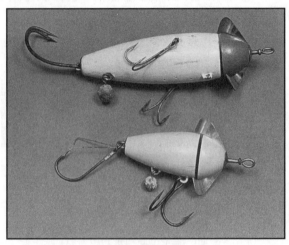

"Nemo" Muskie Bait, top, and "Nemo" Bass Bait

Jersey Expert

E.C. Adams
Morristown, New Jersey

Also, Ideal Minnow
William E. Davis
Morristown, New Jersey

There is some confusion surrounding these two very similar lures. Both were patented in 1907. The two were so close that there has to be some connection. The Davis patent was an improvement over the Adams patent in that there was a preventer device at the tail to keep the trailing hook from becoming entangled in the spinners and the hooks were readily removable. **$900-$1,200**

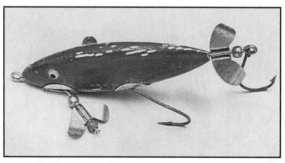

Jersey Expert

Johnson Automatic Striker

Carl A. Johnson
Chicago, Illinois

Very little is known about Johnson or distribution of the Automatic Strikers. Patented in 1935, they are quality-made and somewhat complicated. On all but the smallest size, the design allowed for the hook to swing away from the body upon strike. One ad listed the following colors for the Junior size: ivory body with red stripes; ivory body with black stripes; ivory body with green stripes and yellow tail; ivory body with green head. Only a silver scale finish was listed for the larger size in the ad. When found new in the box, there is also a bucktail included that could be used at the tail instead of the wooden tail piece. **$400-$600**

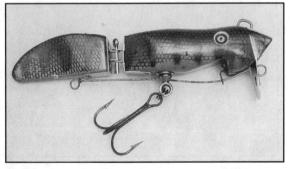

Johnson Automatic Striker

K & K Manufacturing Company

Toledo, Ohio

Little is known about this Toledo company, but it is generally accepted that it marketed one of the first, if not the first, jointed animated minnows in about 1907. Collector value range for any K & K lures: **$900-$1,200**. To find one in the box can as much as double that.

K & K Animated Minnows

#1A Golden Shiner (female type), 4 1/2", for black bass, 3 double hooks, jointed body.

#2A Golden Shiner (male type), 4 1/2", for sea bass or muskellunge, 3 double hooks, jointed body.

#1B Deep trolling, 4 1/2", for bass, 3 double hooks, jointed body.

#2C Deep trolling silver shiner, 4", for bass, large lake trout, land-locked salmon or striped sea bass, double hooks, jointed body.

"The Minnoette", 3", silver shiner, for small bass, rock bass, trout, small pickerel, white bass, etc., 3 double hooks, red devil finish, jointed body.

#3 King of Casting Bait (a surface bait). Swims about 3"
under the surface, 3 double hooks, 4 1/2", jointed body, red devil
finish (bright red and gold on back and side, silver belly).

K & K Animated Minnow

Unjointed K & K Minnows

#1 Rainbow Ghost - one double hook on body, feathered
trailing treble, variegated colors.

#2 Moonlight Ghost - same as above with white body and red
stripes.

#4A The Wriggler - one double hook mounted under the nose
and a realistic tail fin. Also with 3 double hooks. Silver shiner.

Fred C. Keeling and Company

Keeling Bait and Tackle
Fred C. Keeling
Rockford, Illinois

Keeling came on the scene about 1914 and was in business until the 1930s when the company was sold to Horrocks-Ibbottsom. Keeling's early history is tied to the F.C. Woods Company, the first makers of wooden Expert minnows.

Many Keeling lures had spinners or metal diving/wobbling planes that were made with holes in the blades. The Keeling Experts were nearly identical to Woods or Clark Experts at first, but they began to change a little. Keeling made them in 2 1/2", 3", 3 1/2", 4 1/2", and 5" sizes with hooks on the sides and in a few cases, on the belly. They were round, shaped, and flat-sided. All had holes in the propeller blades.

The Keeling baits are extensive. What is covered here are the most commonly known of them. There are many more.

King Bee Wiggle Minnow

This is the king of Keeling lures in scarcity. The two blades were made adjustable allowing the fisherman to impart spinning, wiggling, wobbling, jumping, surface spray and deep-running motions. It was probably not around long. It was made in four sizes: 2", 2 1/2", 3", 3 1/2". **$250-$350**

*King Bee
Wiggle
Minnow*

Tom Thumb Wigglers

This bait has a metal plate on the belly, the front and rear portions ending in metal spoon shapes. These spoons have holes in the center and the metal belly portion has "KEELING" stamped in it. The lure came in five sizes, 12 colors and has one or two belly trebles and a trailing treble hook. Size: Baby Tom, 2"; Little Tom, 2 1/2"; Pike Tom, 2 3/4"; Big Tom, 3"; Surface Tom, 3 1/4". Colors: dark back, aluminum belly; dark back, red belly; green back, white belly; green body, bronze speckled; aluminum body, red head; gold body, red head; white body, red head; dark back, red sides, white belly; rainbow striped; yellow with red and green spots; black with white head; yellow with black head. **$20-$30**

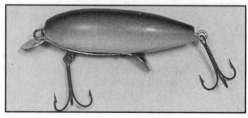

*Little
Tom*

Kent Frog and Kent Double

Spinner Artificial Minnow
F.A. Pardee and Company
Kent, Ohio
Samuel H. Friend
Kent, Ohio
Enterprise Manufacturing (Pflueger)
Akron, Ohio

F.A. Pardee and Co. was doing business as early as 1900. There was an ad that year for the Double Spinner Artificial Bait. This wooden plug is most likely the forerunner of Pflueger's Trory Underwater Minnow or Trory Wooden Minnow. By 1904, Pardee was calling it the Double Spinner Artificial Minnow.

Double Spinner Artificial Minnow

Pardee used aluminum props on the lure. The plug and one from Pflueger are otherwise almost identical. All the hardware on this newer Double Spinner is through-body and strong. There are heavy duty soldered side hook hangers also. **$1,500-$3,000**

Double Spinners

Kent Frogs

Samuel Friend Kent Frogs (as they are commonly known) were listed in catalogs and ads variously as Kent Champion Floater, Kent Frog Floater, Kent Floating Bait, Manco Floating Frog, and finally the "Pflueger Kent-Floater Bait." The Samuel Friend Frogs all have glass eyes and twisted wire through-body hook hangers. **$1,500-$2,000**

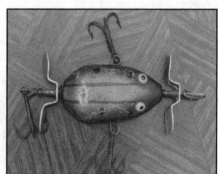

Kent Frog. Photo courtesy of Chris Crawford

Kimmich Mouse

Kimmich Bait Company
Ellwood City, Pennsylvania

This lure is actually called the "Kimmich Special Mouse" according to the pamphlet packed in the box with the lure. It was patented by Harry Kimmich in 1929. The pamphlet said it was available in several colors, but did not specify them. Not known to many collectors is the lure was also available in wood body without the hair. **$200-$300**

Kimmich Mouse

Kingfisher Wood Minnow

Edward K. Tryon
Philadelphia, Pennsylvania

This lure is actually a Pflueger 2 3/4" Neverfail with unmarked propeller spinners. The Edward K. Tryon Company was a large fishing tackle dealer that did not manufacture any lures. There were several other lures in the Kingfisher line. It bought the products of other companies and sold them under the Kingfisher brand. **$50-$100, with the box $200-$300**

Kingfisher Wood Minnow

Kinney's Bird Lure

H.A. Kinney Company
Grand Junction, Michigan
Bangor, Michigan
Sulfur Springs, Florida
Old Hickory Rod & Tackle Co.
Tampa, Florida

Kinney's Bird Lure was patented in 1927 by Herbert A. Kinney. The lures were painted fairly realistically, representing various species of birds. At some point there was a connection to the Heddon Company. An example has the stamped words "HEDDON FINISH" at the upper left corner. It has cup hardware with the Heddon "L-rig" hook hanger. **$1,200-$1,800**

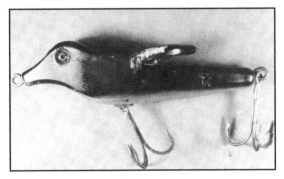

Kinney's Bird Lure

Koepke Lure Company

Frank L. Koepke
Ridgefield, Washington

Frank Koepke obtained three patents for his lures. The first was granted in 1922. Made of soldered brass, the lure was fashioned with three compartments. The forward or rear or both could be filled with water making it a floater, diver or imparting different action depending on how it was filled and the speed of retrieval. They were made in two versions. One was pointed in a cone shape at both ends. This one was available in four sizes, 2 1/4", 2 3/4", and 3 1/2" each with a single hook and the fourth, a 4" model available with either a single or double hook. The second version was available in a 3 1/2" single hooker and a 4" long double hooker. The other two patents were for spinner type lures. The company closed near the beginning of the Great Depression. **$75-$100**

Koepke
Lures

Lake George Floater

Very little is known about this little beauty. It is believed that it is a Michigan lure. The lure has a metal blade at the nose causing the whole body to revolve on retrieve. It measures 2 1/2" and 3" across the front including the cork ball. **$500-$700**

Lake George Floaters

Lane's Wagtail Wobbler

Lane's Automatic Minnow
Charles W. Lane
Madrid, New York

The Wagtail Wobbler is a wood-bodied lure with a fluted metal swinging tail fin. The hook hardware is cup and screw eye. A 1924 ad stated it was available in three sizes, but listed only the one illustrated, 2 7/8". It came in two finishes, brown with gold sides and green back with silver sides. Sizes smaller are considered quite rare.

An earlier Lane product, Lane's Automatic Minnow, was patented in 1913. The tail propeller spinner is mounted on a camshaft so that when turning on retrieve it would make the pectoral fins move. Wagtail Wobbler: **$200-$500**, Automatic Minnow: **$500-$750**

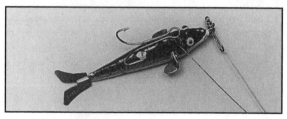

Lane's Automatic Minnow

McCormic Mermaid

McCormic Bait Company
Kalamazoo, Michigan

This plug was found advertised in a 1917 magazine. It has a 3 5/8" body, two belly trebles, and a trailing treble. One unique feature is a small cupped-out area at the nose in which a short wire line tie is mounted (countersunk). The lure was apparently made for Shakespeare later, or perhaps they bought the patent. The same lure shows up in a 1920 Shakespeare catalog as the Mermaid Minnow. Colors: white, yellow, red, white or black with a red head. **$75-$100**

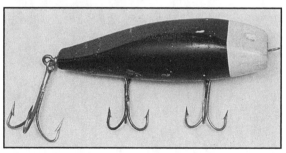

McCormic Mermaid

Manitou Minnow

Bailey and Elliot
Rochester, Indiana

Simon K. Bailey invented this lure about 1904. They were sold boxed with instructions for assembly using a little wrench. The lure was offered for only a short time. Colors: solid red, dark green with yellow belly, pale green with white belly; dark green with white body. **$1,500-$2,500**

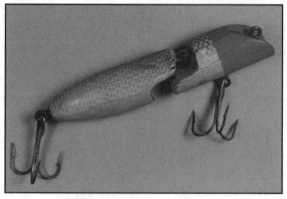

Manitou Minnow

Medley's Wiggly Crawfish

F.B. Hamilton
Pasadena, California

Patents were issued in 1919 and 1920. Both show the same body, but the metal lip blade design is different. The earlier patent shows a metal lip much more like the actual product. Both patents were filed by Harry L. Medley of Los Angeles, and the manufacturer of the lures was F.B. Hamilton Manufacturing of Pasadena. The lures were made in two sizes. The larger (3") has two belly double hooks and the smaller (2 1/2") has only one double. All had glass eyes and were equipped with two flexible rubber antennae. They were reverse running plugs and came in 12 color combinations according to an ad. **$100-$200**

Medley's Wiggly Crawfish

Michigan Life-Like

Adolph Arntz
Muskegon, Michigan

The origin and history of the Michigan Life-Like remains cloudy. The patent was granted to Jacob Hansen of Muskegon in 1908. It has been assumed that he was the manufacturer, and a friend, Adolph Arntz, distributed the lure. They are well made four-section jointed lures. The forward section is the largest, ending with three smaller sections jointed so that there is a life-like motion to the plug. There are two sizes, 2 3/4" and 3 3/4". The smaller had three treble and the larger, five treble hooks. Both have glass eyes and propellers on the nose and tail. The tail propeller has three blades. Colors: light green, speckled back, white belly; dark green, speckled back, white belly; dark back, aluminum color; brook trout; dark back, yellow belly; aluminum color, natural wood finish; perch; green bark, yellow sides, red belly. **$800-$1,200**

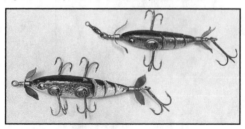

Michigan Life-Likes

Miller's Reversible Minnow

1913-1920
Union Springs Specialty Company
Cayuga Springs, New York

This extremely rare lure can be found in two variations. The earliest model (c. 1913) had simple screw eye or screw eye and washer hook hangers. It also had a slightly longer, much slimmer rear body section. The later one (c. 1916) uses the Pflueger type Neverfail hook hangers and a fatter rear-body section. An agreement was struck between Pflueger and the Union Springs Company whereby Pflueger either bought the company or a license to produce the lures.

The lure is quite a wild looking contraption. Its propellers are colored gold and silver. The body is made of cedar, 4 1/2" long. Colors: No. 1, yellow with gold spots; No. 2, white belly, blended red and green spots; and No. 3, white body, red head with gold spots. **$2,000-$2,500**

Miller's Reversible Minnow

Moonlight Bait Company

Paw Paw, Michigan

The Moonlight Bait Company was formed in 1908. From 1909 to 1922-23, Moonlight enjoyed success and expanded its line considerably. In the two years after the company was founded, it added a weedless version of the Moonlight Floating Bait, the Trout Bob and the Fish Nipple. By 1918 there were at least a dozen in the lineup.

In 1923 Moonlight began a transition period by merging with another lure company, the Silver Creek Novelty Works, becoming the Moonlight Bait and Novelty Works. This transition continued with various acquisitions of the manufacturing rights to other lures until the company evolved into the famous Paw Paw Bait Company.

The Moonlight Floating Bait No. 1

The Weedless Moonlight Floating Bait No. 2

This plug was first mass-marketed by the company about 1909. The earliest versions were coated with a luminous paint and were 4" long with two belly trebles and a trailing treble hook. A second, smaller size soon became available. Sizes and configurations: luminous white, 4", 3T or 2T; luminous white, red head, 4", 3T or 3D; luminous white, red head, 3 5/8", 2T; luminous white, red head, 3 5/8", 2T (weedless); luminous white, red head. The only difference between the No. 1 and the No. 2 was the presence of weedless hooks on the No. 2. **$30-$60**

The Trout Bob

This small 1 1/8" plug first showed up in a 1911 ad. The only color known is solid white. It sports a feathered trailing treble hook and is sometimes known as the "Little Bob." **$100-$200**

Trout Bob

The Fish Nipple

Another of Moonlight's earliest lures, it first appeared in the same 1911 ad as the Trout Bob. There is a Fish Nipple look-alike that was made in the late 1940s and early 1950s with the brand name DuraFloat. **$75-$125**

Fish Nipple

The "1913" Special

Apparently first available in 1913 (an ad said it had been thoroughly pre-tested in 1912), this plug was advertised as available in only one finish. It is painted and covered with a glitter-like material to make it sparkle. It has a treble hook on each side and a trailing treble. There is one nose-mounted propeller and one tail-mounted. **$500-$600**

The Paw Paw Fish Spear

This plug was first found advertised in a 1915 magazine. The size was not given, but colors were red, white, yellow, or fancy spotted. **$200-$400**

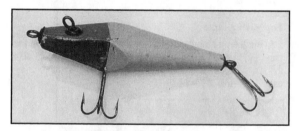

Paw Paw Fish Spear

Lady Bug Wiggler No. 800

The patent for this lure was granted in 1917. It has an odd-shaped diving plane head, a belly treble and trailing treble hook. Colors: white with red head and black legs, yellow with red head and black legs, green back with red and yellow decorations and black legs. **$200-$400**

Ladybug Wiggler No. 1800

This lure was not listed in any of the Moonlight catalogs. It measures 2 1/2". **$100-$200**

Polly-Wog

Polly-Wog Junior

A Silver Creek Novelty Works catalog was the first found to list the Polly-Wogs. It is 4" long, weighs 4 3/4 oz. and colors listed are: solid yellow, white with black spots, white with black stripes and moss back. A 1924 Moonlight catalog listed two sizes as available: 4", 3/4 oz.; and the Junior size 2 1/2", 3/4 oz. The illustration showed glass eyes and the copy listed nine colors: yellow; moss back; white, red striped; yellow, black spots; rainbow; white, black stripes; white; yellow perch; horned ace. **$150-$300**

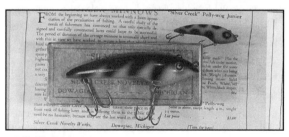

Polly-Wog Junior

The 99% Weedless

A 1926 Moonlight catalog is the first to list this lure. It is actually the Comstock Chunk or a slightly modified version of it. Frederick Comstock received the patent in 1926. It looks as if Moonlight obtained the rights from Comstock at about the time it was in transition to the Paw Paw Bait Company name. Colors: white with green back, white, red head, luminous, white with black head, perch, all black. **$15-$40**

Bass Seeker

Bass Seeker Junior

This is another acquisition of an outside company's lure during the Moonlight to Paw Paw transition period. The Bass Seekers were originally from the Hastings Sporting Goods Company, which called them Wilson's Cupped Wobblers. The lure has a scooped nose, heavy wire link leader, a belly treble and trailing treble. Colors: gold color body with red head, white body with red head, green scale finish, gold scale finish, blue scale finish and perch finish. **$25-$50**

Moonlight Whirling Chub c. 1929

This lure was made by Moonlight for Abbey and Imbrie. It measures 4 1/4". **$100-$150**

Moonlight Crawdad c. 1929

There are two different configurations. They both have external belly weights hanging from the belly. There is no belly hook on some lures and a belly treble on the other. They both measure 2 7/8". **$100-$200**

Wilson Wobbler

This lure was originally made by Hastings Sporting Goods and acquired at about the time of the Moonlight to Paw Paw transition. The lure was actually Wilson's Fluted Wobbler. **$50-$75**

Little Wonder No. 2100 Series c. 1925

The Little Wonder was found in a Moonlight ad that stated: "Brand New for 1925." No size or colors were listed in the ad but a 1926 catalog listing did contain six colors. They are: red head with gold body; gold scale; green scale; blue scale; white body with red head; yellow perch. **$50-$100**

Pikaroon

Baby Pikaroon

Jointed Pikaroon

If you were to compare these to the Pikaroons in the Silver Creek Novelty Works section you may note a subtle difference in the style of the nose area. The Moonlight versions have a little more refined looking, slightly turned up nose than those produced by Silver Creek before the 1923 Moonlight acquisition of the company. The Pikaroons were made in a Baby size, 1000 Series at 4 1/4" with two trebles, a regular size at 5 1/4" found most commonly with two treble hooks, and the jointed version. **$150-$300**

Pikaroon

Bass-Eat-Us c. 1920

Babe-Eat-Us c. 1920

Trout-Eat-Us c. 1920, 1926

Bug-Eat-Us c. 1920

Three of these were found listed and illustrated in a c. 1920 Moonlight catalog. The Trout-Eat-Us was listed as 1 3/4", and a 1926 catalog illustrated a Trout-Eat-Us, but no size was listed. It was described as a fly rod size in the 1926 catalog. The Silver Creek Bass-Eat-Us is 3". The Babe-Eat-Us is a smaller version at 2 1/2" with only two treble hooks. The tiny lure is the Bug-Eat-Us. All four of the lures were part of the Silver Creek Novelty Works at the time Moonlight acquired the company. Colors: yellow; white, green head; rainbow; yellow, black head; moss back; white, blue head; white, red head; yellow perch; yellow, red head; horned ace. **$25-$50**

No. 1900 Series

This unnamed, jointed lure was listed and illustrated in a 1926 Moonlight catalog. It was available in the same six colors listed with the Little Wonder. No other references were found. **$35-$75**

Casting Baits No. 1100 Series, No. 1200 Series

These two Moonlight lures are beautiful examples of the classic, glass-eyed, floating, propeller spinner minnow style of Heddon, Shakespeare, South Bend and Pflueger. Found listed and illustrated in a c. 1924 Moonlight catalog only, they came in two styles. Both were listed as 3" in length. There were also two underwater models of the Casting Baits. Colors: Yellow; yellow body, black stripes; rainbow; white; moss back; yellow perch; white body, red stripes; horned ace; white body, black stripes. **$80-$175**

Light Bait Casting Feather Minnow

No. 1400 Series

A 1920 and a 1926 catalog each listed this lure and the small version of the Weedless Feather Minnow. The catalog entry reads: "Light casting Feather Tail Minnow for light bait casting. No. 1-0 single hook, weight 1/3 ounce, length of body 1 3/4." Colors: yellow, white, orange, brown, red, gray. **$75-$150**

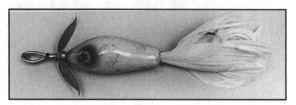

Light Bait Casting Feather Minnow

Weedless Feather Minnow

No. 1500 Series - 3-1/2" overall, 1/6 oz.

No. 1800 Series - 3" overall, 1/10 oz.

Colors available are the same as the No. 1400 Series. These two were also listed in the c. 1920 catalog, but only the No. 1800 was in the 1926 catalog. **$75-$150**

Feather Minnow No. 1600 Series

This lure was found in the c. 1920 catalog, as were all the Feather Minnows. It was listed as 3 1/2" overall length, 1/8 oz. and available in the same six colors as the others. This little beauty came packed with a separate weight to be used on the line in front. The weight is painted in typical Moonlight style and has painted eyes. To find the lure with this weight is extremely rare. **$75-$150**

The "Bug" No. 8

This curiously shaped plug weighs 3/4 oz. and came along around 1915-16. It has only one treble hook, mounted toward the tail, but on the belly of the lure. Colors: Solid black; yellow and black with red head; yellow with red head; white with red head; white with red and black stripes; yellow striped white body. **$300-$400**

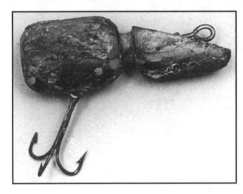

The "Bug"

The Dreadnought

First found advertised in 1912 and called a "Fish Pirate," it was a "... new departure in bait design" and "makes a wake 'like a battleship.'" It has five treble hooks and two propeller spinners. The body is 4" long. Colors: red and white, black and white. **$500-$800**

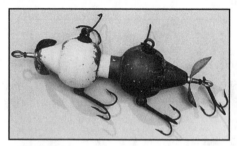

Dreadnought

The Paw Paw Underwater Minnow

This lure was first found advertised in a 1913 magazine. It was available in white, red or yellow. It has a nose-mounted propeller spinner and trailing bucktail treble hook. **$200-$300**

Mud Puppy

C.C. Roberts Bait Company
Mosinee, Wisconsin

This lure was first made in 1918 and the company is still in business. Constance Charles Roberts invented the lure and won a patent in 1928.

This very unusual lure was designed so that the lure body would separate from the hook and line once the fish was hooked.

The lure was made in two basic sizes, the Little Mud Puppy at 5 1/2" and the regular size at 7". Each could be had in "natural" or white body with red head. In 1951-52 the Pupette was made. These are being made again in limited quantities.

One rare finish is the sucker scale. Other colors: black, black and yellow, blue, gold, green, green perch, orange, purple, silver, tiger perch, yellow, and yellow natural. **$25-$75**

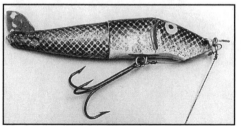

Mud
Puppies

Mushroom Bass Bait

J.A. Holzapfel
Jackson, Michigan

This unusual lure was made around the 1910s. It is known to have appeared in at least three different paint patterns: all red, all white, and a frog finish with some red. It has also been found in 3 1/2" and 3 7/8" sizes. All the line ties and hook hardware are large brass screw eyes. **$275-$375**

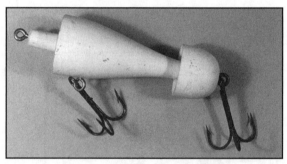

Mushroom Bass Bait

Myers and Spellman

1914-16
Edward D. Myers
Jack Spellman
Shelby, Michigan

These two have had a dozen or so lures attributed to them over the years but it is now thought they produced only one or two. The lures of Jacob Hansen and a man named Keller were erroneously lumped under their name. It is easy to mistake a Myers lure for a Keller unless it is stamped with the name on the back. Myers and Spellman were partners in an automobile dealership. Local historians believe that the lures were made in the dealership garage. The number of them made is not known, but they did advertise the lure.

The lure is quite similar to the Keller Gets-Em. The name "Myers" is usually found stamped along the back of the plug.
$275-$375

Myers and Spellman Lure

Neon Mickey Bait Company

A single reference to the Neon Mickey indicated that the lure was from the mid-1950s and the company was based in Oregon. The lure measures 4" and has what appears to be a glass vial of mercury in the clear plastic mid-section. It is also filled with neon gas. When it wiggles, it actually lights up. It is red with indented painted eyes. This is a scarce bait, difficult to find intact and operational. **$50-$100**

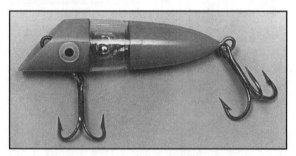

Neon Mickey

Niftie Minnie

Joseph M. Ness Co., Mfgrs.
Minneapolis, Minnesota

A 1915 magazine has an ad for a lure that was thought to be another of the several different glass minnow tubes that have been found. Advertised by Joseph M. Ness Co., it is called the Niftie Minnie. It is a transparent tube with a metal cap and propeller spinner at the nose and tail. It sports two sets of opposite-mounted side treble hooks, a trailing treble and a 5 1/2" body. The ad states it was patented in 1913. **$1,000-$1,500**

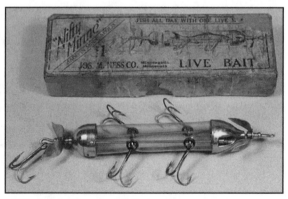

Niftie Minnie. Photo courtesy Jim Muma

Nixon Underwater c. 1914

Frank T. Nixon
Grand Rapids, Michigan

The Aristocrat is known to have been offered by Nixon because it was found in its original box. The box has a 1914 copyright date. The box further stated that the lure was made of "Persian Ivory" though this seems unlikely. It is more likely an early plastic. They are handsome and look like ivory. Other lures have been labeled as Nixon products because they are made of virtually the same material and utilize the same type of hardware. **$600-$900**

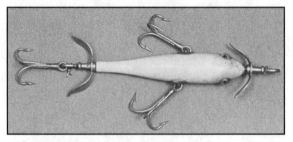

The Aristocrat

North Coast Minnow

William Hoegee and Company

This 2 1/2" glass-eyed lure is extremely similar to three other lures: the H.C. Royer South Coast Minnow, the Pflueger Catalina, and the South Bend Coast Minnow. It has a through-body wire twisted on each end forming the line tie and the trailing hook hanger. There are three flush internal belly weights. **$175-$275**

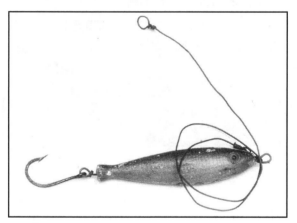

North Coast Minnow

O'Brien Artificial Minnow

R.F. O'Brien

There is very little known about this interesting lure. The lure and patent are so unusual and share so many characteristics it is reasonable to match them up. The body, painted red, white and black, measures 3 5/8" and rotates around a through-body wire armature. "PAT APPD FOR" is etched into the lower wire hook hangers and painted white. **$250-$500**

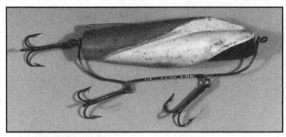

O'Brien Artificial Minnow

Oscar the Frog c. 1947

T.F. Auclair and Assoc. Inc.
Detroit, Michigan

This is an animated frog made of metal. It has a belly treble and a single hook mounted in each leg. It probably caught a lot of weeds. **$350-$450**

Oscar the Frog. Photo courtesy Jim Muma

Outing Manufacturing Company

Elkhart, Indiana
Heddon Outing
James Heddon's Sons
Dowagiac, Michigan

Clarence L. Dewey is the inventor of the Floater Getum. The Outing Company manufactured at least six different hollow metal lures made of bronze and painted in various patterns. It also manufactured a nice tackle box, a rod and reel combo, decoys, camping gear and more. The company was bought by Heddon in 1927 to get the rights to the tackle box. The lures came with the purchase and they were inventoried and sold until the supply was exhausted. Heddon never manufactured them.

Du-Getum Outing

Size: No. 700, 3 1/8", 3/4 oz., No. 750, 2 3/4", 1/2 oz. Colors: white with green head, white with red head, solid black, aluminum with red head, unpainted metal with green head. **$90-$125**

Bassy Getum

Size: No. 1200, 3 7/8", 5/8 oz. Colors: black bass, large-mouth bass, smallmouth bass, rock bass, calico bass, silver bass. **$75-$125**

Piky Getum

Size: No. 1000, 3 5/8", 1/2 oz. Colors: white and red, rainbow, red and green spots, green scale, pike scale, perch scale, silver shiner, red throat and silver back, mullet scale. **$100-$200**

Floater Getum

Size: No. 400, 4 1/8", 3/4 oz. Colors: white with red head, yellow with red head, aluminum color with red head, black with red head, yellow with green head. **$140-$200**

Floater Getum

Bucky Getum

Sizes: 1/2 oz., 5/8 oz., 3/4 oz. **$50-$75**

Porky Getum, Feather Getum

Lucky Getum

These three use the same body as the Bucky Getum. The Feather Getum has a weed guard and attached feathers. The Lucky Getum has a trailing bucktail hook and the Porky Getum has a rigid-mount single hook with a tiny single hook pork rind attachment. **$50-$75**

Payne's Humane Woggle Bug

Payne Bait Co.
Chicago, Illinois

This 3 1/4" plug was available only in a white body, red head finish. It was first found advertised in a 1915 magazine. There are metal clips in the body slots to hold the hooks in until a strike, then the fish would pull the hook away from the lure body. **$500-$1,000**

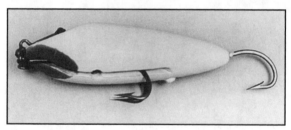

Payne's Humane Woggle Bug

Joseph E. Pepper

Rome, New York

It is difficult to sort out all known and suspected Joe Pepper lures. Some are readily identifiable by obvious characteristics and/or the Pepper name stamped on metal parts. Others are a result of his peculiar habit of painting gill strips on the lure opposite to the direction of actual fish gills.

The Pepper name is connected with fishing tackle back to 1860 when Joseph Pepper's father, John Pepper, went into the rod-making business. In the late 1890s, Joseph began his own tackle company. Joseph E. Pepper Jr. took over the company upon his father's death in 1936. The company is known to have continued in business into the 1950s, but advertising for Pepper lures seems to disappear around 1923. Pepper products run the gamut from crude to high gloss with quality hardware. They are found with no eyes, painted eyes and glass eyes and several quite dissimilar body styles. Often the glass eyes are placed in the head so that the lure appears to be looking forward, forward and up, or cock-eyed. This arrangement is a unique Pepper characteristic. Many of the metal parts are stamped with his name and/or patent dates. The metal fins he used are most often found painted bright red. Pepper seemed to have used whatever propeller spinners were readily available, for many different types are found.

Roman Spiders

These came along prior to 1915. The large (4 3/4") Musky size has no notched or split head as do the two smaller sizes. The Bass or Pickerel size is 3 1/4" and the Baby Roman Spider is 1 3/4". Most found have a crackle back finish. All will have string or twine legs or at least the holes through the body where they once were. Each has painted eyes. All are very scarce. **$400-$500**

Roman Spider

Revolving Minnow

The Revolving Minnow was introduced in 1911. It is extremely well made with high quality paint and hardware. A unique feature is the removable fins. If you didn't want the lure to revolve you simply unscrewed the fins. They are soldered to screw eyes to facilitate their removal without a screwdriver. The side hook hangers are twisted wire through-body. The large size is 3 1/2" and the small, 2 1/2". **$900-$1,200**

Revolving Minnow

Yankee Aero

The belly of the Yankee Aero shows the same method of providing adjustable or removable fins. The fins are soldered to screw eyes. The lure was said to be available in four colors in an ad, but the only one listed was white with red tail. This well-made 4 1/2" plug was also available in a jointed version, with painted eyes or no eyes. **$1,500-$2,000**

Roman Redtail Minnow

The Redtail came along about 1912. Another well-made quality lure by Pepper, it too has adjustable side fins. In addition it has another fin fixed at the bottom of the tail. It was made in two sizes, 2 1/2" and 3 1/4", has glass eyes and through-body wire line tie and tail hook hanger. **$900-$1,200**

Roman Redtail Minnow

The Roamer Bait

A 1912 Pepper ad said that this was "The latest Bait on the Market." The ad text also said the legs were white. Some of these were made with a slant cut on the top of the head where eyes were painted. They were made in two sizes, the standard at 3" and the Baby Roamer at 1 3/4". Colors: yellow body with green head, and green back with yellow belly. **$400-$500**

Pfeiffer's Live Bait Holder

Pfeiffer's Live Bait Holder Co.
Detroit, Michigan

The only place this one was found advertised was in a 1915 magazine. The ad was illustrated and stated "None genuine unless Pfeiffer's name on stopper." The stopper is metal and it is stamped. The ad goes on to say "… it is the original bait of its kind. Patented March 3, 1914." Except for the metal stopper (cap), this Pfeiffer lure is remarkably similar to the Detroit Glass Minnow Tube. The Pfeiffer bait is found in two sizes, 4 1/4" and the rarer 3" size. **$700-$1,000**

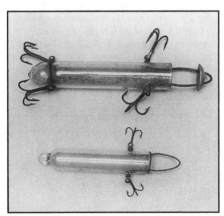

Pfeiffer's
Live Bait
Holder

Pontiac Radiant

Pontiac Minnow

**Pontiac Manufacturing Co.
Pontiac, Michigan**

An article in a 1958 periodical takes an historical glance back 50 years and reprints an article headlined "1908æLuminous Lures Big News in Latest Lineup of Tackle Items." The article describes "the Radiant Minnow developed by the Pontiac Mfg. Company." Pontiac produced these lures in two sizes, plus the same lures in other non-luminous colors.

There are three distinct and unique hook hanger hardware styles to be found. Each of them was designed to make the side hooks stand away from the body of the lure. Pontiac lures sport glass eyes and round propeller spinners fore and aft. There are two sizes to be found, a 2 7/8" and 3" three-hooker, and a 3 3/4" five-hooker. The latter is the most difficult to find. Non-luminous colors available were Red, White, Yellow or Green. Three-Hooker, **$300-$500, Five-Hooker, $400-$600**

Pontiac Minnows

J.W. Reynolds Decoy Factory

Chicago, Illinois

Spike-Tail Motion Bait

References were found in a 1915 ad and in a Schmelzer's catalog also dated 1915. The lure came in a red body, white fin, or a white body, red fin finish. It measures 3 5/8" long, has no eyes, and sports cup and screw hook hardware. The catalog entry also states that the single hook is detachable and reversible. **$150-$200**

Spike-Tail Motion Bait

Swan Lake Wiggler

A 1915 ad said this lure was available "... in any color desired," that it was patented, and the hooks were detachable and reversible. The ad illustration shows a lure with double hooks. The metal flange is made of aluminum. **$150-$200**

Rhodes

Bert O. Rhodes
Jay B. Rhodes
Kalamazoo Fishing Tackle Manufacturing Co.
Fred D. Rhodes
Kalamazoo, Michigan

There is some confusion about the relationship between Fred D. Rhodes, his uncle Jay B. Rhodes, Bert O. Rhodes, Frederick C. Austin and the Shakespeare Company. They are all tied to each other by a family or a business relationship.

Fred D. Rhodes was the inventor of The Perfect Casting Minnow, patented in 1904. Jay Rhodes, Fred Rhodes' uncle, was the inventor of the Kalamazoo Minnow and the Kalamazoo Frog. He sold rights to the Kalamazoo Frog to Shakespeare in 1905.

Most, if not all, of the Rhodes lures ended up in the Shakespeare line early on in that company's development years. The Perfect Casting Minnows have five treble hooks (5T), but the company made a shorter 3T model, which is seldom found. **$600-$900**

Perfect Casting Minnow

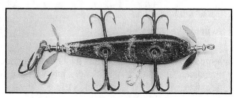

Rotary Marvel

Case Bait Company
Detroit, Michigan

This strong, well-made 3" lure has a nickel-plated rotating head. They appear to have hard staple-type side hook hangers. A 1914 ad said they were available in red, yellow or white bodies.
$400-$600

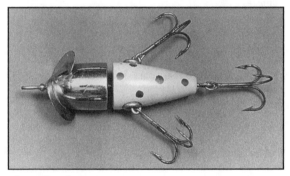

Rotary Marvel

Rush's Tango Minnows

J.K. Rush
Syracuse, New York

LeRoy Yakely was credited with the invention of the Rush Tango Minnow. There were several simultaneous revelations regarding the invention of an at-rest, floating plug with a sloped nose (flat planed) making it dive upon retrieve. This gave rise to a dispute.

Fillmore M. Smith held rights to two patents filed in 1912 and granted to a Henry S. Welles in 1913 and 1914 that described "... floating artificial baits ... which shall dive beneath the surface when drawn through the water ..." Believing the Rush Tango Minnow infringed upon his patents, Smith filed a lawsuit in 1915. The Welles patent lure was declared the first and from that point on Rush Tango boxes incorporated the words "Fully recovered patents include Welles basic patents." The earliest Rush Tangos had a unique line tie. It was a brass screw eye that was actually a machine screw eye that went all the way through the lip, secured on the bottom of the lip with a nut. Hook hardware was the simple screw eye. Later the line tie was simplified to the regular screw eye and hook hangers were cup and screw eye type.

Rush Tango Minnow

A 1916 listing in an Abbey and Imbrie catalog calls this lure "Rush's Swimming Minnow." It was offered in two sizes (4" and 5") and three colors; white body with red head; white body, green and yellow mottled back; and yellow body with red head. Later, other colors were added. It has two belly trebles. Smaller and larger sizes were added to the line under different names. Colors: luminous; white with red head, white, yellow and green mottled back; yellow with red head, yellow, red and green mottled back; red with white head, solid white; white, red and green mottled back. **$25-$75**

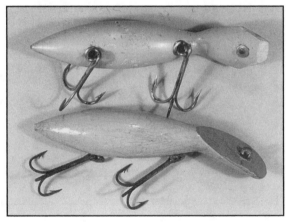

Rush Tango Minnows

Schoonie's Scooter

John Ray Schoonmaker
Kalamazoo, Michigan

This lure was made in two sizes: 3 1/2", 5/8 oz., and 4 1/2", 1 oz. It was a floater at rest, but on retrieve it rode just below the surface, weaving from side to side. It was consistently advertised until about 1920 when it disappeared from periodicals. The Junior size has only one belly treble. They were available in a rainbow finish and white with a red head. **$100-$200**

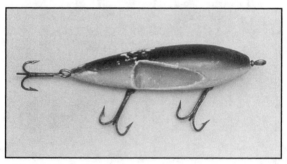

Schoonie's Scooter

Scooterpooper

Scooterpooper Sales, Inc.
Columbia, South Carolina

This odd lure was born in a jewelry store. Alex Woodle first made the lure from metal watch crystal containers or other round metal parts containers. The company was formed and the first commercially manufactured lures were made available in 1947-48. The lure measures 3" and the name is stamped on the spinner blade. **$50-$75, with box: $175-$275**

Scooterpooper. Photo courtesy Jim Muma

Sears, Roebuck and Company

Chicago, Illinois

Sears sold lures under the J.C. Higgins brand, Meadow Brook Lures, and Winner Wooden Minnows. We know that Sears seldom, if ever, manufactured anything for sale in its stores. We know that Creek Chub made some in the Shur-Strike line and sold under the Sears Meadow Brook Brand. We also know that Shakespeare made the Winner Wooden Minnow, but there were bound to have been more.

The Winner Wooden Minnow

This lure came in a wooden box. The 1908 Sears catalog describes it as the "... New Winner Wood Minnow." Perhaps it is an earlier model and the "new" in the catalog refers to the lure with the new hook hanger. This one has opaque yellow glass eyes, tube-type propeller spinners, and is 3" long. **$350-$450**

The Winner Wooden Minnow. Photo courtesy Clyde Harbin

Silver Creek Novelty Works

Dowagiac, Michigan

Silver Creek Novelty Works started doing business in the 1910s and continued until 1923 when the company and the Moonlight Bait Company merged. The Silver Creek Company was making a number of lures at the time and many were carried on in the Moonlight line. Those originally made by Silver Creek and continued in the Moonlight line include: Wiggler, 3 1/2", **$200-$300**; Polly-Wog, 4", **$3,000-$5,000**; Pollywog Junior, 3 1/4", **$250-$500**; Bass-Eat-Us, 3"; Babe-Eat-Us, 2 1/2"; Trout-Eat-Us, 1 3/4"; Bug-Eat-Us, 1 1/2", all **$50-$125**; Pikaroon Minnow, 5 1/4", **$300-$700**, and Baby Pikaroon, 4 1/4" **$200-$500**

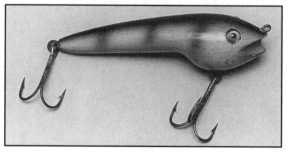

Polly-Wog

South Coast Minnow

H.C. Royer
Los Angeles, California

The South Coast Minnow was first offered advertised around 1910-11. A search turned up no patent, but the ads identified the inventor and source as Dr. H.C. Royer of Terminal Island, Los Angeles. About 1913, the Heddon Company began offering a very similar lure in its catalogs. The similarity of the Royer lure and the name leads to speculation that Heddon obtained the rights to the lure around 1912-13, and renamed it the Coast Minnow. **$125-$225**

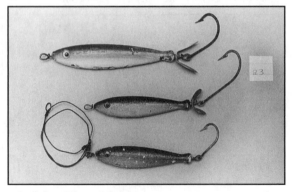

South Coast Minnow

Speed Bait

Walton Products Company
Rochester, New York

This is a crazy metal assemblage of 16 tiny propeller spinners all "… flashing, whirling and humming," according to a 1931 ad. They were made in three sizes: Trout at 1 1/4", Bass size at 2", and Musky at 4". They are all hard to find with the largest being the most difficult. **Large: $200-$300, smaller sizes: $100-$150**

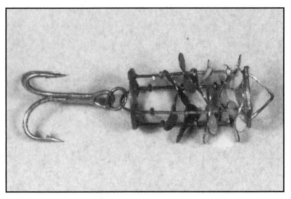

Speed Bait. Photo courtesy Jim Muma

Spider Lure

The Turner Company
Ed and Delbert Turner
Hale, Missouri

This lure was developed by the Turners, who were father and son hardware store owners, around 1950. Only about 150 were made and they didn't sell well. They are 3 1/2" in diameter overall. **$50-$75**

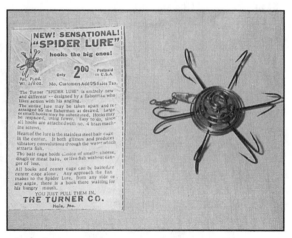

Spider Lure

Springfield Novelty Manufacturing Co.

Springfield, Missouri

The "Reel" Lure and Charmer

The Springfield Novelty Manufacturing Company was founded in 1932 by Stanley F. Myers and Adolph A. Kunz. With the help of Kunz's son and Myers' two sons, they produced 8,000 lures in a garage in the first four months of operation.

The earliest Reel Lure bodies are 1/8" slimmer than those produced later. The lure body was 2" in length. It also started to make a musky size at 3 1/8", but failed to place them into full-scale production and made only about a dozen examples. These are very rare.

The lures made by Springfield Novelty were very high quality. It used select cedar, brass bushings, German silver hardware and imported hooks. It did not advertise widely. The lures were marketed only in Northeastern Missouri, East Oklahoma and East Texas so to find one outside that area would be unusual. There isn't suffi-

cient trade data to establish a realistic collector value for either the Musky Reel Lure or the 1/2 Charmer. Reel Lure: **$75-$125**

Reel Lures

Stewart Tackle Company

Elman "Bud" Stewart
Flint, Michigan
Fenton, Michigan

Bud Stewart is a legend in his own time. Stewart began making lures when he was 17, and was in the business commercially by the time he turned 20, back in the early 1930s. He retired in 1981 and has been designated a "preeminent folk artist" by the Smithsonian, and given the Michigan Heritage Award by Michigan State University. He has also been inducted into the Fishing Hall of Fame.

Stewart's lures are characterized by bright and realistic colors, often looking wounded or bleeding. He traveled the sporting and tackle show circuit hawking his wares for many years. He did hire a few people to help assemble his lures, but he says he painted them all himself. He produced ice fishing decoys as well. Stewart still makes lures, but they are limited and snatched up by collectors. **Musky Duck: $200-$400, Crab Diver: $100-$200, Surface Sucker or Diving Sucker: $50-$70**

Musky Duck. Photo courtesy Jim Muma

Strike-Master Lures

Strike-Master Tackle Company
Versailles, Ohio
Sure-Catch Bait Company
Versailles, Ohio

During the late 1920s in Union City, Ind., A.T. Death was producing lures under the name Sure Catch Bait. In 1928, he traveled to Versailles, Ohio, to raise money to open a lure manufacturing facility. With partners, he opened a bait factory. In 1930, the company's name was changed to the Strike-Master Tackle Co. The company's success was short-lived and it shut down in 1931.

Although Strike-Master lures were produced for a short period, numerous variations of the same lure appear from time to time.

Mr. Death

Although not found in any catalog or brochure, these 3 3/4" no-eyed lures have long been attributed to A.T. Death, dating to his early Indiana days. They use screw-eye hook hangers, around which are surface-mounted round wire bands. Silver (aluminum) and yellow are the only colors that have been noted. **$75-$175**

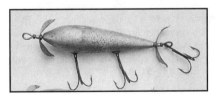

Mr. Death

Surface Killer No. 45/4SXX

These 3 3/4" top water baits were a mainstay product of Death from his Union City days. The No. 4550 has black glass eyes. During the Sure-Catch period, this lure was also offered in a two-hook (No. 35) rendition. The No. 45 was listed as available in white with red head (No. 46); all silver with red head (No. 51) was added; and all yellow, deleted. The No. 35 series was offered in scaled and striped, all silver (No. 50), and white with red head (No. 46). **$50-$150**

Night Hawk No. 36XX

The No. 6352 is 3 1/4" in length and has no eye detail and a mouth. During the Sure-Catch period, the company offered a similarly shaped model No. 63; however, the brochure shows glass eyes but does not illustrate the notched mouth. The No. 63XX was offered in colors No. 52 (white with black spots) and No. 46 (white with red head). **$60-$160**

No. 33 Surface Minnow-Type

Sure-Catch produced two groups of surface minnow-type lures. This style has a taped rear half and was described as "slightly underwater." The No. 45/45XX series was full bodied and referred to as "surface." The No. 33 (Perch) measures 3 1/2". A larger size was known as the No. 47 and the smaller No. 55. The No. 33 colors include natural perch scale and white with red head. The No. 47 was offered in similar colors plus all silver and all yellow. The No. 55 was listed in white with red head, all silver, and white with blue back. **$50-$150**

Injured Surface Killer

This 3 5/8" lure is a modified No. 45XX Surface Killer, which has been shaved on one side and has hooks mounted in injured minnow fashion. The lure is in perch finish. **$50-$150**

Hellgrammite No 91XX Series

One of the company's most famous baits, which was only offered during the Strike-Master era, is the Hellgrammite. There are three sizes: Large No. 9153 (3 3/4") black with gold head; Medium No. 9146 (measures 2 3/8", catalog states 3") white with red head; and Fly Rod No. 9147 (2") black with white head. This lure was also available in color No. 48 (orange with black head) and has been found in the bullnose variation. **$50-$70**

Crab No. 71/77XX Series

The Sure-Catch catalog shows this lure with bead eyes, a metal lip, two trebles, and available in one size. The Strike-Master brochure reflects a no-eye slant-head model with a single double hook available in two sizes: Large (3 1/4") and Fly Rod (2 1/8"). The only available color is No. 23 natural crab (dark green). **$50-$75**

Crab lure

No. 31

Only described as "slightly underwater," the No. 31 is a handsome wood-tailed lure with bulging (a SureCatch characteristic) glass eyes. This 3 1/4" lure is shown in the catalog as having a single forward propeller only, although there are variations. Available in the "scaled" color pattern only. **$75-$175**

Bug No. 19

This 3" wooden plug was offered during the Sure-Catch period only. Depicted in the brochure with black glass eyes, it may have been produced with regular glass eyes as well. It was available in one size and three color patterns: White with red head (No. 46), black with gold head (No. 53), and all silver (No. 50). **$75-$120**

Mouse No. 65/65XX

This 2 1/2" lure with bead eyes and rubber ears is missing its rubber tail. Note similarity to Creek Chub's Lucky Mouse, which was introduced in 1930. The Mouse was available in three colors during the StrikeMaster era: No. 27 (natural mouse), No. 46 (white with red head), and No. 47 (black with white head). **$80-$110**

Frog 67/67XX Series

This 2 1/4" lure has rubber legs and glass eyes in an early version. A later version is a no eyed, no legged rendition. This lure was offered in one size and color (No. 25 green with black spots) only. **$80-$120**

Rolling Diver No. 43/43XX

There are several versions of this bait. The perch colored lure has a short flute, standard glass eyes, and red spots (a Strike-Master trademark) in the flute. The other two are all silver. One uses black glass eyes while the other has standard eyes. The Rolling Diver was offered in one size (4") and in colors: No. 46 (white with red head), No. 15 (silver flecked natural perch), No. 49 (rainbow), No. 50 (all silver), No. 51 (silver with red head), and the un-cataloged No. 62 (above, white with green back, striped). **$75-$100**

Underwater Lures

During the Sure-Catch era the company marketed a number of nameless underwater plugs, including the No. 23 and 53 series.

No. 23: This lure measures 2 7/8", has black glass eyes and employs a lip which is stamped with a cup like depression, very similar to those found later on Paw Paw lips. This model was offered in three colors: red with silver head, black with gold head (No. 53) and white with black spots (No. 52). **$50-$75**

No. 53: This 2 1/8" bait with black glass eyes is identical to the Sure-Catch brochure illustration. These lures were cataloged as available in white with red head (No. 46) and yellow with black spots and white with red spots. Other colors include all black and black scale with red spots. **$50-$75**

Death's Pride No. 29/29XX

This lure provides an excellent example for comparison between Sure-Catch era (the eye placement, next to line tie), eye usage (standard glass eye) and line tie (no washer). The No. 2953 is also 3 1/2" but has a rear mounted black glass eye and washer line tie. The No. 29 was offered in white with red head (No. 46), black with gold head (No. 53) and all silver (No. 50). In addition to these colors, the No. 29XX could be had in No. 15 (silver flecked, natural perch), No. 47 (black with white head) and No. 51 (silver with red head). **$125-$200**

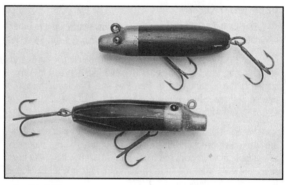

Death's Pride

Water Waltzer No. 19XX

The 3" Water Waltzer was available in colors: No. 46 (white with red head), No. 47 (black with white head), No. 48 (orange with black head), No. 51 (silver with red head), and No. 54 (all black). **$100-$175**

Bass King No. 85XX

This 3 1/2" lure is one of four similarly shaped Strike-Master products. It can be most readily confused with the 3 1/2" 89XX Witch. The later has a more tapered rear and a grooved head. The Bass King was offered in color patterns No. 46 (white with red head), No. 47 (black with white head), No. 48 (orange with black head), No. 49 (rainbow), and No. 53 (black with gold head). The No. 89XX was available in the same colors plus No. 62 (white with green back, striped). **$100-$150**

Muskie Minnow No. 75XX

The largest of these near surface swimmers, the Muskie Minnow was available rigged for either bass or musky (different hooks). The No. 7551 measures 3 7/8". It was offered in the same colors as the Bass King plus No. 51 (silver with red head). **$125-$200**

Surface Spraying Glider 8746

Most notable due to its similarity to the Creek Chub Jigger, this 3 5/8" lure has standard glass eyes and bears characteristic Strike-Master spots on the belly. Available color patterns include: No. 46 (white with red head), No. 47 (black with white head), No.

48 (orange with black head), No. 51 (silver with red head), and No. 53 (black with gold head). **$125-$200**

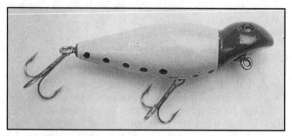

Surface Spraying Glider

Surface Teaser No. 21/21XX

Offered in both the Sure-Catch and Strike-Master eras as a front prop plug, it was available in other configurations. Generally measuring 2 3/4", this lure has been noted in the no eye variation. The No. 21 was offered in: White with red head (No. 46), white with black spots (No. 52), all silver (No. 50) and all black (No. 54). The No. 21XX series dropped color pattern No. 50 and added No. 47 (black with white head) and No. 62 (white with green stripes). **$75-$100**

Smith Minnow

The Wiggle Bait
LaGrange Bait Company
LaGrange, Indiana

Known as the Smith Minnow to most collectors, this rare little beauty sports glass eyes and a fairly complicated wagging tail fin. Smith was granted a patent for this lure in 1905. Apparently Jim Heddon was interested in this particular lure. There is a slightly different lure, but nevertheless a copy, that was obtained from the Heddon factory and has Heddon hardware. **$5,000-$7,000**

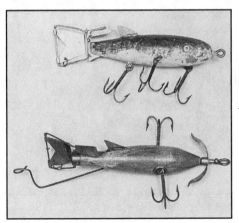

Smith Minnow

Spiral-Lure

Calumet Tackle Company
Detroit, Michigan
Spiral Tackle Company
Detroit, Michigan

The first name and address was revealed upon removal of a paper label on the box. The lure is fluted, has no eyes, and rotates around a heavy wire armature on retrieve. The line tie and both hook hangers are integral with the wire armature. The plug measures 3" and is thought to date around the 1930s. **$100-$125**

Spiral-Lure. Photo courtesy Clarence Zahn

William Stuart & Co.

Canton, Ohio
Eclipse Minnow

The Eclipse is a wooden lure that was in production as early
as 1905. It has been found with yellow glass eyes and unusual
white glass eyes with black pupils. It was made in two sizes, 5T at
3 5/8" and 3T at 3". It sports fore and aft propeller spinners and a
unique style of raised aluminum cup hook hanger hardware. They
were available in white, green, red, and yellow colors. It is thought
to be the forerunner of an early Shakespeare plug. **$500-$800**

Eclipse Minnow

Slim Sweeney's Twinminnow

Twinminnow Bait Company
Fresno, California

A c. 1939 glass eye, wooden 3 3/8" lure, this is a surface or subsurface running lure depending upon which of the line ties used. Colors: red head/white body, green perch scale, yellow perch scale, black back with gold sides and a white belly. **$50-$100**

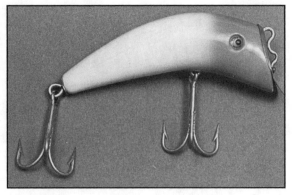

Twinminnow

Tempter Frog c. 1935

Tempter Bait Company
Pittsburgh, Pennsylvania
Akron, Ohio

Three references to this bait were found. Two put the company in Pittsburgh and the other placed it in Akron. There are at least two sizes to be found: 3 3/4" and the 2 1/4" fly rod size.
$175-$375

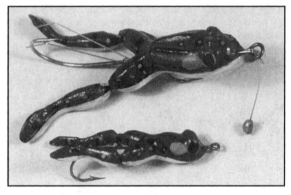

Tempter Frogs. Photo courtesy Jim Muma

Thoren Minnow Chaser

A. H. Thoren
Chicago, Illinois

This is actually two lure bodies mounted on a wire. The flyer states: "A silvery minnow swimming for dear life chased by a fish." It also called the lure "The latest 1940 lure." What is puzzling is that the rear lure on the wire has hardware for attaching to the end of the wire fixture from the smaller forward minnow body. The smaller forward minnow measures 2", the rear measures 2 3/4" and the whole rig from tail to nose of the forward lure measures 5 1/4". The forward lure was always a "Silvery Minnow" but the larger "Chaser" was available in the three finishes: red head with white body; red head with yellow body; Pikie scale finish. It has tack painted eyes. **$200-$400**

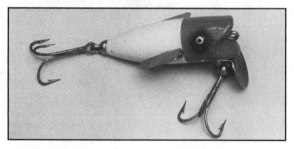

Thoren Minnow Chaser

Toledo Weedless

Toledo Bait Company
Toledo, Ohio

An old but undated ad states that this lure was "famous" and that it was patented in 1925. It is a wood body lure with slot and spring-loaded single hook. The hook point is concealed in the body so as to come out when the fish bites down on the lure. **$200-$300**

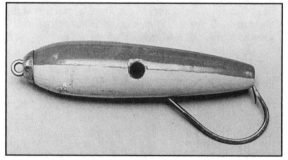

Toledo Weedless

L.J. Tooley Tackle

Kalamazoo, Michigan
Detroit, Michigan

The company was owned by Lloyd J. Tooley of Kalamazoo and Detroit. Tooley was a champion bait caster in 1904, 1905 and 1906, setting a world record in 1905 with the then newly developed shorter Shakespeare bait casting rod called the "Kazoo" rod. The company manufactured silk lines and fishing rods as well as a few lures. Lures included the Tooley Minnow Tandem, the Surface Bunty Darter and the Spinnered Bunty. There are two sizes of the Bunty Darter: 2" and 2 1/4" long, and three finishes: red head, white body; red head, gold body; white head, red body.

The Spinnered Bunty is 2 1/2" long with a nose mounted propeller spinner. Tooley didn't prime them before painting and the finish is very fragile after nearly a century. **$150-$250**

Surface Bunty Darter

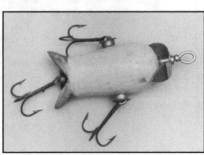

Torpedo Bait

George Jennings
Newark, New Jersey

This lure was found in Abercrombie & Fitch catalogs as early as 1907, but it is reported to date back to 1899 in an Abbey and Imbrie catalog. They do not list any sizes, but they have been found in 2 1/4" and 2 3/4" lengths. The catalog also said the fins were drilled to attach extra hooks if desired. All came fitted with one feathered treble hook. **$300-$400**

Torpedo Bait

Turbulent Fishing Lures

Oscar C. Schaefer
Racine, Wisconsin

The box that the wooden lure came in had a couple of inserts. One was a comprehensive list of both saltwater and fresh water game fish and which Turbulent Lures were best suited, how to rig them with bait such as worms, minnows, cut bait, crabs, mullet, etc. The other listed 11 lures that were available: Surface Lure, Giant Surface Lure, Diver Lure, Giant Diver Lure, Tiger Lure, Giant Tiger Lure, Penetrator Lure, Giant Penetrator Lure, Excitor Lure, Headless Lure, and Wet Fly Lure. Colors: red-yellow, black dotted, red-white, white dotted, black-yellow, green dotted, black-white, yellow dotted. The Turbulent Giant lures were available only in red and white. **$150-$200**

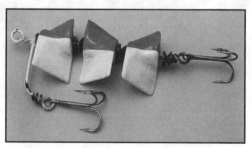

Turbulent Giant

Turner Casting Bait

Turner Night Caster
Zachary T. Turner
Coldwater, Michigan

The Turners ran their lure making business out of their barbershop. The 4 1/8" wooden plug dates from the 1920s. A unique feature is the removable lead belly weight. The weight was cast with a spring wire so that it would have the weight firmly in the hole, but by squeezing the spring against the weight it could be removed. This feature made the plug a floater or sinker at will. There is a second, probably older, style where the belly weight is free swinging from the belly. The hook hardware is cup and see-through Gem-clip type hook hangers held fast by pins inserted from the belly. Colors: frog back, orange and black, brown and white, mauve, dark back and orange belly, gold, aluminum, yellow white, orange, yellowish lemon. The Night Caster was luminous white. The company ceased operating in 1927. **$500-$600**

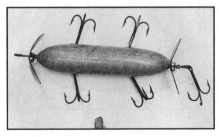

*Turner
Casting Bait*

Vaughn's Lure

Vaughn's Tackle Company
Cheboygan, Michigan

This lure has a green body and fully rotating head with three flutes. The flutes are painted red, yellow, and white respectively. The body of this wooden lure measures 3 1/2". It dates from the early 1930s. It was made "... in Six Different Colors, Red, White, Orange, Green, Black and Metallic Gray with contrasting colors in spiral." **$90-$125**

Vaughn's Lure

Viking Frog

Viking Bait and Novelty Company
Oscar Christiansen
St. Paul, Minnesota

This very rare wooden frog was patented in 1936. It is sometimes called the Christiansen Frog by collectors. It measures 4 1/2" long. There is a variation where the first leg section behind the body is absent and the bent legs are attached to the body with the feet pointing inward instead of out as in the normal two joint model. **$300-$400**

Viking Frog. Photo courtesy Jim Muma

Welch & Graves

Natural Bridge, New York

The glass minnow tube was invented by Henry J. Welch and he was granted a patent in 1893. This is certainly the earliest of this curious style of lure. You were supposed to put a live minnow in the glass tube and it would stay alive all day, presumably catching fish over and over. A glass stopper was used to keep the minnow from escaping. The Graves in the name is Calvin V. Graves who manufactured the lures. His literature states that there were three sizes available, 3 1/2", 4 1/2", and 5 1/2". It has been reported that there was a fourth size offered. There is clear identification molded into the side of the glass body with the company name. **$900-$1,200**

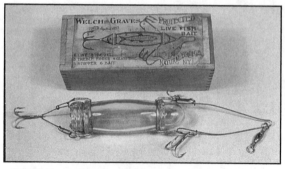

Welch & Graves Glass Minnow Tube

Wilcox Wiggler

Charles M. Wilcox
New Paris, Ohio

Two Wilcox ads were found for this lure, in 1909 and 1915 magazines. It is a very strongly constructed lure with single joint articulation, yellow glass eyes, and one surface-flush internal belly weight. **$2,500-$3,500**

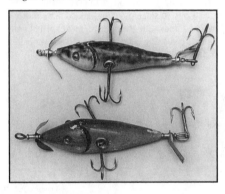

Wilcox Wigglers

Wilcox Red Headed Floater

This very rare lure measures 2 7/8" long. It has raised cup and screw eye hook hanger hardware, three trebles around the body and one trailing with a propeller spinner. **$300-$600**

Clinton Wilt Manufacturing Company

Springfield, Missouri

The earliest advertising was in a 1922 magazine. When first released the Little Wonder Bait and Champion Bait were available in eight color patterns: white, orange, or gold body with red stripes; white, orange, gold, or red body with green stripes; green body with orange stripes. At some point they added three more finishes: copper-plated body with green stripe, nickel-plated body with a green stripe or red stripe. There are three-blade propeller spinners aft. **$600-$900**

Little Wonder and Champion bait

Winchester Bait & Manufacturing Co.

"Lucky Hit Bait"
Oliver H. Williams
Muncie, Indiana
Winchester, Indiana

The lures of the "Lucky Hit Bait" numbered 12 models. They were all hand-crafted wood floaters. The bodies were turned on a lathe, hand-detailed and painted in Williams' home in Muncie, Ind. Williams and his daughters comprised the whole employee force. The lures were marketed from his father-in-law's home in Winchester, Ind. There were 17 different color finishes used on the lure, but not all colors were available on each lure. Each individual lure was available in choices of four finishes. Williams discontinued lure making in 1937. **$200-$300**

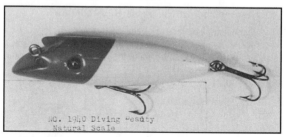

Winchester Bait

Winchester Repeating Arms Company

New Haven, Connecticut

The famous Winchester Company got into the fishing tackle business in late 1919 and ended in 1931. It made many flies, metal spinner baits and a few wooden baits. It also bought out the Hendryx Reel Company. The wooden lures are limited and almost any would be quite a find.

Winchester Multi-Wobbler

This is a teardrop shape, reverse running lure measuring 3 1/2". It sports two adjustable metal nose-mounted side planes and has two belly-mounted double hooks. It is a surface lure or underwater swimmer depending upon how you adjust the planes. **$250-$500**

Winchester Three/Five Treble Hook Minnow

These lures have glass eyes and the distinctive Winchester nose and aft-mounted propeller shapes. The colors are the eight standard listed. They each have a trailing treble and opposite side mounted trebles (2 or 4).
$300-$600

Winchester Minnow

Winnie's Michigan Stump Dodger

Albert Winnie
Traverse City, Michigan

Winnie was a barber in Traverse City who handcrafted all his lures on a lathe and painted them himself. There are a tremendous variety of colors and sizes to be found as well as several different types of hardware. He first patented his Stump Dodgers in 1914. There were two simple screw eye line ties, one at the top and the other beneath the head. There is a second generation line tie. This lure is made of metal with a cork interior body.

The only references were in a 1916 Abbey and Imbrie catalog and in a mixed company section of a 1921 Shakespeare catalog. There have been 35 colors found so far. **$100-$300**

Michigan Stump Dodger

Winter's Weedless Surface Bait

N. G. Souther & Company
Chicago, Illinois

Two ads were found for this lure, both in 1921 publications. They were made in 1 1/4" and 1 7/8". Colors: green, white and red; yellow, red and black; tan, red and white; white, red and black. **$300-$600**

Winter's Weedless Surface Bait. Photo courtesy Jim Muma

Wright and McGill Company

Denver, Colorado

This well-known firm has been doing business continuously since 1925. Their "Eagle Claw" products are widely used and respected, but the number of artificial lures they have made is quite limited. They are heavily into fishing reels, rods, and hooks and currently produce no lures. The 1930, 1951, and 1956 Wright and McGill Company catalogs represent the majority of the plugs marketed by the company.

Bass-O-Gram

This is a minnow-like lure with a large open mouth and two belly treble hooks. It appeared in the 1930 catalog as available in three sizes and two finishes. Sizes: No. 1101, 4", 1 oz., Colors: red and white. No. 1102, 3 1/2", 3/4 oz., Colors: red and white. No. 1103, 3", 1/2 oz., Colors: red and white. No. 1106, 4", 1 oz., Color: natural. No. 1107, 3 1/2", 3/4 oz., Color: natural. No. 1108, 3", 1/2 oz., Color: natural. **$400-$500**

Bug-a-Boo

The Bug-a-Boo is a 2 3/8", 1 oz. plastic body lure with two belly trebles and a metal lip. It has scooped-out (concave) eye sockets and the line tie is at the nose above the diving lip. Size: No. 303, 2 3/8", 1/2 oz.; No. 467 (600), 1 3/4", 3/8 oz. Colors: red and white, pike scale, perch scale, silver scale, gold scale, chub scale, yellow with silver scale, black and white, frog, rainbow, pearl, pearl with red stripe. **$5-$15**

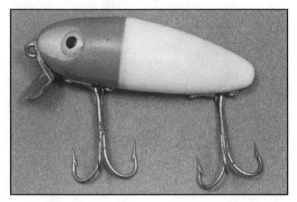

Bug-a-Boo

Basskil

This is almost exactly the same plug as the Bug-a-Boo but longer (3"). Colors unknown, but probably the same. **$5-$15**

Crawfish

This lure was found in the 1930 catalog as available in only one size (2 3/4", 1/2 oz.). It was a reverse running plug with rubber legs and bristle antennae at the nose of the crawfish body. It has one belly treble. **$100-$150**

Dixie Dandy

This is a surface spinning plug with a belly treble, trailing treble hook and a tail-mounted propeller spinner. Size and colors unknown. **$6-$12**

The Flapper Crab

Found in the 1930 catalog this lure was made in two sizes, one color. They have glass eyes, one treble, rubber legs and pinchers, and are reverse running. Small fly rod size: 1/2 oz. Large, casting size: 1 oz., 2 1/2". **$50-$75, Box alone: $80-$120**

The Flapper Crab

Zink Screwtail

Zink Artificial Bait Company
Dixon, Illinois

This peculiar looking lure measures 2 1/2". The body rotates around a wire armature that makes up the line tie and tail hook hanger. The metal device at the head is adjustable rendering it a surface or diving plug. The eyes are painted and located in a depression. It is a 1940s era lure. Colors: Pearl white body and a red head; orange, brown and black; yellow and green, black and silver gray. **$50-$75**

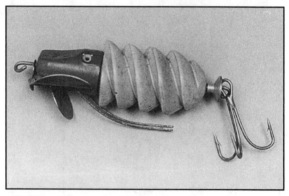

Zink Screwtail